CRITICAL WRITING

A Guide to Writing a Paper Using the Concepts and Processes of Critical Thinking

Gerald Nosich

ROWMAN & LITTLEFIELD

Lanham • Boulder • New York • London

Acquisitions Editor: Mark Kerr
Assistant Editor: Courtney Packard
Sales and Marketing Inquiries: textbooks@rowman.com

Credits and acknowledgments for material borrowed from other sources, and reproduced with permission, appear on the appropriate pages within the text.

Published by Rowman & Littlefield
An imprint of The Rowman & Littlefield Publishing Group, Inc.
4501 Forbes Boulevard, Suite 200, Lanham, Maryland 20706

www.rowman.com

6 Tinworth Street, London SE11 5AL, United Kingdom

British Library Cataloguing in Publication Information Available

Library of Congress Cataloging-in-Publication Data
Names: Nosich, Gerald M., author.
Title: Critical writing : a guide to writing a paper using the concepts and processes of critical thinking / Gerald Nosich.
Description: Lanham : Rowman & Littlefield Publishing Group, 2021. | Includes practice and self-assessment exercises and self-assessment tests. | Includes bibliographical references and index. | Summary: "The main goal of this book is to provide students with a set of robust, integrated critical concepts and processes that will allow to them think through a topic and then write about it, and to do so in a way that is built on, and permeated by, substantive critical thinking"—Provided by publisher.
Identifiers: LCCN 2020045292 (print) | LCCN 2020045293 (ebook) | ISBN 9781538140901 (Cloth : acid-free paper) | ISBN 9781538140918 (Paperback : acid-free paper) | ISBN 9781538140925 (ePub)
Subjects: LCSH: Academic writing—Study and teaching (Higher) | Critical thinking—Study and teaching. | Creative writing.
Classification: LCC LB2369 .N68 2021 (print) | LCC LB2369 (ebook) | DDC 808.02—dc23
LC record available at https://lccn.loc.gov/2020045292
LC ebook record available at https://lccn.loc.gov/2020045293

∞™ The paper used in this publication meets the minimum requirements of American National Standard for Information Sciences—Permanence of Paper for Printed Library Materials, ANSI/NISO Z39.48-1992.

To Linda Elder, and to Matthew, Nicole and Artemis.

Contents

CHAPTER 3 Constructing the Paper: Planning, Researching, Writing 73

CHAPTER 4 Other Minds, Other Views: Addressing "the Other Side" and Cultivating Critical Thinking Traits of Mind 113

Critical Writing: A Guide to Writing a Paper

Using the Concepts and Processes of Critical Thinking

Brief Overview

"To the Instructor" introduces the main features of the book and the benefits that a robust approach to critical thinking brings to the enterprise of writing a paper. First, it briefly lays out for instructors the framework for critical writing that constitutes the structure of the book, and then, second, it highlights main features of the book, eleven of them. Pervading everything else is the intensive focus (and often the resulting insight) that critical thinking brings to writing. The Paul-Elder approach to critical thinking, unlike more piecemeal approaches, aims at being not only flexible but also *comprehensive*, which allows it to illuminate all aspects of writing papers in virtually any non-fiction genre.

The main features describe processes that allow students to engage critically with the fundamental tasks of writing a paper: getting an idea in the first place; analyzing a topic to generate a coherent plan for the paper, including a viable thesis statement and main points; writing the actual paragraphs; taking account of how others might disagree; using Socratic questioning and the standards for critical thinking to enrich and further develop the paper; cultivating the traits of mind that are so essential to writing papers that are both well reasoned and compelling; and internalizing the fundamental and powerful concepts—content, communication, audience, and criticality—that guide writing in any genre or kind of writing, including writing that takes place long after the course is over. Additional main features of the book include in-depth and extended examples of students planning, clarifying, and structuring a paper using the processes of critical writing; self-assessment exercises, with feedback, at the end of each chapter; and finally an elucidation of "the spirit of critical thinking" and of how it runs through and motivates the entire process of writing a paper using the concepts and processes of critical thinking.

"**To the Student**" provides three self-assessment pieces to help students make a realistic assessment of three far-ranging skills that are essential for writing something even moderately well. Later in the book, there are sections containing feedback on each of the three self-assessments. The concepts and processes of critical writing help dramatically in developing these and other crucial skills.

This section further provides reasons and motivations for a student to use the concepts and processes of critical thinking while writing a paper. It thus serves as a motivation for students to work through "To the Student" (and, more important, the book as a whole).

The emphasis in **Chapter 1** is on laying out the components of a paper. These components are fleshed out in two extended examples that show students constructing an actual plan for their papers. The students start off with an initially unfocused *topic*; they work their way to finding a *thesis statement* and then the *main points* that will constitute the *structure* and *outline* of their papers; they identify the *research* they will need to do; they *give credit* to the sources they will use, and, as they proceed, they *revise*. The plans in these examples are fairly strong ones, and in that sense they show good or careful thinking. Still, they do not contain the key features that characterize *critical* thinking: They do not carry the necessary emphasis on reflectiveness, on process, or the focus on standards. Even more pointedly, they don't show *how* to do the actual thinking that will result in a well-thought-out paper.

Near the end, Chapter 1 outlines the systematic (but non-linear) framework for critical writing that will be developed in the succeeding chapters, a framework that focuses on a critical thinking approach to planning, writing, researching, and revising. It is this framework that shows the "*how*" of critical writing: it guides and focuses writers so that they can think through all the parts of constructing and writing a well-reasoned and compelling paper.

Chapter 1 also spells out a process for writing for clarity (one of the standards of critical thinking). The process—tagged "SEE-I"—is a structured way of writing the actual sentences and paragraphs of the paper directly from the critical thinking plan. SEE-I (*stating, elaborating*, giving *examples* and *illustrations*) provides a concrete way to engage in critical writing from the beginning of a course. SEE-I is amplified in Chapter 3 and substantially expanded in Chapter 5.

Chapter 2 introduces the "elements of reasoning." The eight "elements" are critical thinking concepts (such as *assumptions*, *question at issue, conclusions, implications and consequences*) that allow the writer to analyze a topic with much greater depth, breadth, and clarity. The elements bring *focus*. Analyzing a topic "around the circle of elements" gives a person an effective, concrete procedure, one that generates the specificity that is essential for turning a vague topic into a crisp, well-defined, reasoned plan for a paper, one that is suitable for writing in virtually any non-fiction genre or kind of paper. The chapter contains three differently oriented examples of students analyzing a topic and thinking their way through it.

Each chapter (after the first) begins with a "GPS" showing the topics within the framework that will be highlighted in that chapter. A second, related GPS shows pervasive aspects of critical writing that will be specifically addressed in the individual chapter. (In the chapters, these traditional components and vocabulary of writing are given renewed vigor by the concepts and processes of critical thinking.)

GPS
- topic →
- analysis →
- plan: thesis, structure, outline →
- writing →
- "the other side" →
- improvement →
- flow

Pervasive aspects
- research
- critical thinking standards
- revision
- fundamental & powerful concepts
- giving credit

Chapter 3 is on planning, researching, and writing the paper. It begins by showing students how they can straightforwardly use their analysis "around the circle of elements" to produce virtually a full critical thinking plan for the paper. Their analysis generates not only a focused thesis statement but also the other main points (and additional supporting points) that constitute the structure and outline of the paper. Chapter 3 also shows how the analysis generates a way to research a paper far more effectively. An extended example shows a student starting with an initially unpromisingly general topic—stereotyping—constructing a focused plan (thesis, main points), polishing it, revising it, reasoning through how to research it, and, finally, showing how the student can use the clarification process SEE-I to write the paper itself directly from the plan.

Chapter 4, "Other Minds, Other Views," highlights two closely related facets of critical writing. First, being a critical thinker involves developing critical thinking "traits of mind," such as *intellectual humility, intellectual empathy, fairmindedness,* and *intellectual integrity* (nine of them in all). Second, though these traits enter into all phases of critical writing, they come out in an especially pointed way in addressing "the other side" of an issue: how someone with a different point of view might reasonably see the topic in a different or conflicting way. The extended examples here bring back some of the examples from earlier chapters (such as the one on stereotyping) and show how considering the other side adds richness, fairness, and realistic thinking to a paper.

Chapter 5 is devoted to making the paper better, to revising it. It begins with critical thinking *standards*—such as *clarity, accuracy, relevance* (ten of them in all). People invariably assume (or at least hope) that what they think or write is clear, relevant, accurate, important, and so forth. But focusing on the standards *explicitly, consciously,* brings with it a much more focused and effective way of thinking and writing. The standards come to the forefront in a highly specific and focused way in Socratic questioning, a way to address flaws and pitfalls, to sharpen things up, to limit or expand the writing, and to enhance pacing and coherence. Virtually any of the Socratic questions (see p. 165) are directly helpful in enabling writers, at any level of expertise, to enhance and expand their writing almost at will. The chapter contains several examples of students enriching their papers with Socratic questioning.

Chapter 6, on making the paper "flow," highlights the "fundamental and powerful concepts" of critical writing: *content, audience, communication,* and *criticality.* The chapter shows how those four concepts allow someone to think through unanticipated difficulties that come up when writing papers (including issues that will inevitably come up long after courses are over). Specific writing issues addressed in Chapter 6 include some aspects of rhetoric, grammatical correctness, practical guidelines for writing, and giving credit to sources. The book ends with a section on taking writing seriously, engaging with what you write.

To the Instructor

The main goal of *Critical Writing* is to provide students with a set of robust, integrated critical concepts and processes that will allow to them think through a topic, and then write about it, and to do so in a way that is built on, and permeated by, substantive critical thinking.

The critical thinking tools and concepts in the book are built on the Paul-Elder approach to critical thinking.[*] A major advantage of the Paul-Elder approach is that, in contrast to other approaches to critical thinking, it aims to be *comprehensive*. By going through "the elements of reasoning" (see p. 36), you will be addressing *all* the major "parts of thinking." In other approaches, you address some aspects of thinking but unintentionally leave others out entirely. Thus, with another approach you might identify, say, the *assumptions* someone is making or the *point of view* the person holds, but it may never come into your mind to examine how you are *interpreting* the issue, or the main *questions* you or the person should be asking about the issue, or the *implications and consequences* of it. Those are serious omissions: the key points you may need to address in your paper may well fall into categories that you overlook simply because nothing in these approaches draws your attention to them.

Saying that the Paul-Elder approach aims at being comprehensive does not mean that it is linear or step-by-step. It isn't. (See the note on p. xvi.)

---

[*]*Critical Writing: A Guide to Writing a Paper Using the Concepts and Processes of Critical Thinking* lays out the main dimensions of the Foundation for Critical Thinking's articulation of critical thinking (www.criticalthinking.org) as they apply to writing. The approach was developed by Richard Paul, Linda Elder, and myself. Probably the best overview of it is contained in Richard Paul and Linda Elder, *The Miniature Guide to Critical Thinking: Concepts and Tools*, 8th ed. (Lanham, MD: Rowman & Littlefield, 2020). Though Paul and Elder's book is highly condensed, it spells out the essential components of a robust conception of critical thinking.

It also does not mean that using the elements is cold-bloodedly rational (with the negative overtones this word sometimes carries): addressing the elements gives great scope for imaginative thinking and writing. Finally, it also does not mean that it in any way guarantees success. The elements of reasoning direct you to what you need to address—but they don't guarantee that you will address it *accurately* or *clearly*, or that you will identify the most *important* responses, or that you will be as *precise* as you need to be.

The italicized words in the last sentence are four of "the standards of critical thinking" (see p. 151), and something roughly similar applies to them. The standards are not comprehensive in the way the elements of reasoning are—but they are close. The ten standards highlighted in this book—clear, accurate, relevant, important, logical, precise, deep, broad, sufficient and fair—are the ones that apply most often and in most circumstances.

One further note about the Paul-Elder approach is that, because of its comprehensiveness, it applies to all varieties of non-fiction writing. By contrast, other critical thinking approaches tend to be built on a tradition of informal logic, and as a result, they apply almost exclusively to writing argumentative (persuasive) papers, or papers that center on reacting to something read or viewed. That makes for a highly limited approach to writing. There are, of course, many different forms of non-fiction writing, and many of these are neither argumentative nor reactive. (This book contains several examples of these.) Students will write different kinds of papers not just in courses specifically centered on writing but also in courses in different disciplines. Moreover, once school is finished, most of the writing people do is not argumentative or reactive. A virtue of the framework in this book is that it lets you think your way through different kinds of papers and adapt your writing to them. Good thinking applies to writing *anything*.*

A major part of the goal of the book is to provide not only the "what" of writing a paper but also the "how" of it. The "what" comprises the essential components of a well-thought-out paper: thesis statement and main points, an articulated structure, development, research, the need for clarity, grammatical correctness, and several others.

---

*This should be clear from the fact that *all* non-fiction modes or genres of writing have or embody assumptions, implications, concepts, questions at issue, and the other elements of reasoning; all rely on accuracy, clarity, relevance, and other critical thinking standards; all would benefit from traits such as intellectual perseverance and intellectual empathy; all can be enriched with Socratic questioning. (In a very different way, most of those apply even to writing many genres of fiction as well.)

Addressing the "how" of these occupies a significantly greater part of *Critical Writing*. The aim throughout is to show:

- how you can actually construct a thesis statement and the other main points that constitute the structure of the paper;
- how you can write the actual paragraphs that make up the body of the paper;
- how you can engage in productive research and do so in a planned, self-directed way;
- how you can make a point clear—not just grammatically or stylistically clear but also clear in thought and clear in communicating that thought to an audience;
- how you can think your way through the numerous unanticipated issues (including aspects of grammatical correctness, transitions, as well as many other aspects of rhetoric) that arise in the course of writing papers.

The book aims to provide close and careful processes for carrying out each of these, always through the use of one's best reasoned judgment—through critical thinking.

A closely related goal in the book has to do with the *standards of critical thinking*, mentioned above. It is not enough simply to recognize that a well-thought-out paper needs to be clear, accurate, relevant, and so forth. With the critical thinking standards, the "how" is again paramount. *Critical Writing* provides concrete, usable ways for students to make their paper more accurate, more relevant, and so forth, and to communicate its accuracy, relevance, and the rest to the writers' audience. Perhaps just as important, the book gives specific prompts that direct writers toward the thinking required to help them meet those standards.

The specific focus in the book is on writing a paper, but the concepts and processes of critical writing apply in a direct and useful way to virtually any kind of non-fictional writing.

A Framework for Critical Writing

The central unifying concept in *Critical Writing* is a framework for creating, planning, structuring, researching, and writing a paper. The main components of the framework include the elements of reasoning, clarification and elaboration tools (called "SEE-I"), procedures for using intellectual empathy to address the other side of an issue, the standards for critical thinking, Socratic questioning techniques to enrich the paper, critical thinking character traits, and several others. The framework is intended to function as an organic whole, with the parts of it integrated. But each of the components can work independently of the others, and instructors can incorporate any of them, wholly or in part, into their own ways of teaching writing. This approach yields considerable flexibility for both instructors and students. In addition, the extended examples in the book allow students to engage imaginatively with how someone might actually reason through crucial issues in writing.

Working through the concepts and processes in the book can have deep and far-reaching consequences for students. Some of the outcomes are immediate and dramatic, and some, because they allow students to experience the dynamism of the critical thinking concepts, lay a groundwork for helping students re-think and re-imagine the goals and rewards of writing well.

Main Features of the Book

The main features of the book grow out of the techniques and goals inherent in critical writing.

First, **focus**. A crucial advantage of using a critical thinking framework in writing a paper is that it allows for a focused, incisive, informed analysis of a topic, question, problem, issue, situation, response to a reading—virtually anything. The framework begins with a critical thinking analysis of a topic using the "elements of reasoning": *purpose, assumptions, implications and consequences, information, question at issue, conclusions and interpretations, concepts, points of view*—eight of them (each with several near synonyms), arranged in a circle. The elements of reasoning focus a person's thinking. Analyzing a topic by "going around the circle of elements" both generates and guides critical thinking about the topic. It also generates and guides the purposeful research a person needs to engage in to write about a topic in a responsible way.

The elements give students a systematic (but non-linear*) set of tools to analyze a topic using their best critical thinking. They help dramatically even if the topic is too general, or if it is as ill defined as initial topics so often are. Analyzing "around the circle" is not something students do only *after* they have found a focus for their paper. It is something they do to *find* that focus.

---

*Again, it is not a step-by-step method in which, for example, you first go through Step 1, then through Step 2, and so forth. It *can* be used that way, and this is often helpful for students who may need such a structure. But, in fact, the elements of reasoning can be used in any order, because reasoning itself does not exist in a given order. Often the problem or topic itself will suggest the most helpful elements to begin with.

Take a topic as unpromising as "college life." As it stands, it is far too general to write a paper on. But when students analyze "college life" by going around the circle, it is almost as if the topic starts to focus itself. As they work through the main *purposes* of "college life," the main *questions at issue* or *problems* that come up around it, the *assumptions* it embodies, the *concept* of what they mean by "college life" in the first place, and so on around the circle, they will be in a position not just to focus their thinking but usually to focus it to the point where they can generate a plan for the paper they will write.

The elements of reasoning bring a similar kind of focus to *research*. A dysfunctional concept of research often sidelines paper-writing for students. But with the elements as a guide, research and reasoning work together. Rather than research being just a haphazard process, analyzing around the circle helps students focus more exactly on what they need to research. The goal is for students to begin to see research not just as something to report on but as a major part of thinking through an issue or question in a way that is deeply informed by reliable sources, so they can then write about it with authority and insight.

The *process of focusing* is a major part of the learning and the understanding that is such a key factor in planning out a paper. It lays the groundwork for formulating a focused thesis statement, and also for identifying the main supporting points writers will structure their papers around.

Second, **planning out the paper as a whole: thesis statement, main points, structure, outline.** Analyzing a topic with the elements of reasoning puts students in a position to identify the main thing they will be saying in the paper, its thesis statement. Students' thesis statements will very often emerge directly out of their analysis. As students analyze their topic (and do relevant research on it), they will be identifying one or more central *assumptions* within it; they will be finding and elucidating one or more major *implications* of it, and so on around the circle of eight elements. With that analysis in front of them, what usually happens is that they just "see" that their response to one or more of the elements *is* in fact the main thing they want to say in their paper. It *is* their thesis statement. (With my own students, about 60 percent of them just "see" the thesis statement among the responses they've written in their analysis, and that percentage grows dramatically as they begin to trust the process.) Though it may still need to be refined and polished, the thesis statement will often be right there in their analysis.

Even if it doesn't emerge directly in one or more of their responses, the framework provides a straightforward way for students to *construct* a focused thesis statement. They can do this by closely examining their responses to the elements and then choosing those responses that, in their best judgment, are the most important. They can then combine those responses, re-state them as a coherent whole, and thereby construct what is in effect a composite thesis statement.

In much the same way, the main points students need to explain or support their thesis statement will emerge from their analysis (or at least most of them will). Thus, by working their way through their topic, and using the eight elements of reasoning to guide them, there is a strong likelihood that students will have not just a viable thesis statement but the structure and outline of their paper as a whole. Creativity plays a strong role in this process: it is students themselves who are creating the content of their papers. When students work their way through their analysis in an engaged and genuine way, they will be in the best position to generate, out of their own informed critical and creative thinking, a reasoned plan for the whole paper.

An aside on **the vocabulary of writing**: This book uses a good deal of the traditional vocabulary of writing and composition courses: topic, thesis statement, main points, outline, and so forth. But it allows for using that vocabulary in a great variety of ways. Instructors may choose to use these terms in a carefully defined, restricted way or to use them, as the book tends to, in more flexible and far-ranging ways. Thus, for instance, in this book the term "topic" is used in the broadest possible sense. A topic can, of course, be a specific, already-focused issue the student is discussing or it can be a response the student has to an article the student has read and carefully summarized. But, far more flexibly, the topic in question can be virtually anything that can be written about: situations, problems, questions, arguments, decisions, and something simply wondered about are just some examples. "Topic" is extremely sensitive to context, to audience, and to the writer's goals, as well as to the role the writer sees that writing will play in her or his life after formal schooling is over. (The reason the term "topic" can be used so broadly, with so little initial focus, is that, as mentioned above, the focusing of the topic is accomplished by analyzing it with the elements of reasoning.)

Similarly, "thesis statement," as used in this book, is not a highly restrictive term. It is roughly just the main thing (or things) the writer is saying in the paper (though constructing a crisp, clear, interesting, imaginative, plausible thesis statement is a far more challenging matter: see the third main feature of the book). Even the term "paper" itself does not have to apply only in a narrow sense. In fact, at the instructor's discretion, short papers can be generated from the state-elaborate-exemplify-illustrate technique (SEE-I) described in Chapter 1.

Third, **reasoning and "getting an idea."** The earlier point about *focus* is worth emphasizing. One of the frustrations of teaching critical writing is that students often just hope "to get" an idea for their paper. They often believe that the idea for the paper is just supposed to come to them, and that the main supporting points for that idea should also just come to them. Alternatively, they hope that reading something or doing some research will simply give them the idea for their paper.

One problem, of course, is that very often in fact no idea comes. Trying to come up with one by associational thinking (such as brainstorming or clustering) is typically too hit-or-miss to be reliable. Even after they have thought about a topic, say, or written a summary of something they have read or viewed, no idea may come to them, let alone a well-focused idea—and waiting for an idea to come is the opposite of a reasonable strategy. Moreover, without a *process* to analyze a topic critically, even if students do magically "get an idea," it doesn't carry over into getting an idea for the *next* paper they write. Getting an idea is often an unhappy and discouraging process for students.

But from a critical writing point of view, students need more than just a focused idea, more than just a well-circumscribed thesis statement, more than something that just comes magically to mind. They need a thesis that is *clear, accurate, relevant,* and as *deep* and *broad* as appropriate in that context. These are standards for critical thinking. Maybe the student's idea will not in the end meet all those standards, but it has to be examined with enough care and attention for the writer to be able to say that, in her or his best judgment, it genuinely seems to meet those standards.

With a framework for critical writing, the ideas students use to structure their paper are the product not of what just happens to spring magically to mind but of their own best reasoning and research, prompted and guided by the central concepts of critical thinking.

Fourth, **other minds, other views.** Part of being a critical writer is seeing, acknowledging, and often describing how someone with a different point of view might see the issue in the paper differently. That is true whether the issue is a situation, argument, description, interpretation, report—really, anything the person is trying to figure out, understand, and write about.

Said another way: writers cannot really construct a well-thought-out critical paper without being aware of how their paper might go wrong. Part of being a critical writer is actively searching for how people with other points of view might see the issue or situation differently, noting what they might object to, or what they might see as seriously missing in the paper.

Often, this "other side" may need to be brought into the paper itself and addressed there with intellectual empathy and integrity. Addressing other minds and other points of view, honestly and in a forthright manner, is a key part of the framework in this book.

Fifth, doing the actual writing: SEE-I. Doing the writing itself, putting down the actual words, sentences, and paragraphs, is often a major challenge for students. In my college-level classes, for example, students sometimes have a point they want to make about an issue and they state that point in a sentence or two. But then they find themselves at a loss about how to say more. This is one kind of common problem, but there are many others: facing a blank screen, having a dysfunctional model of how to write (such as cutting-and-pasting), making actual paragraphs, "filling the pages" (i.e., expanding, but in a way that's relevant), incorporating research (and citations), keeping their thinking and their writing authentic, creative and coherent—all of these problems and others present distinct challenges, and they often undermine students' skills and motivation.

The framework helps with these problems in several ways. Perhaps the most direct way is through "SEE-I." The acronym stands for *state, elaborate, exemplify,* and *illustrate.* SEE-I is a critical thinking technique for clarifying something, and it serves as a major mechanism for writing actual paragraphs and developing the paper.

If I'm a student, I can use SEE-I again and again. I take each important point in my paper and *state* it: crisply, concisely, in a sentence or two. Then I *elaborate* on it, explaining it at greater length, in a paragraph or two. Then I give an *example* of it—a good example—spelling it out in as much detail as is appropriate. Then I can give an *illustration*: a metaphor or simile, an analogy, a comparison, a picture-in-words, something to convey my point to my readers as vividly and clearly as I can. As I continue through with SEE-I, my paper itself is building, expanding in a way directly relevant to the thesis and structure of my paper.

Also, though, I continue developing my paper by "staircasing SEE-I": I use it to clarify, expand and make vivid not just major points themselves but any important aspects of those major points as well. So, to take a schematic case, one of the main points in my paper might be "The only humane way to address the problem of feral cats is to neuter or spay them and then set them free." In accord with the critical writing framework, I start the writing by giving an SEE-I for that statement itself. But, in addition, I can staircase the SEE-I. That is, I can look within the statement, focus on the concept of "humane," and give an SEE-I for *it*. I can state what it means to be *humane*, elaborate on what makes a practice humane or inhumane, give an example (perhaps more than one) of different kinds of humane treatments, and come up with an illustration that conveys what I mean by describing a treatment as "humane."

I can continue staircasing by giving an SEE-I for what the *problem* of feral cats is; for what makes a cat *feral*; for what constitutes *setting them free*; for the effects of *neutering and spaying* them. Thus, SEE-I provides a major process for both clarifying and developing a paper and for expanding it in ways that make it richer.

SEE-I provides a vehicle in which students creativity can come to the forefront. They are choosing—often creatively choosing—forceful ways to *elaborate* and striking *examples* of points they are making. They are creating vivid *illustrations*—metaphors, analogies—to convey what they are trying to communicate to the reader. In Chapter 3, SEE-I is expanded to include other related ways of developing the paper, and a third much more extensive process for enhancing the writing is presented in Chapter 5 with Socratic questioning (see the seventh main feature below, p. xxiii).

From an instructor's point of view, one of the further virtues of SEE-I is that it gives students a process to begin writing productively right from the beginning of the course. (In my own courses, I often have students engage in SEE-I on the very first day of class. I ask them, for instance, to state, elaborate, exemplify, and illustrate a defining moment in their personal lives, an important concept in the course as they understand it now (such as *"fairness"* or *"writing a paper"*), a key part of the syllabus, or what they take to be the purpose of the course.)

As a separate point, it is worth noting that a substantial part of writing a well-reasoned paper can be accomplished by mastering just two critical thinking techniques: *analysis* around the circle of elements and *SEE-I*. The analysis part allows students to think their way through a topic or issue and then construct a focused plan for their paper. SEE-I then allows them to write out and develop the main points and sub-points of all parts of the plan. It is not the whole of writing a paper, but those two techniques form a strong core on which other critical writing processes can then be built.

Additionally, the two techniques have rich consequences for addressing some perennially problematic aspects of student writing. Giving an analysis with the elements of reasoning directly yields a good part of both the introductory and concluding sections of the paper. And it and SEE-I together straightforwardly suggest not only a natural division of the paper into paragraphs but also specific topic sentences or ideas for those paragraphs.

Moreover, the book strongly recommends that students do the analysis *in writing*—not just in their heads. (In my own classes, it's a requirement.) Though my students tend to feel a pronounced resistance to doing any preparatory work such as this, the resulting success they experience is clear and immediate enough to make many of them more willing to invest the time it takes.* In line with this process, there is a section of the book called "Writing Before You Write." It recommends that students take written notes, as much as possible, in the form of at least partial SEE-I's. There is a strong motivational factor in this: if students can be induced to do this writing as they plan, while they are only preparing, they will often find that they have already written a substantial draft of their actual paper before they start to compose paragraph one.

Sixth, **models of reasoning through issues.** Students in my own courses have difficulty knowing what actually *to do* when asked to reason something through, and a mere verbal description of what to do helps only to a limited degree. To give a more first-hand experience of reasoning things through, this book contains a number of extended examples (sometimes with a commentary) of how a student might work through crucial aspects of writing. Though the students themselves are fictitious, the examples depict genuine issues of critical writing, and genuine ways of thinking through those issues. The extended examples are set off from the main text in contrasting shades. The examples in Chapter 1 show students thinking about a topic and constructing a plan for their papers, but without a framework for critical thinking. The plans these students come up

---

*Students' resistance is often, of course, much more generalized than this. A question they face in relation to writing a paper is "Why do this? Why do the work of thinking critically about a topic, planning out the paper, and the rest?"

The opening section of this book, "To the Student," is intended to help address that resistance. (In my own classes, I assign it right at the start.) It contains three self-assessment pieces to help them confront three central skills they need if they are to write something even moderately well, and thus why they might need a framework for critical writing. There is a section of feedback on each to allow them to do some serious self-assessment of their responses.

with are, at least in this preliminary way, strong ones, but—because they are not generated by using the concepts and processes of critical thinking—they don't give the focus, guidance, and reliability that the framework for critical writing provides. Though they show people who, in a sense, *happen to* come up with a strong plan, they don't show *how* to do it. They also don't give any guidance in how to carry out the rest of writing a paper.

In the remaining chapters, by contrast, the extended examples display how people can, reliably, come up with a full logically organized plan and then carry out all the rest of the tasks of writing a paper based in the concepts and processes of critical thinking. They show how someone might actually go about identifying assumptions, implications, and the other elements of reasoning, and how someone can generate a focused thesis statement starting from a vague, general topic. They show people checking for accuracy, giving illustrations, doing authentic research, enriching a paper with Socratic questioning, and doing many other tasks. The examples are intended to show not just the finished *product* of the critical writing but the thinking *process* a student might engage in on the way to that finished product. They show people sometimes having to face the confusions and conflicting ideas inherent in critical writing. A goal for actual students using the book in a course is for them not just to read through the examples passively but also to imagine themselves working through the process along with the student in the example.

The responses in the extended examples are not chosen because they are perfect or the best way. They are chosen as genuine and reasoned ways to address challenges anyone faces in writing something significant. Some show students coming up with exciting new insights, but it is important to note that some show students creating a solid but not an extraordinary paper. Moreover, with many of them, instructors and students may find themselves disagreeing strongly with the thesis and/or supporting points in those papers. They may find relatively serious inaccuracies or a failure to go deeper into the issue.

Thus, this book does not endorse the positions or arguments put forward in the examples. (Indeed, some of the positions are ones I myself profoundly disagree with.) The examples in the book are to be seen rather as sincere, good-faith efforts to reason through a topic, to come up with a defensible thesis, one with at least initially reasonable points to support it.

Seventh, **Socratic questioning and enriching a paper using the standards for critical thinking.** The framework gives concrete tools specifically for enriching and expanding a paper. "Socratic questioning," as the term is used here, is metacognitive questioning that is based primarily in the *standards* for critical thinking. The standards include *clarity, accuracy, relevance, precision* (the book emphasizes ten of them). When fashioned into specific Socratic questions, they allow students, almost at will, to make "interventions" that enhance the paper, enrich it, give it more substance, and expand it in ways that fill it out and make it more complete.

The Socratic questions (based in the standards) prompt students to ask (and then answer) questions such as:

- How is this relevant to the main point of the paper?
- In what way is this important?
- What are the details of this?
- What are some complications that might arise?

To give just a schematic example: Think of yourself as a student who is having the familiar student problem of "filling the pages." Your paper seems finished. In it you've said XYZ, and one of your main points is X. Using SEE-I, you've already elaborated on X and given examples and perhaps an illustration.

But the instructor has assigned an eight-page paper and you have only six.

What can you do? How can you expand the paper in a way that is directly relevant and enriches the paper? (Or, to put it in terms my students often use, how can you get two more pages?)

Socratic questioning gives you a clear way to proceed, to take the next steps. You can ask yourself, "How is X relevant to the thesis of my paper?" You then spell out how X is relevant, and you do that not just in your head but at the keyboard, in your actual writing. If you choose to, you can further ask, "How is X an important point?" "What are some of the details about X?" "What are some of the complications that arise in considering X?" In each case you write out your best answer and judiciously add those paragraphs to your paper.

Notice the way the Socratic questions function. For any given paper, most of them work by fastening on aspects already there in the back of your mind, waiting to be accessed. By answering one or more of the questions, you make explicit what was before only implicit in your thinking. You *already* thought that X was relevant to your thesis; you *already* made the judgment that X was important. That's why you chose to include X in the first place. The Socratic questions prompt you to spell out the relevance and the importance in the paper itself. With the other two questions, you may or may not already be aware of *details* in X, or of *complications* surrounding it, but with the question posed directly in front of you, you can pause to focus on them now, and thus generate a wealth of new ideas and paragraphs. You end up "filling the pages" in ways that enhance the paper and give it more substance. Indeed, one of the most striking benefits of Socratic questioning interventions is the sheer abundance of paths they open up for any form of writing.*

Eighth, **traits of mind.** The book provides concrete guidelines for internalizing and exercising the critical thinking character traits that are so necessary for writing an authentic, creative, compelling paper. These traits of mind—*intellectual courage, intellectual humility, intellectual empathy, fairmindedness, intellectual integrity,* and several others—pervade, in different ways, the entire enterprise of critical writing. It takes *intellectual courage* to try, genuinely, to think one's way through an issue, especially when time pressure, self-doubt and frustration get involved. It takes *intellectual empathy* to capture the other side of an issue or topic, to put oneself into a perhaps alien point of view, to think one's way through it as that person would, and then to describe it fairmindedly in the paper. It takes *intellectual humility* to engage in genuine research, *intellectual perseverance* to both write and enrich the paper, and *intellectual integrity* to give credit to one's sources not just because an instructor requires it but because it is a part of being fair.

Ninth, **fundamental and powerful concepts: content, communication, audience, criticality.** One of the most far-reaching features of the book is a compact set of concepts and processes, ones that a writer at any level can use to think through writing-issues that lie outside the limited purview of any book or course on writing. The *fundamental and powerful concepts* of writing are emphasized all through the book: *content, communication,* and *audience*; adding *criticality* highlights the distinction between merely writing and writing critically.

Students standardly encounter the concepts of *content, communication,* and *audience* as part of a writing course, but too often students see those concepts just as details, or as no different in kind from any number of other important writing concepts, such as sentence fluency, finding your voice, writing vividly, and many others.

---

*I find in my teaching that there is a danger of overload. The sheer abundance of questions can sometimes feel like a burden to students. Even though they can just pick one or two, having so many possible questions to choose from can feel overwhelming.

In my classes, I have students practice using only one or two of the Socratic questions, taken from just a few of the standards. Then, gradually, as students start to see the Socratic questions as helpful rather than burdensome, they can select questions from a greater number of standards.

But *content, communication, audience* and *criticality* are significantly different from other important concepts in writing. It's not exactly that they are somehow more important. It's that they are *structural*. These four can be used as conceptual tools that allow writers to think through questions or problems that come up with regard to writing about anything or in any context. That is what makes them the fundamental and powerful concepts for writing. In Chapter 6 they are applied to using transitions, to some issues of grammatical correctness,* and to other rhetorical aspects, as well as to giving citations and references.

A main goal of this book, then, is for students to start acquiring the habit of thinking issues through using those fundamental and powerful concepts, and then to carry those four with them as conceptual tools beyond the course, whenever they are needed. When students are out of school, and they are writing an important memo in an office where they work, or writing a letter of recommendation for someone, or writing a lesson plan, or anything else, they will be able to carry it out far better if they think it through in terms of how they can best *communicate* their *content* to their *audience*, and do so in a way that brings *criticality* to bear.

Tenth, **practice and assessment exercises, with feedback.** At the end of each chapter there is a set of exercises that prompt students to work through and apply the concepts and processes of critical writing and apply them to their own writing. Many of these (marked with a *) have feedback and commentary by the author, allowing students to engage in the self-assessment that is such a necessary part of becoming an autonomous critical writer.

Finally, there is one more main feature of this book: **The Spirit of Critical Thinking.** Running through everything else in the book, there is an attempt to foster the spirit as well as the skills and dispositions of robust critical thinking and critical writing. That spirit involves:

—a willingness on the part of students† to think their way through a topic, understand it as well as they can, engage in open-minded research about it, and then write about it as clearly, accurately, and fairly as they can. The main goal is not just to report on what

---

*In accord with communicating to an audience, *Critical Writing* is written in a relatively informal style, though there is a note to students advising that an informal style is not appropriate for many academic papers.

†Though these are written with respect to students, the same "willingnesses" apply really to everyone.

some source has said, not just to prove a point, still less to jump to a conclusion and then defend it at all costs. The goal is to write a paper that is compelling, trustworthy, and well reasoned and to feel the rich pleasure that can come from that endeavor.

—a willingness on the part of students to re-think their writing. In the book, re-thinking the issue or topic is a built-in part of the process all the way through: critically analyzing the topic, recognizing and including other relevant points of view on an issue, using the standards explicitly, putting an emphasis on fairmindedness, intellectual humility, and other traits of mind. (This book gives several examples of students re-thinking, or questioning, or changing their mind in relation to a topic they are writing about.)

—a realization that improvement in critical writing and critical thinking does not require *mastery* of critical thinking concepts or processes. It requires their repeated use so that, ideally, they become internalized. This can occur at almost any level of expertise.

—a willingness to take their writing seriously, to engage with it and make it their own, to see it as an expression of who they are and of what their best thinking is.*

A consequent goal in the book is to build in students an increased confidence in their ability to reason and write better. One thing the processes of critical writing reveals is that we often possess an implicit ability to think things through that is greater than we sometimes suppose. The elements of reasoning, intellectual standards, and critical thinking traits of mind bring out this untapped ability. There is a profound and telling difference between just thinking about a topic and asking oneself the focused critical thinking questions: What are its implications? What are my assumptions about it? In what way is this point relevant to the topic? Is this the most important aspect of the topic? How can I bring more of my intellectual courage to bear as I explore it?

---

*There is a section near the end of the book on "Taking It Seriously" (p. 202). In my own classes, I have my students read the first pages of that section right at the beginning of the course.

To the Student: Before You Begin

This book offers a way to write a paper using critical thinking. The framework it provides gives you the best chance to write a paper that has substance to it, that is clear, focused, and logically organized. It helps you avoid a paper that is haphazard, thrown together, based on unfounded or momentary impressions or on unreliable sources.

Some of what is ahead of you will involve working in a different way from what you may be used to, but the real key step is making a mental shift in how you think about writing. If you make that mental shift, much of writing a critical paper will fall into place. Sometimes it may actually be easier, but even when it's not, it will usually be easier than you might anticipate beforehand. (And even in those parts that are not easy, you may find it rewarding to accomplish writing a well-reasoned paper.)

As an analogy, think about going on a job interview. The usual way people go to a job interview is *they just go*. The interviewer asks them questions, and they respond with whatever happens to jump into their mind at that moment. But if you *prepare* for a job interview, you substantially increase the chances that you'll do well in it.

How could you prepare? Though this is a book on writing, you could actually prepare for a job interview by using any number of aspects of this book. That would mean asking yourself:

What questions are they likely to ask me at the interview?
What information about me will be most important for them to hear?
What are their goals in hiring someone for this position? And how do I fit with those goals?

(These and other questions, you will see in Chapter 2, are based on the "elements of reasoning.") Notice how straightforward, helpful, and sometimes almost easy such questions are. If there is a hard part to them, it's not mainly in answering them; it's in thinking to ask them of yourself ahead of time. Preparing, even a little, is completely different from just going to the interview.

Why go through the work of preparing and writing a paper using the concepts and processes of critical thinking? Why not just sit down and write the paper?

You may be able to answer these questions for yourself. Suppose you are assigned to write a five-page paper on some topic X. How would you do it? What would you do?

Here are three of the most common ways people tend to write papers:

1. They start writing about X and see how it goes. They see how many pages they get. (After that, they hope for the best.)
2. They find some articles about X. Then they cut-and-paste from them.
3. They find some articles about X as in (2), but they take what those articles say and put it into different words to avoid plagiarizing.

It may be hard to realize it at the beginning, but each of those responses is likely to be weak—maybe even disastrous for your paper. Compare it to a situation where, after you graduate, you have to do some writing as part of your job or your profession. It might be a proposal to a client, a way to address a problem that's been referred to you, a progress report, an important letter to your supervisor, anything. Suppose the person who assigned the writing expects it to be done in a certain number of pages.

The hope is that you see immediately the weaknesses in approaches (1), (2), and (3). Writing off the top of your head, or relaying the thoughts that just happen to come into your mind, or just stringing together a bunch of only marginally related articles about X—those are almost sure-fire ways of producing writing that will be seen as shallow, superficial, and un-thought-out. Almost certainly, you'd be seen as someone who doesn't take your job or your profession seriously.

These methods in writing for a class, or indeed for any purpose, are not helpful and may mean doom for your grade or your job.

Test It Out

You can test it out for yourself, at least roughly, by trying out some crucial aspects of writing a paper, just to see how you do before you begin to immerse yourself in the critical writing processes detailed in this book. Again, each of these aspects is crucial not just for writing a paper for school but for almost any professional writing you do after school is over. The three aspects are, roughly, (a) *being clear about the main thing you'll be trying to say* in your paper as a whole, (b) *identifying the main points* you will be making in the paper and organizing the writing logically, in a way that makes sense, and (c) *being trustworthy* in what you are saying—knowing what you are talking about, having enough knowledge and understanding of what you are saying so that the reader can rely on what you are saying.

Test It Out #1: Being clear about the main thing you will say in the paper. Writing instructors often use the term "thesis statement" (or "thesis"). Not everyone uses that term, but the basic idea of it is straightforward: it's the main thing you will be saying about whatever topic you are writing on. It's the (a) mentioned in the previous paragraph. Part of the challenge in coming up with a thesis statement is coming up with one that is specific and focused enough for you to build a meaningful paper around it.

The self-test, then, is about writing down a thesis statement for a paper of an assigned length—five pages would be a good length to choose. Start by picking some topics that matter to you. Maybe global warming is one, or a favorite writer, or a personal issue in your life. It might be your reaction to something you've read or viewed, or it might be some topic related to your course material. Try it out with just one topic at first, then try it with several others just to get the feel of it. For each one, the self-test is:

Write a thesis statement.
(That is, write out a single specific, focused statement that expresses the main thing you will say about your topic.)

[When you have a few candidates written, you can get feedback by looking at the Self-Assessment section "Test It Out #1," located right after Chapter 2. But don't shortchange yourself: don't look ahead until you've given it an honest try—in writing, not just in your head.]

Test It Out #2: Organizing the main points of the paper. A thesis statement is not enough. You're not literally trying to say just one single thing in a paper (or really in anything else that you write). If that was all you were doing, your paper would be just a single sentence. Instead, your paper needs to be organized logically around a set of main points you will be making in it. Main points can work in different ways: they might, for example, be the main aspects of the thesis statement that you want to explain or emphasize, or the way you support it, or the main information you are giving about it, or the main conclusions you are drawing from it.

In effect, you will be saying something like this:

Here is the thesis of my paper_____, and here are the main points I'll be making in relation to that thesis:

A. _____,
B. _____,
C. _____,
D. _____.

This second self-test #2, then, is related to the first one: to figure out the main points you'll be making in your paper:

Take the best thesis statement you just came up with and decide on the main points you will make about it in your paper.

Again, try it more than once, for more than one thesis statement, and for each one, look for three or four such main points—so you can get the feel of the task facing you. (If you don't like the thesis statements you've already come up with, you can try out some new ones.)

[As with the previous test, there is a Self-Assessment section on "Main Points." This time it's located right after Chapter 3. You can use it to get feedback on how well you did. But, above all, don't look at it until you've actually tried writing out your own main points.]

Test It Out #3: Being trustworthy. Most of the time, writing a good paper involves at least some research. That's because you have to know what you're talking about. If you say X, Y, and Z in your paper, readers need to be able to trust it. That's true whether your readers are your teachers, your employers, your colleagues or clients, or people who are important in your personal life. People have to be able to rely on what you are saying.

That means that you either already have to know what you're talking about or have to find out about it. Finding out about something is *research.* Probably, you need to do some research as part of both identifying a solid thesis statement and figuring out the main points you will be making.

But research doesn't do the work for you. It won't "give you" your thesis statement, and it won't give you your main points either. It may give you information that helps you choose your thesis and main points, but it won't give you the points themselves. You yourself have to find them, select them from among many possibilities, choose the ones most worth emphasizing, organize them, elaborate on them, and explain them.

The third self-test, then, is different from the first two. You can think of it as being about research, but it actually taps into your concept of what writing a paper is all about. Being trustworthy involves owning up to the realization that whenever you say anything in your paper, you are *vouching* for it.

Sometimes people's concept of writing a paper is that it's just jumping through hoops, something you have to get through to get to what's important. Writing a paper using critical thinking is different. It involves taking ownership of your paper and of the ideas in it.

The focus of this self-test is on how to go about writing a paper that someone can trust. To make it concrete, imagine that you are taking a course that has a required paper, and your assigned topic is on "the stages Lincoln went through on the way to issuing the Emancipation Proclamation." **Important:** If this was an actual paper you were writing, you would, of course, actually have to *do* the research and actually *find* information, but that's not what this self-test is about. Also, to try this self-test, you don't already have to know anything about Lincoln or the Emancipation Proclamation.* Instead, this is a self-test on the *process* you would go through. It's a self-test on what you see yourself doing in order to write the paper.

Self-test #3, then, is:

Describe how would you go about writing the paper.

[There is a Self-Assessment section on "Being Trustworthy," located right after Chapter 4. But again, don't look at it until you've described what you would do.]

All three of the self-tests focus on aspects essential to writing a paper. When you write, you have to have at least one central thing that you're trying to convey. There have to be main points in what you are saying, ones that fit together. And you have to know what you're talking about.

So some questions may be coming up for you now, such as:

- I get that I should have a thesis statement. But how do I come up with one? (Especially one that's specific and focused enough?)
- How do I figure out the main points?
- Even if I come up with a thesis statement and all the rest, how do I do the actual writing? How do I fill X number of pages?
- What about writing-problems not covered in this book? How do I deal with *those*?

---

*If you feel at a complete loss about the Lincoln example, change the assignment to some other important event in the past, one that you would have to research. It could be the stages on the way to a discovery in science, a national or international event, a ruling in law: almost anything.

- I understand that my writing needs to be clear, but how do I make it clear? (It looks clear enough to me.)
- Isn't it going to take too long to do this? (I have a lot of other things I have to do besides writing this paper.)
- And what about references, and plagiarism, and other points of view, and good grammar, and all the other parts of writing?

The aim of this book is to spell out directly usable concepts and processes of critical thinking that enable you to do all of those.

So, back to the question "Why do this?"

The starkest answer is that what people usually do when they write papers just doesn't work very well. Their papers often go all over the place, with no central thing they are trying to say, or only a very unfocused one. They often don't have a logical organization in their paper, or start off with a plan for their main points, and so they often don't know what they are going to say until they say it. They often don't write based on their understanding, but rather on bits and pieces they've picked up somewhere, and they end up saying things that people might never want to rely on or trust. If there is a page requirement, they often run out of things to say before they reach it. They often don't revise, and if they do revise, they often don't know how or what to revise. They frequently use unreliable sources.

But there is reassurance that comes in using the concepts and processes of critical thinking:

- You will find that it is well within your ability to write papers that show rich critical thinking.
- You will find that though some parts of critical writing may be hard, many are not. Some will even be easier.
- You will begin to see how critical thinking skills will benefit you in all the writing you do, not just in one course but in others as well, and in the writing you do professionally long after school is over.
- You may find that even the harder parts are well worth it, in terms of both grades and self-empowerment.

A Few Things to Keep in Mind as You Work through This Book

First, there is no formula for writing well. This book guides you through a framework for critical writing, one that can help in a deep and direct way. But with every aspect of the framework, you have to *think through* what you're doing, maybe considering alternatives, maybe looping back and forth or changing your mind. There is no linear, step-by-step procedure.

Why not?

Well, for many reasons, but mainly because step-by-step mechanical processes are unrealistic when you are dealing with complex issues and problems. In other words, any real situation that is even slightly complicated has too many variables and subtleties for it to be captured in a mechanical formula. Complex, real-life situations require critical thinking.

Another thing to keep in mind as you read the book is to make the best use you can of the extended examples by using them as ways to prompt your own thinking. The examples show students working through the process of writing critical thinking papers, but the examples are designed so that you yourself can work through the same processes along with the student. Though the students are fictitious, their responses are chosen to bring out important aspects of writing a paper. The examples are intended to depict not just the *results* of their thinking but the actual *processes* they might go through to arrive at those results. The student responses show only one way of thinking through the issues they confront. Your own way would be different and might in fact be better than theirs. Their responses were not chosen because they are perfect or the best way. They were chosen as genuine and reasonable ways to address challenges anyone faces— students as well as professionals—in writing something significant.

To get the most out of them, try not to read the examples just passively. Their value lies not so much in the specific answers the students come up with, but in the way they go about coming up with their answers. Again, the best way to use them is to put yourself in the mind of the students in the examples, to see how they are working through a given aspect of critical writing, and to follow along with their train of reasoning (while maybe being aware of how you might respond differently). You can get feedback on our own thinking from the students' thought processes, and also from the commentary that accompanies some of the examples.

Finally, a major way to approach critical writing is the one mentioned at the beginning: to let your concept of writing a paper change and deepen. In this book, it is called writing with engagement.

What that means, roughly, is taking it seriously. It's the opposite of just going-through-the-motions. It means trying to get something valuable from the process.

Though you may not use the word *engagement*, it is something you know from other contexts of your life. In almost any domain, you see people who are just going through the motions. You may have friends who are like this: they do the things that are part of being a friend—but still their heart isn't in it. They are not *engaged* in the friendship, and it means that you probably can't rely on them in a real crisis. You can probably think of similar instances from any important domain of human experience, in politics, religion, science, parenting—in anything that makes for a meaningful life.

This book advocates *engagement*. It involves seeing writing as a way of enriching your life, and thus as something worth taking seriously.

Acknowledgments

It gives me a rich sense of pleasure to extend my deepest thanks to those who have generously given me invaluable help on the ideas and the writing of this book: Barash Ali, Rachael Collins, Francis Coolidge, John Draeger, Nicole Fargo Nosich, Annemarie Franzyk, Amanda Hiner, Balaji Janamamchi, Jon Kalagorgevich, Ann Kerwin, Andy McCaffrey, Matthew Nosich, Karthik Orukaimani, Patty Parsons, Ann Pearson, Wil Smith, Jean Walker, Chuck Witte, and Marlys Witte; to the members of NOMC; to Mark Kerr, Courtney Packard and Patricia Stevenson at Rowman & Littlefield; and, of course, to Richard Paul and Linda Elder.

CHAPTER 1

Thinking about Writing

Writing and Critical Writing

Thinking is inseparable from writing. And critical thinking is inseparable from critical writing.*

In writing you are expressing thoughts in written form. The thinking, and the writing that expresses that thinking, can be reasonable, or not; coherent, or not; well thought out, or not. "Criticality" is what turns writing into critical writing.

Critical writing is not writing that emphasizes the negative side of things, and being a critical thinker does not imply that the person is coldly rational or is putting aside all emotional considerations. It is not merely writing out thoughts that happen to come to mind, even if you are a pretty good thinker. Instead, being a critical thinker means paying attention, in an explicit way, to what is

---

Before You Begin

Using concepts and processes of critical thinking can have immediate and far-reaching results for your writing, and the new skills you'll develop can start to feel natural. But this makes it easy to lose sight of the advances you've made. You need some way to see the changes in your writing and thinking.

The suggestion, then, is that you write a baseline paper now, before working through any of the techniques in the book. Choose some topic to write on, one that's of interest to you, or one that fits with the goals of the course you are taking, or maybe an instructor will assign you a topic.

Afterward, put the paper away and don't look at it until the end of the course.

---

*In this book, *footnotes* (such as this one) give information that is intended to be directly helpful. They are designated by a symbol such as *. *Endnotes* (designated by numbers) are primarily used to list references, but they also sometimes contain further explanatory information. They are listed in a section at the end of this book.

important in coming to a well-thought-out judgment about the issue at hand, including thoughts, facts, data, emotions, passions, and anything else that is relevant, including both positives and negatives, along with aspects you may have overlooked.

In writing, the result of this critical thinking process is a paper that has strong reasoning at its center. It is a paper that is powerful both in ideas and in the communication of those ideas to the audience. It is a paper that takes the reader to the heart of the issue the writer is addressing. It is a paper that gives insight. It is fresh, compelling and convincing. What gives these results is paying close attention to the reasoning in the paper.

In your own papers, then, the difference between "just writing" and "critical writing" will depend on how explicit and focused you are on making your writing well reasoned or well thought out. It will depend on how aware you are of the factors that make a piece of thinking or writing reasonable, on how clearly you think through the issue, and on how explicit and mindful you are in addressing those factors.

What are those factors? What exactly do you pay close attention to when you write critically?

There are several of them, and key ones will be spelled out in this book.[1] They fall into different categories. First, when you write something critically, one major dimension you pay attention to is your thinking itself: you're aware of what your *purpose* is in your paper, what *questions* you are addressing, what the *implications and consequences* are of saying X rather than Y, and so forth. These are the parts of your thinking or reasoning. They are called *the elements of reasoning.*[2]

A second factor you pay close attention to is the quality of your thinking. Using your best judgment, you ask yourself whether what you're saying is *accurate*, whether it is *clear*, whether it is *relevant* to the issue you're addressing, and so forth. Quality terms, such as these, are evaluative terms. They are *standards for critical thinking.*[3]

In addition to these two categories, in critical writing you also pay attention to *yourself* as you write. You may ask yourself, "Do I need to think about this point at greater length?" "Should I say X (which I believe is true), or should I say Y (which is what I think the teacher agrees with)?" "It seems risky to write this idea—should I say it anyhow?" "Am I approaching this issue in a biased way?" These are questions about *intellectual perseverance, intellectual integrity, intellectual integrity,* and *fairmindedness.* They are critical thinking *traits of mind* or *critical thinking character traits.*[4]

Closely linked to the traits, you may ask yourself about *impediments* you face as you reason through the paper you're writing. These can be practical difficulties, such as the limited amount of time you have for writing, or the knowledge that there are other things in your life that compete for your time and attention. But they can also be challenges directly related to the thinking in the paper, such as the strong tendency we all have to find reasons to justify our own beliefs and actions and those of the groups we belong to, often just because they are *our* beliefs and actions. Impediments such as egocentrism and sociocentrism can undermine even good-faith attempts to think things through.[5]

Finally, as you engage in critical writing, you pay close attention to the fundamental and powerful concepts that are central to all writing: *content, audience,* and *communication.* Adding *"criticality"*— the factors that make for critical thinking—as the fourth fundamental and powerful concept turns writing into critical writing. These four concepts enable you to address virtually any question or issue, in virtually any kind of writing. They are the concepts to keep in the front of your mind, shaping everything you do in writing: the *content* or message you are trying to convey in a particular context or situation, the *audience* you are trying to convey it to, the kind of *communication* you need to use to convey it, and the critical thinking concepts that guide you.

"Writing a paper." This book focuses on writing a paper. The emphasis is on the kind of paper you might write for a course or class, including courses specifically on writing or composition, as well as in courses in a subject matter (e.g., in the sciences, humanities, arts or professions). In addition, though, the concepts and techniques of critical writing apply to virtually any other writing you do: reports, essay exams, case studies, reviews, speech writing, personal statements for employment or graduate school, all the professional writing you will do in your future career, and so on.[6] Indeed, critical-writing skills, concepts, and habits of mind are central to virtually any writing people do in their lives. These concepts and habits may have to be adapted to fit other areas, but one of the great benefits of both critical thinking and critical writing is the way skills and habits of mind learned in one area can, with reflection, transfer across the domains of a person's life. In fact, people who come to embrace critical writing as an important part of their lives often find that it gives both a measure of personal power and a range of choices that vastly enrich their lives.

The Components of a Paper

One way of describing a paper is to look at the components that make it up.

It begins with **planning**. You start off with a **topic** and then with a far more focused **thesis statement**. The topic is the general subject you'll be writing about, and the thesis statement (often called just the thesis) is, roughly, the specific claim you want to put forward about that topic. It is stronger than that though: the thesis statement is not just the claim you'll write *about*: it's the claim your whole paper will be centered on.

In addition, your paper will have **main points**. These will usually explain, support, or elaborate on your thesis statement. (Sometimes you also back up those main points with further supporting points.) Altogether, the thesis plus the main points constitute the **structure** of your paper. (There is a sample diagram of a structure on p. 10.) As you write out the points of your paper's structure in words, you have an **outline** of your paper. (There is a sample outline of a paper on p. 13.) This outline—the composite of thesis and main points—is really the **plan** for your entire paper (though, of course, you can change it later).

Planning
    topic
    thesis statement
    main points
    structure/outline

Researching

Writing the Paper
    introductory section
    body
    concluding section
    giving credit

**Revising: Making the Paper
    Better**

Research is another essential part of writing a paper. People need to be able to rely on what you say in the paper. A good deal of your trustworthiness will depend on finding out about the topic, enough so you can stand behind the points you make about it. Research is not as separate from the other components as the diagram suggests. It will often play a role in the planning stage, in choosing a topic, as well as in coming up with a thesis statement and the main points of the paper. You may also need to do research while actually writing the paper (you may realize you need additional supporting points, for example) and sometimes when you revise.

Next you write the paper itself (or at least a draft of it). The paper begins with an **introductory section** and ends with a **concluding section**. Everything in between, the bulk of what you will be writing, is the **body** of the paper. There, you turn your plan—the thesis and each of the main points—into the actual paper.

There are two more components of writing a paper. One is **giving credit** to those whose ideas you have used in your paper. (This is not only a basic part of the writing process; it is also part of intellectual integrity.) You give credit usually with citations in the text of your paper, with references in footnotes or endnotes, and with a page titled "Works Cited" or "Bibliography" at the end (see p. 199). In addition, you will need to **revise** the paper, making changes, adding, subtracting, and sharpening it up. A good way to think about revising is that it's "making the paper better." This isn't something you do only at the end. It's something you do all the while you are writing.[*]

Benefits of writing critically. These components are essential, but they do not automatically turn your paper into a piece of *critical writing*. (An analogy: Your body may have all its essential components, but that doesn't automatically mean that it is healthy or that it functions effectively.)

The concepts and processes of critical thinking are what turn ordinary writing into critical writing. Most of this chapter centers on the components of a paper, whether it is written using critical thinking or not. The emphasis on *critical* writing comes in strongly from Chapter 2 on. The critical thinking tools are what give you the means to construct not just a thesis statement but a cogent, focused one—not just a plan but a logically organized plan, one built upon clear, accurate, relevant main points and based on both strong reasoning and sound research. The concepts of critical thinking similarly transform and re-shape all other components of writing a paper.

With practice, you will internalize many of the critical thinking concepts and processes and concepts so that eventually they will become simply part of the way you write, and part of the way you think as well. They will become part of your "voice" as a writer and thinker. For instance, part of what makes a point clear is giving *examples* of what you mean. So instead of just making an abstract point or writing out an idea you have, you will also give one or more examples of it. Giving examples makes the point more concrete and understandable

---

[*]Different instructors and other writing professionals use this traditional vocabulary of writing—topic, thesis statement, outline, structure and the rest—in different ways. There is no standard, set-in-stone way to use these terms. The goal is always to have a vocabulary that captures what is important in writing a paper. As with many other fields, you may have to adapt the vocabulary to your context. Some instructors and others dislike this vocabulary, seeing it as too limiting. Two central premises in this book are that the vocabulary is helpful rather than limiting and that the processes of critical thinking (from Chapter 2 on) give great flexibility and new vitality to these terms.

for your reader. It also makes your points more convincing. An enduring benefit, then, is that you may start giving examples as a matter of course, without even having to remind yourself to do so. You may start to give examples not just in writing a paper but when writing anything, or when speaking or just thinking as well. You will have internalized the practice of giving examples, and as a result everything you try to communicate will likely become clearer.

You already use the components of a paper. Seeing the components of a paper laid out in a box as on p. 4 can make them look too complicated. But don't let the terminology get in your way. They are not really complicated at all. It may not be easy to do all of them as well as you would like, but the components themselves are not complicated. A good deal of what makes it seem that way comes just from giving separate names to things you do almost automatically, not just in writing but also in casual conversation. (If you write out all the components of something as ordinary as playing a guitar or shooting pool, they also might seem overwhelming.)

As a comparison, suppose you are just talking about an issue, one that is personally important to you. Suppose you're talking with someone about whether Will is really a trustworthy friend to you. Your side of the conversation might go like this:

> I've been thinking about whether Will is really trustworthy as a friend, and I want to talk with you about it because more and more it seems to me that I shouldn't trust him as much as I thought I could. He's been talking about me behind my back, and he always seems to do what's good for *him*, without taking into account what's important to me.
>
> Last week he said some negative things about me to Susan. He said I hadn't lent him money when he asked for it. He also said that I was weird. That's not the way you talk about a friend.
>
> And every time we hang out, it has to be somewhere *he* likes. When we go to a movie, he wants to be the one to pick the movie. There are a lot of other examples too.
>
> That's not what friends do. They don't talk behind your back and they don't always put themselves first. I just don't think that Will is really trustworthy.

Think of this as an ordinary part of a conversation you might have with someone. You're trying to explain what you think about Will as a friend, and why you think so. Really, you're just talking about it. But if you look more closely, you can see in it virtually all the components of a paper. They are present in an abbreviated form, but they are still there:

Your **topic**: Will as a friend.

You have a **thesis statement**: Will isn't trustworthy as a friend.

You give three **main points** to back up your thesis. Two are about Will, and one is about what friends do and don't do:

> (#1) that Will talks about you behind your back;
> (#2) that he always seems to do what's best for him, without tak-
> ing into account what's important to you; and
> (#3) that that's not what friends do.

Though you probably didn't think of it this way, there is a definite **structure** to your explanation, and there is a sense in which you **outlined** it mentally as you spoke.

You also gave sub-ideas to back up your main points: you backed up #1 with the two things Susan reported to you (those were pieces of *information*); you backed up #2 with two personal experiences (more *information*); you didn't back up #3, but you could have spelled out more of your *concept* of what a friend is.

As you spoke, you gave an **introductory section**; you gave the **body** of your conversation by elaborating on the ideas in the thesis and main points; and you gave a **concluding section**. Because you were just talking casually, all these sections were very brief, but they were there. If the person you were talking to had asked questions, your treatment of these sections would probably have been filled out (or developed) a good deal more. You even—in an informal way—**gave credit** to one of your sources of information.

You didn't make any **revisions**, but that too was probably because it was just a casual conversation. But even that is something you could have done in a very natural way. For example, if you paused after the conversation, you might have qualified your account a little. You might have added:

> Well, Susan is the one who told me what Will said. I know that she's not always reliable. But in this case I believe her.

You might have revised your concluding section as well. You might have added:

> At the end, I said he wasn't trustworthy, and I know Will is your friend too. I really just mean that I think he isn't trustworthy as *my* friend.

Writing a paper may be a challenge for you. But the challenges are not built into the components themselves. Many times in writing you won't be exactly clear about what you're trying to say at the beginning of the process. That's something that also happens in conversations: we say the wrong words, we alienate someone we care about, and it is sometimes too late to take it back. Luckily, in a paper you can go back and make the changes to say things better—more clearly, more accurately, and more fairly—before you turn it in.

You will likely face difficulties in actually carrying out the planning and writing, or carrying them out well; there may be difficulties having to do with time, or motivation, or with your individual skills; there may be difficulties in getting clear in your own mind about what you are trying to say in your paper, and then in expressing it clearly to others. It is natural to have genuine difficulties like these. Many of them will be addressed in this book. But you should note that the methods and tools of critical writing (the ones that will be addressed more fully starting in Chapter 2) are intended to make the process of writing not only more successful and more reasonable but *easier* as well.

Getting Familiar with the Components of a Paper: Extended Examples

You can get a better feel for the components of a paper with a couple of examples. The examples are intended to help give an initial workable understanding of the components, particularly those in the planning stage. They are not intended as examples of *critical* writing: they do not show someone using the concepts and processes of critical thinking to write a paper. Rather, they show writers who get an idea for a *topic* that interests them and who then work to formulate a *thesis statement* and *main points*, who recognize where they need to do *research*. The result is an *outline* of the *structure* of the paper they plan to write.

As you read through the examples, try not to be affected by whether you think the example is well reasoned, or by whether you agree or disagree with the writer. Concentrate instead on seeing how the components take shape in the student's mind. Both of the examples go on for several pages, showing not just the end results but the thinking the writers engaged in to reach those end results. Note that there is a serious danger that you may be misled by the examples. First, having all the components of a paper is only a *minimal* requirement: they do not by themselves make a plan (or a paper) a good or a well-reasoned one. Second, though the examples show students thinking about a topic and constructing a plan, the examples do not show *how* to go about doing this in your own paper.

Example #1. Some background: James has a friend whose father recently was recently hospitalized for lung cancer (though he also has cirrhosis of the liver). It was clear that the diseases were the product of long-term use of alcohol and cigarettes. Though James felt bad about his friend's father, he was also shocked at the enormous medical expenses involved in treating the diseases. He saw that many of those expenses were covered by Medicare, and he concluded that this meant that he and other people like him were the ones who were really paying for all those expenses. To James, there seems something unfair about this situation. James has heard about what are called "sin taxes"—special taxes on harmful substances such as alcohol and tobacco. He reasons that sin taxes are a way to get people who smoke and drink to pay a bigger share of the money used to pay for their medical treatment. In the case of his friend's father, he is torn about where he finally stands on the issue, but, for now, he decides to pursue *sin*   **topic** *taxes* as the **topic** of his paper.

The main reason James chooses this topic is that he thinks that people like him—people who don't smoke or drink excessively—should not have to pay for medical care for the people who do smoke and drink. He writes down this basic idea and then decides that it is the main thing he wants to say in his paper. All he has to do is bring "sin taxes" into it, and he'll have it:

> **Thesis statement**. We should raise "sin taxes"
> on alcohol and tobacco and then use the money   **thesis statement**
> raised through these taxes to pay for the treat-
> ment of people who abuse those substances.

James realizes he may have to sharpen up his thesis statement, but he thinks he has made a good start. It is something he believes, and it is an issue that seems clearly important.

He now looks for the main points he will use to back up his thesis. He finds that he already has some of them. One is the statement he began with:

> **Main point #1**. People who don't smoke or drink   **main points**
> excessively should not have to pay for medical care
> for the people who do.

Next, though, James sees that he has to say why sin taxes would help with the problem. He writes several versions so that he will get the wording right, and he finally says it this way:

> **Main point #2**. The money from sin taxes can be used to pay
> for medical treatment that abusers of those substances bring on
> themselves.

The last phrase catches his eye, that it is something they "bring on themselves," and he realizes that this is a key part of his position. He reasons that people who abuse alcohol and tobacco do so by their own choice. It is *voluntary*. So they should pay for the effects of their substance-abuse themselves—by paying "sin taxes"—and not make other people pay for them. As he sees it, the "voluntary" part will make another good main point:

Main point #3. People *choose* to smoke and drink. It is voluntary.

James realizes that he needs to have some real data about how much it costs taxpayers to pay for medical treatment for people who smoke and drink. For this he needs to do some research. When he does a search on Google, he finds he has to bypass several websites because they might be biased or not reliable. He needs to find a *reputable* source. He finds one from the Centers for Disease Control. It is a ".gov" site and so likely to be more reliable than a political or a 12-step website. From one CDC site he finds that "the direct medical costs" of smoking tobacco are $96 billion per year, and he follows a link there to another article and finds that the healthcare costs of excessive drinking are $25 billion per year.

research

Main point #4. The healthcare costs of tobacco and alcohol in the U.S. amount to $121 billion per year.

It also occurs to him that he could calculate roughly how much individual Americans have to pay as their share of the total cost. That would give him a possible supporting point to back up #4.

The **structure** of his paper consists of the thesis, those four main points, plus the possible supporting point he came up with:

structure

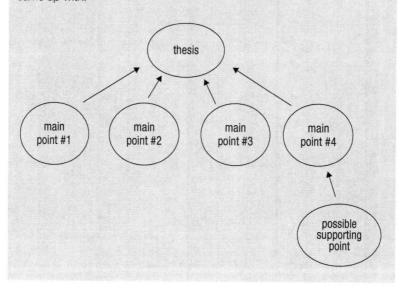

The structure and the outline of a paper convert naturally into one another. Thus, James's **outline** will consist of his thesis statement, plus his four main points, plus the possible supporting point as soon as he formulates it.

outline

With the thesis, structure and outline in front of him, James makes the judgment that he is in a strong position to write the paper itself. He now has a definite **plan**. In his **introductory section** he will state his thesis and summarize the main points he will address in the paper. To write out the **body** of his paper, he'll explain his thesis and each of the main points in turn. He figures that he will devote at least a paragraph to each of the points, probably more. In the **concluding section** he will again state his thesis, and he'll re-state the points he has developed in the body of his paper.

Back when he did the research for his main point #4, James carefully cut-and-pasted the reference information for the two websites he used. He needs that information in order to **give credit** to his sources, and having it already recorded will make his life easier. James is required to use an MLA format (see p. 198–201 for more on giving credit to sources). In accord with MLA guidelines, he will cite the sources in the actual text of his paper, and then he will include the full reference information in a "Works Cited" page at the end. His in-text citations and Works Cited references are in the endnote.[7]

giving credit

Example #2. Background: Sheila sometimes listens to NPR (National Public Radio) as she rides home from school, and she heard recently that tuition at public universities in some European countries has been going up. But what really surprised her was how low tuition was at those universities compared to the state university she is attending in the U.S. She heard that some German universities, even world-class ones, charge no tuition at all! She started thinking about the possibility of attending a university in Europe (some have classes in English) and working for her degree there. The countries she'd most like to study in are France and Germany, and she's heard that both of them have very low tuition. So she looks at some websites that list the costs of a university education in various European countries. The websites she consults also direct her to sites that rank universities around the world, and she notes that many universities there are very highly ranked, and many of them rank far higher than the state university in the U.S. she now attends.

She thinks about it and decides to write a paper for one of her classes on the topic of *tuition differences between public universities in the U.S. and Europe.* This is her **topic,** but she considers

topic

different versions of it. In the first version, the one·that had an impact on her, she would explain the main differences.

But a slightly different topic comes to mind: *the advantages and disadvantages of going to a European university versus a university in America.* With this topic, she would be not just explaining the differences but also analyzing the main advantages and disadvantages of each.

But she finds that she is upset by the idea that students in the U.S. pay so much more to go to a university than Europeans do, and so she moves to a third version. She decides to write a paper saying that American public universities should be as inexpensive as European universities are. (This is her **thesis statement**.) She reasons that if European countries can manage to provide a low-cost university education for their citizens, the U.S. should be able to do that too.

> **thesis statement**

She thinks of a number of points she could use to back up her thesis. She realizes that she's given one main point already in the reason she just came up with. Another point will contain the factual information from the research she's already done (such as the differences in tuition) and some further research she knows she'll have to do. (In passing, she also considers possibly trying to find out if there are differences in the availability of scholarships.)

> **main points
> research**

Sheila also thinks of additional points to back up what she is saying. One is that when people receive a university education, it benefits the society as a whole, so society should pay for at least a large part of it. Another is that American students leave the university with a huge student debt that burdens them for years to come. Another possible main point is that elementary, middle, and high school education are free in public schools, and she thinks that there is no good reason for free education to stop after high school.

Putting all these together, she has a specific **plan** for the paper she will write. The **structure** consists of her thesis statement plus the five main points to back it up, and the **outline** is just those six statements written out clearly. By following the outline, point by point, she will write out the **body** of her paper. In both the **introductory section** and the **concluding section** of her paper she will summarize those six points in a paragraph or two. But she recognizes that her thesis statement is the heart of her paper, so in both those sections she'll put the main emphasis on it.

> **structure
> outline**

Sheila's outline

#1. American universities should be as inexpensive as European universities are. [Her thesis statement.]

#2. If European countries can manage to provide a low-cost university education for its citizens, the U.S. should be able to do that too.

#3. In this point she'll give the information she's gathered from research: the different costs of a university education in Europe and in the U.S., the rankings of both European and American universities, plus any other relevant information she finds from further research.

#4. When people receive a university education, it benefits the society as a whole, so society should pay for at least a large part of it.

#5. American students leave the university with a huge student debt, one that burdens them for years to come.

#6. Elementary, middle, and high school education are free in public schools. There is no good reason for free education to stop after high school.

Sheila's efforts to **give credit** turn out to be more complicated than James's. She looks over at least half a dozen sites before she finds the ones she actually ends up using, and as a result she doesn't take down the reference information for them.   **giving credit**
She has to spend some frustrating time before she finds the references again. She is required to use Chicago-style formatting. The endnote here shows the way she cites her sources.[8]
She recognizes that she will have to **revise** her ideas and her writing as she works her way through the paper. She will   **revision**
also have to work on saying her points more clearly, and she is already considering dropping her main point #5 about student debt. (She thinks it's a good point, but she realizes that she has more than enough information supporting her thesis without this point.)

The two examples above bring out some essential features of a paper.

Topic. In this book the word "topic" is used in an intentionally broad way. Roughly, it just refers to whatever you choose to write about (though, of course, not every topic is worth writing about). Both James and Sheila start out with topics that are definite and fairly specific. But that will not always be the case. In fact, there was an element of luck in it for them: they both just happened upon something they wanted to explore or understand better. Many times you will start off with something much less definite than theirs. In this book, the topic you start from, subject to one or two conditions noted below, can be general or specific or anywhere in between. Readings are often a good source for topics, especially if you carefully summarize or analyze them. The topic you choose can come from ideas a writer is discussing in an article, or the topic can be the article itself. But there are other potentially rich topics as well: social issues, interpersonal situations, TED Talks and other videos, life problems, people's behaviors, and school subjects are just a few examples.

Many approaches to writing stress the importance of narrowing your topic down right from the beginning. There are great benefits to doing that, but often it just doesn't happen. You decide that you want to write something about dieting, say—a really general topic— but it just doesn't narrow down for you, especially not right at the beginning.

One of the great advantages of using the framework for critical thinking in this book is that it enables you to take even a vague, general topic and turn it into something definite, crisp, and focused. That is where the narrowing down takes place. Chapter 2 spells out a reliable, concrete way to focus your topic using the concepts of critical thinking. It's not a fool-proof process, but it is one that will yield focused results the way almost nothing else can. (Moreover, it is a process that not only narrows your topic down but also, as you'll see in Chapter 3, helps substantially in giving you a thesis statement, the main points you will be making, and most of the outline of your paper.)

Though the topic you start with can be general, there are two factors to keep in mind when choosing one. First, it is essential to choose a topic that is important to you and that you believe will be important to your audience as well. Both James and Sheila do this. Second, James and Sheila choose topics that they think might give them an *insight*. They both think that by exploring the topic they might come to some new understanding about it.

This second factor is not absolutely essential in choosing a topic—when you use the processes in Chapter 2, you might well gain insights that you hadn't envisioned at all—but it is highly advantageous. As much as possible, you should choose a topic where you have a reasonable chance of gaining some insight, an insight that you will be able to communicate to your audience.

Thesis statement. By contrast, thesis statements are radically different from topics. A thesis statement *says* something. It's not just a subject or area or topic you are writing about: it's a *statement*, one that says something specific and definite *about* the topic. But more than that, it is *the* main thing you are trying to say in your paper. Again, it is the statement your whole paper is built around.

The thesis of your paper can start out as an idea in your mind (as in James's case), or it can be something that comes to you only after research or after thinking about it for a while (as in Sheila's). It will very likely evolve and change as you think about it and write about it. Almost certainly you'll have to refine the wording of it. Both James and Sheila have already done some revision of their thesis statement, and they will probably do more as they work through the actual writing.

Main points. There is no set number of main points you need. Often they are based strongly on research (as in James's main point #4); at other times they are based in your own thinking (as in Sheila's main point #1).

Sometimes it's crucial to *refrain* from having a thesis statement until you've done the necessary research. In doing many kinds of research (a research paper in marketing, for example), having a thesis or hypothesis in your mind at the beginning can unconsciously lead you to distort the information you gather. It's called confirmation bias or researcher's bias.

There is another danger in having your thesis already established in your mind before you begin to plan out your paper. It's that your thesis should be the *result* of your reasoning process. Critical writing is not merely giving reasons in favor of beliefs you already hold. It also involves *coming to* reasonable beliefs as you think critically about your topic. So, for example, whether you are for or against capital punishment, it might be better to begin with the *question*: "*Should* capital punishment be abolished or retained?"

The plan for the paper: Its structure and outline. You can think of the structure of a paper as like the structure of a person's body: the bones fit together and interlock, forming a frame that enables the parts of the body to function as a coherent whole. In a similar way, the thesis statement plus the main points form the **structure**, the skeleton, of a paper. The **outline** of your paper is really just the same structure, but written out in sentences. The result is like a blueprint: a practical, definite plan you can follow as you do the actual writing.

This book strongly recommends the critical thinking processes in Chapters 2 and 3 as the best way to come up with a clear, accurate, important thesis statement, main points, as well as the structure and outline of your paper. In fact, since the processes in those chapters are based in substantive critical thinking, they are more reliable than the thesis statement that just pops out at you.

Reflecting on the Process of Critical Writing

There are also some things to notice about the *process* James and Sheila went through as they planned out their paper. These bring up themes that will be developed later in this book.

"Getting an idea." Notice that both James and Sheila just "get an idea" for their papers. They start with a topic, but then their thesis statements just seem to come to them before, during, or after research.

But that brings up some good questions to ask:

- How can you go about getting a thesis statement for your paper? (That is, not just a topic but a *thesis statement*: one that says something specific and limited enough to write about in the time and space available to you.)
- What if no idea for a thesis statement comes to you? What can you do?
- And suppose you do "get an idea" and a thesis statement just comes to you. What if it doesn't work out? Sometimes an idea can flash into your mind and seem brilliant, but in the end it doesn't pan out as accurate or logical at all.
- It is not enough for an idea just to be focused. How can you tell if it actually makes sense?

Kinds of writing. Different kinds (or modes) of writing can enter your paper.* Sometimes, your paper may be written using only one of them, but often more than one will play a role. Both James's and Sheila's papers are intended to be **persuasive** (or **argumentative**). They are both arguing for a position—trying to persuade someone to accept a conclusion they have come to. (James is arguing in favor of the view that sin taxes should be increased; Sheila is arguing that American universities should be as inexpensive as European universities.)

In **expository** writing, by contrast, the primary goal is to explain (rather than to argue for) something. Sheila's first idea for a paper is an example of this: her main goal was to explain tuition differences in the U.S. and Europe. (Her thesis statement in that expository paper would probably be: The main differences in tuition costs between European and American public universities are X, Y and Z.) Expository writing tends to present the writer's understanding of a topic.

---

*Some people use the term **genres** for these kinds of writing. More often, though, the term genre refers to broader categories (such as fiction, poetry or drama) or to more specialized categories (such as movie reviews or lab reports).

Analytic writing is similar to expository, but there is a difference in emphasis: in expository writing, you explain something; in analytic writing you explain the thing by breaking it down into its component parts. For example, much of this book is expository, but when it lists the components of a paper, the writing is more analytic. Similarly, Sheila's second idea for a paper—on "the advantages and disadvantages of going to a European university versus a state university in America"—would probably also have been mainly analytic. In it, she would not just explain the differences but also analyze and evaluate the advantages and disadvantages of both. **Research papers** tend to be primarily expository or analytic, usually a combination of both. (An extended example is on p. 52–55.)

Beyond these, other varieties of writing often work well in papers. In **descriptive** writing you are trying to convey a scene or experience by describing the way it looks and sounds, the way it feels, the tastes and smells that are present. Sensory details such as these communicate the experience to the reader in a way that abstract descriptions seldom do.

In **narrative** writing you tell a story. While this is, of course, central to fiction, in writing non-fiction (such as papers for classes) stories can set the scene for the content of the paper, help the reader empathize, and create striking examples and illustrations of points you are making. Both descriptive and narrative writing can bring vividness and expressiveness to your papers.

The terminology for such different modes of writing is less important than realizing that you have different kinds of writing available to you for making your papers better. Though there are important differences among them, critical thinking, as it is developed in the chapters that follow, helps with all of them.

One of the most empowering things about bringing critical thinking into your writing is that it gives you a way to address all four questions.

Research. Both James's and Sheila's papers involve research.

James does research to back up a major point in his paper with reliable data. Notice that he searches for *reliable* data. He doesn't just choose the first website that comes along. He searches for a reputable one. In any writing you do for school or in a profession, you are in fact vouching for what you say, giving your word about it: you have to have reliable information, and that almost always means research.

Both James and Sheila take the trouble to record the reference information about the sources they use. They **give credit** not just for data, and not just when they quote from a source. If they used ideas they got from a source, they would give credit for that as well.

"**Critical writing.**" Both James's and Sheila's plans seem in many ways to be well thought out. But an important thing to note is that both of them lack an account of *how* to come up with a well-thought-out plan. Because of this, to repeat something mentioned earlier, neither of them is an example of *critical* writing, of using the concepts and processes of critical thinking to write a paper. For example, neither writer examines the assumptions they are making or explores the implications of what they are saying in their papers. Similarly, they don't look for possible flaws in their own ideas or in their reasoning about those ideas, and they don't consider how other people, with different points of view, might reasonably see the issues in a different way.

This doesn't mean their papers are "bad." Indeed, they were chosen for this book because the plans, at least in a preliminary way, seem pretty strong and might result in solid papers. But there is a sense in which the strengths they have may be merely accidental. It looks as if both James and Sheila just *happen* to come up with strong main points. Nothing in their process shows how they might come up with an effective plan for their next paper. Moreover, though they display the various components of a paper, nothing in the examples shows you *how* to construct a well-thought-out plan for your own paper.

One of the great virtues of critical thinking is that it *does* show you how: how to come up with a strong thesis statement, main points and a logical outline of the whole; how to take account of your assumptions and implications; how to address flaws and different points of view; how to expand and enhance the quality of your papers; and much more besides. Critical thinking is the "*how*" of writing a strong paper.

Adapting Critical Writing to Your Own Individuality

The process of critical writing is not linear or rigid. The components (laid out on p. 4) logically have to be there in a paper, but nothing dictates the order in which you actually have to proceed. For example, some accomplished writers save writing the introductory section for last, when they are clearer about the structure of the paper they have just written. There has to *be* an introductory section in the paper, and of course it has to *be* at the beginning, but that doesn't mean it's the first thing you have to *write*.

But more than that, critical writing is a back-and-forth process in which your own strengths and your own goals play an essential part. The ideas you begin with strongly influence the writing of the actual paragraphs later on. But, just as strongly, writing the actual paragraphs will often show you how you need to change your initial ideas. As you proceed, the components—planning, writing, getting ideas, and making changes—all interact. You will often find that you start with some ideas of your own and from research; you put them together into a concrete plan with a thesis and main points, and then you start to write. But then as you write, you get new insights, your way of viewing the topic develops and matures, you end up changing the plan, revising the thesis, coming up with new main points, or pursuing an additional line of research—and that, in turn, changes the paper (which in turn generates still other new insights, and so forth).

This reverberating process is one of the main benefits of critical writing. It happens because effective writing involves your individual creativity in a major way. Writing is not just a matter of passively putting thoughts on paper, or cutting-and-pasting, or writing down what other people have said. Instead, writing is a way of constructing your own thinking about a topic. It is in fact a way to go about understanding something, making it a part of yourself. Research papers involve creativity just as much as other kinds of papers. A research paper requires something very different from just reporting what you find in an article or on a website. It involves putting sources together, integrating information, selecting what to include, coming to see how different aspects of the topic fit with one another, and then finally creating a whole.

As a result, papers you write will have a lot of "you" in them— your ideas, your research, your ways of putting ideas together, your creativity, your ways of constructing a whole. The methods in this book are open-ended: they may ask you to find an example for a point you are making, but the example will be one you yourself come up with; they may ask you to identify assumptions or draw conclusions, but the assumptions will be ones you yourself see, the conclusions are ones *you* come to. The concepts and processes in this book give a framework in which both criticality and creativity can work most effectively together.

Still, it is important to notice that, although the methods of critical writing are open, they are not "wide open." Some ways are more effective than others. It's not as if one way of writing is automatically as good as another. Compare it to a sport. There are many different ways of being a good tennis player. And among good tennis players, styles differ: the amount of running to the net, preferences for top-spin, reliance on counter-punching, and so forth. But this, of course, doesn't mean that one way of playing tennis is just as good as any other way. There are many *bad* ways of playing tennis. With both tennis and writing, even though you may have always done it in one way, or you're used to doing it that one familiar way, that doesn't mean that it is an effective way.

The methods and techniques in this book need to be adapted to the subject matter, to your personality and your skills as a writer, to the kind of writing you are engaged in, and to a host of other variables. The methods presented here are *good* ones. They enhance reasonableness, critical thinking, and organization. They make any paper you write more powerful and compelling. They address key steps in writing a paper. The suggestion, then, is that you make a good-faith effort to try the methods and concepts presented here, see how they work for you, and then evaluate whether using them makes your writing and your thinking better.

The Tasks That Lie Ahead

Think again about the components of a paper. What do you have to do with them to write a *good* paper? There is still the challenge of finding a topic that matters, one where you are likely to have something important to say about it. But beyond that, you have to:

- Topic
- Thesis, main points
- Researching
- Writing the paper
- Revising

1. give a critical thinking analysis of your topic so that you understand it and can write about it with authority and confidence.
2. come up with a thesis statement (ideally, a focused, limited, clear, plausible, supportable thesis statement).
3. come up with relevant and plausible main points to back up your thesis statement. Together with the thesis statement itself, these main points will let you construct a logical plan for your paper. The goal is for the whole structure to be coherent, strongly supported, and make sense overall.
4. use critical thinking to do whatever research is needed, first, to find out about your topic at the beginning, and maybe to find or formulate your thesis; and, second, to find information, data, evidence, and further reasons to make your points substantive.
5. identify those aspects of the paper someone might misunderstand, disagree with, or find insufficient.
6. write the paper itself: the introductory section, the body of the paper, and the concluding section, developing your main points,

seeing what is needed to make them coherent, clear, detailed, and substantive. (One way of saying this—a really misleading way—is to ask "How do I fill up X number of pages?")

7. revise and make the paper better (more coherent, more well thought out, clearer, more accurate), noticing what needs more support, elaboration, details, and so forth. (Socratic questioning, in Chapter 5, will help directly with this process.)

Addressing these seven problems is a major part of making your writing *critical* writing. You are thinking about your thinking, reflecting on what will make it better. Specifically, you are starting to address what will make the thinking in it become a more powerful piece of writing.

The explicit concepts and processes of critical thinking help with *all* of these. Moreover, they help not just slightly or tangentially but in a substantive, central way; not just at the beginning, or at this or that stage of the process, but all the way through. Even a little bit of critical thinking helps substantially, but as you increase and refine your skills, the process can be transformative. For some people there is a moment of epiphany: because critical thinking is far more focused than the way we ordinarily think, people often get an "Aha!" moment. Finally, though no one would say that critical thinking is easy, it is *sometimes* easy. A dramatically empowering fact about the tools of critical thinking that will be presented in the chapters ahead is that there is a sense in which they do a lot of the work for you. For this to happen, you can't use them mindlessly, you can't just "go through the steps" on auto-pilot. But if you engage with the concepts and processes, applying them to your writing can be surprisingly easy.

Writing for Clarity: SEE-I

A good way to make a start toward critical writing is to develop your ability to write more clearly.* A prime tool for making your writing (and your thinking) clearer is **SEE-I**. Not only will it make your writing clearer, but it will also give you a main way to fill out the body of the paper. It makes the task of writing not only better but easier. The initials stand for:

State
Elaborate
Exemplify
Illustrate

---

*The *standards* of critical thinking will be addressed in Chapter 5. Clarity is one of them.

- When you **state** something, you say it carefully and concisely, usually in a single sentence in which you try to capture the essence of it.
- When you **elaborate**, you then give further explanation. This takes a paragraph or two, or more (not just a sentence or two). In the elaboration you explain and expand on what you are saying and what you mean by it.
- When you **exemplify**, you give an example, a good one, carefully chosen to show the reader what you are saying. Examples tend to make the meaning concrete.
- When you **illustrate**, you give an analogy, a metaphor, a simile, a comparison, a picture or a picture-in-words of what you mean. A good illustration allows the reader to understand and relate to what you are saying.

Example: An SEE-I: This book talks about *critical* thinking and *critical* writing. But the term "critical" is one that often throws people off. What is *criticality*?

Let me clarify:

To **state** it:

When you are exercising criticality, it means you are reasoning things out, thinking them through, and, as you do that, you are also explicitly paying attention to how you are thinking about it and to whether you are doing it well.

To **elaborate**:

In other words, criticality has two main aspects. First, it involves reasoning something out. It could be something you're writing, but it could also be an issue you are working on, a question, a decision, a subject in school, a problem you face in your profession—almost anything. When you think things through, you are not just following directions blindly, or just hoping things will work out, or just engaging in some vague sense of "good thinking," or doing things because that's the way you've always done them. Rather, you are trying to understand them and figure them out.

Second, there is an explicitness to criticality. It involves paying attention—explicitly paying attention—both to *how* you are thinking and to *how well* you are thinking. When you focus on *how* you are thinking, you pay attention to aspects of your thinking you may have overlooked: You examine your *assumptions*, for instance; you look for the *implications* of what you are saying; you consider other *points of view*; you look at how you are *interpreting* the situation. When you focus on *how well* you are thinking, you ask yourself questions such as "Am I being *accurate* here?" "Am I addressing the most *important* aspect of this?" "Do I need to be more *precise* about this matter?"

When you think about something critically, you pay close attention to both its positives and its negatives, to what is strong about it as well as what is weak about it, to its parts as well as to it as a whole. Thus, engaging in critical thinking means you are not just relying on how you ordinarily think. You are thinking reflectively and consciously, trying to make your thinking better.

To **exemplify**:

For example, take listening to a political debate. If you think critically about the debate—if you exercise criticality—you will identify assumptions the candidates are making (as well as assumptions you yourself are making). In your mind, you will be asking them questions—tough questions: Are they facing up to the complexities of the issues? Are they clearly owning up to the implications and consequences of the actions they say they will take?

You will also focus on whether the candidates are truthful in the full sense of the word: Do they exaggerate in order to score points? Do they spin the issues?

You will also focus on your own judgments. Do you notice only positives about one candidate and only negatives about the other? Do you give weight to minor details such as the way they look, or slips of the tongue they make, rather than focusing on the heart of what they say?

You would make these judgments so that you can come to a well-reasoned and fair conclusion about the "whole": the candidates themselves, the way they will govern overall (not just on one issue); the way their values and abilities accord not just with your own interests but with the well-being of all.

To **illustrate**:

It's like having an MRI scanner. With an MRI scanner you can view organs and other structures in the body. The MRI allows you to distinguish between healthy tissue and malfunctioning tissue such as tumors, aneurysms, and arthritis. An MRI gives you a reliable picture of the way structures in the body are functioning or malfunctioning. Being a critical thinker is like having a portable MRI scanner to carry around with you. It gives you insight into people's thinking the way an MRI scanner gives you insight into people's health.

SEE-I clarifies and fills the pages of your paper. SEE-I is an incredibly useful critical thinking tool in writing almost anything, both in school and in the writing you do after you graduate. Applied to a paper, it provides you with a main way to do the actual writing.

When most people think of writing a paper, they tend to think not of the components of a paper as laid out on p. 4—topic, thesis statement, main points, all the way down to revision. Instead, they tend to think almost exclusively of only one thing: writing the body of the paper. What confronts them then is how to "fill up," say, a five-page paper. They state their thesis, and then they state the main points of their paper, but somehow many pages are still blank.

The problem, of course, is not how to "fill the pages," but rather how to fill the pages in a way that is relevant, that enhances the paper, makes it interesting to read, and communicates the content of the paper to your audience. So how do you do that more challenging task?

Illustrations. The illustration part of SEE-I is interesting. Some people seem to have a special gift for illustrations, coming up with comparisons or analogies that are striking and dramatically clarifying. Other people have to work to develop the skill of coming up with appropriate illustrations. (The author of this book is in the second category.)

Notice that examples and illustrations are quite different in SEE-I (even though the two words are often used synonymously in English). An *example* is an actual instance of the thing. (Take "studying for an exam": an *example* might be staying up all night making sure you understand the key terms in the course.) An *illustration*, by contrast, shifts to a different domain entirely. The illustration uses some other area we are already familiar with to help us understand the idea we are clarifying by giving something like a comparison, analogy or metaphor. (An *illustration* for "studying for an exam" might be: It's like making sure your parachute is well packed and up to specs before you go skydiving.)

The actual writing of the body of the paper is often called development, and SEE-I is a main way of developing the body of your paper. Maybe, in the end, it is *the* way to write the body of a paper. You can give an SEE-I for your thesis statement, for each of your main points, and for your second-level supporting points as well. For each of those, again, you *state* it so as to express the idea as concisely and exactly as you can. Then you *elaborate*. For any main point with any depth to it, this will take at least one full paragraph. Probably it will take several.

Then, again for each point, you give an *example*, one that displays well the point you are trying to make. Often the example also has to be explained, so the reader can follow just how it *is* an example of the point you are making. You may want to give more than one example in order to convey different aspects of the point you are making. Sometimes the example you give will be a story. In a paper about X you might give a story of something that happened to you or someone else in relation to X. Stories often convey points with an immediacy that brings the point home more directly than anything else. Finally, you give an illustration: an analogy, a metaphor, or a comparison that will vividly illuminate what you are saying.

By repeatedly stating, elaborating, and giving examples and illustrations, the pages will fill—the body of your paper will be written—in ways that are not merely relevant but also give substance to the bare bones of the points you are making.

"Staircasing" SEE-I. The usefulness of SEE-I goes further. Often, your thesis or main points will themselves contain important concepts or ideas within them. If you judge that it is valuable to do so, you can give an SEE-I for those concepts and ideas as well. This is called "staircasing" SEE-I. You can give an SEE-I for each point in your paper, but you can also give an SEE-I for every important part *within* each point. As an example, take the following statement:

> It is important to conduct research—even if the results seem obvious—because many of the things we "know" to be true turn out to be false when carefully inspected.

The sentence is actually from a book in psychology,[9] but you can see how it might be a main point in a paper you might write.

As already mentioned, you would develop the point itself with an SEE-I, elaborating on why we need to conduct such research and giving examples of things we thought we knew but that turned out to be false. You might give an illustration (maybe a comparison to trusting people who turn out not to be trustworthy).

But **staircasing** lets you go deeper into the statement and gives you a way to develop your thinking and writing to a much greater degree. You can proceed by drawing a circle around important ideas in the point. Thus you might choose "research" as a focus for staircasing, draw a circle around it, and then give an SEE-I for *it*. You would then state what research is, elaborate on it (by, for example, discussing different kinds of research), give examples of what is and isn't "research," and come up with a good illustration.

That's one thing you could staircase, but there are others as well, all centered on that one sentence. You could choose "carefully investigated" as a focus, draw a circle around it, and then explain what makes an investigation careful versus sloppy, exact versus vague, intensive versus casual. You could also draw a circle around the word "important" and focus on just how it's important: Is it merely finding out new facts, or are there practical ramifications as well?

Just ponder for a moment how it would enrich a paper to state, elaborate, exemplify, and illustrate all the ideas packed into the original sentence. It is conceivable that someone could write an entire paper on the meaning packed into that one statement (in fact, there are whole books that, in essence, do precisely that).

SEE-I gives you choices and opportunities. Again, you don't *have to* do any of this further development—but you can. What SEE-I gives you is *choices*, not obligations. That is part of what makes it so powerful.[*]

Like other critical writing processes, it's not a rigid procedure. Though SEE-I says "*elaborate* in a paragraph or two," you may decide to write more than that. It says to "give an *example*," but you might decide you can make your paper better by giving several. You may decide to give examples as part of the elaboration, or to further elaborate on the examples you give (the SEE-I on *criticality* does both of these). *Illustrations* are in fact another choice, rather than an obligation.

> **SEE—and sometimes I**. Illustrations can make your writing vivid. Problematically, though, having too many of them can be distracting. (That is why illustrations come in only from time to time in this book.) You may find that your paper is becoming overloaded with illustrations or that the ones you've come up with don't really bring home the point you are trying to make. Instead of having an abundance of different illustrations, you may decide to search for one really powerful analogy or comparison that makes not just that main point but the whole paper clearer and more forceful.

Whenever you are communicating with someone, in writing or in conversation, in any context, in school or outside, you can freely choose what you want to make clear, and SEE-I gives you the tools for it.

---

[*]The treatment of SEE-I here will be refined and expanded in Chapter 3 and then again in Chapter 5. When you add Socratic questioning to it (Chapter 5), it will give you an amplified set of tools to fill the pages of your paper and let you write multifaceted descriptions and explanations, with compelling details, greater precision, depth and significance.

SEE-I is so useful that it is hard to overstate its importance. Here's a question:

> How do you actually *do* the writing? After the planning stage, how do you actually go about writing the paragraphs?

A main answer to this is SEE-I:

> You use SEE-I for every important idea in your paper. You use it for your thesis statement, for every main point, and for all second-level supporting points. You use it (staircasing) for every important part within every major point, and for any other concepts or issues that you decide to explain further or that the reader may not understand in exactly the same sense you do.

A Framework for Critical Writing

This book presents a framework for critical writing. Remarkably, a major part of writing a paper comes down to mastering just two critical thinking techniques. One of the things you need is a *plan* for the paper, an outline, the full thesis and main points you will write about. Then, second, you need to turn that plan into the words on the page. You need to *write* the paper.

One of the critical writing processes gives you the plan. It is called "analyzing around the circle" (or "going around the circle"), and it is by far the best way to give a critical thinking analysis of a topic you choose. The analysis helps you take the topic apart, to see the logic of it. Moreover, that analysis will then give you a straightforward way of constructing a well-thought-out plan for your paper: your thesis statement and the main points you need to back it up or explain it.

The second process is SEE-I. Once you have your plan, SEE-I is perhaps *the* main way to do the actual writing. You write the paper by taking every main point and every important aspect of a main point and stating, elaborating, giving good examples and helpful illustrations. As you do that, your paper builds, sentence by sentence, paragraph by paragraph.

You have to use both processes thoughtfully, and using them well is sometimes challenging. You will also have to combine them with other aspects of critical writing. But with them, you will be able to generate a paper that is powerfully reasoned and often insightful. Of course, using critical thinking concepts and processes won't *guarantee* that your paper will be fully sound. Nothing can guarantee that. But it will make your paper the strong product of your best thinking. One additional technique—using Socratic questioning, the subject of Chapter 5—will help expand, deepen and improve your paper significantly.

A Framework for Critical Writing: A GPS

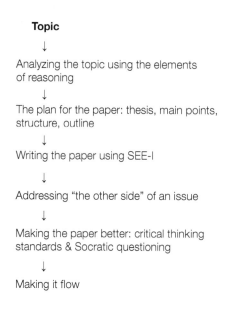

Topic
↓
Analyzing the topic using the elements of reasoning
↓
The plan for the paper: thesis, main points, structure, outline
↓
Writing the paper using SEE-I
↓
Addressing "the other side" of an issue
↓
Making the paper better: critical thinking standards & Socratic questioning
↓
Making it flow

All the way through:
- research
- critical thinking standards
- revision
- fundamental & powerful concepts
- giving credit

You can use the framework as a kind of GPS for your writing. Though it is not really linear, you can use it to locate yourself in the process, giving direction to the enterprise of critical writing. As you work your way through the framework during the course of this book, you may notice how critical thinking concepts re-shape and enrich the bare components of writing a paper on p. 4. As you progress through the planning and writing, you will see how parts of the framework fall into place, inter-weave, and put your writing far more within your own control, your own skill-set, your own expertise.

Walking through the framework. You begin with a topic. Though it is helpful if it is already focused, at this point the topic can even be a general one. It is something you see as worth learning about, thinking about, and writing about. It is something you can engage with.

   Chapter 2 introduces you to the *elements of reasoning*. These elements allow you to analyze a topic. The analysis will give you a deeper, clearer, more specific understanding of whatever issue, situation, or subject you will be writing about, and in the process, it also brings a level of focus that is almost unachievable in any other way. It lays the groundwork for everything that follows.

Chapter 3 takes you through three further parts of the framework. With the critical thinking analysis in hand, you will be able to generate virtually the full plan for the paper. From it you will be able to see or construct a strong workable thesis statement, plus the main points to back it up or explain it. That same analysis will also guide you in your research, making it far more productive, relevant and focused. You write the paper itself—the actual sentences and paragraphs of it—by using SEE-I for every important point and for every important part of every point.

Chapter 4 shows how, as you work your way through planning and then writing the paper, you address "the other side": how other people with a different point of view might disagree with you or find important aspects missing in your coverage of the topic.

Chapter 5 demonstrates how you monitor what you are planning and writing by using critical thinking standards, checking to see that points you are making are clear, accurate, relevant to the issue at hand, and so forth, and you revise as you go along. Socratic questioning allows you to make your paper substantially better, enriching and expanding it almost at will.

Chapter 6 is on making your paper flow. It lays out the fundamental and powerful concepts of critical writing—content, audience, communication, and criticality. These four concepts pervade everything having to do with writing of any kind. They give you the most promising means for addressing any problems or issues that come up for you, not just in this paper but also in any other writing you may do in the future.

Chapter 1: Practice and Assessment Exercises

A note on the exercises. In all the chapters, the practice and assessment exercises are aimed at providing ways to practice internalizing and applying the concepts and processes of critical writing, and then to let you assess how well you did. They will usually require a substantial amount of writing on your part. That's because, as with any other set of skills, to write well, you have to write a lot.

There are themes that will run through the exercises to all the chapters. There are questions asking you to:

- identify and write about the main concepts and processes in the chapter;
- identify and explain what you see as the main intended outcomes for that chapter;
- apply your own criticality and creativity to re-think and maybe improve on the extended examples given in the book (in Chapter 1, for example, to build on James's plan for a paper on sin taxes);

- tell your own story, reflect on your own experiences, and create a personal narrative;
- write about writing.

Notice that the point of the exercises is not primarily to review the concepts and processes in the chapters. The point is to internalize those concepts and processes well enough to use them with assurance. Moreover, as mentioned in Chapter 1, critical writing is organic, not linear. That means that, as in learning to play a sport, you are learning a large number of skills at the same time, not one after the other. Because of the organic nature of writing a paper, the exercises sometimes bring in concepts that extend beyond what is covered explicitly in the chapter, and they sometimes ask you to do some thinking and writing about concepts and processes that will not be explored deeply until later in the book. (These will be concepts and processes that you are already familiar with implicitly. For example, *research* will not be explored extensively until Chapter 3, but you already have at least a rough concept of what it is—in its broadest sense, it is how you find things out—and so you are asked to reflect on it a little in the exercises to Chapter 1.)

Starred questions. To help you assess your writing and thinking, the questions marked by a star (*) have a feedback section beginning on p. 219 at the end of the book. In critical writing (and in critical thinking generally), there will often not be one and only one correct answer to the question, but there will always be reasonable and unreasonable answers. The responses in the feedback section will at least be well-reasoned ones. Sometimes a response will be only a commentary on the question or on one possible way of addressing it, or sometimes only a further question that might arise.

A major problem is that, for most people, it is almost impossible to keep from looking at the answers in the feedback section *before* they give their own responses. Unfortunately, the only way these will really work for you is if you give your own answer first, and only *then* look at the feedback.

*1. **Write about writing.** The title of this book is *Critical Writing: A Guide to Writing a Paper Using the Concepts and Processes of Critical Thinking.* What are the main critical thinking *concepts* and *processes* in Chapter 1? (Try doing this without looking back at the chapter.)

   After you have identified them, write out an SEE-I for each of them.

2. **Tell your own story.** What are some experiences in your life that led you to be where you are with respect to writing? In a page or

so, describe the experiences by using SEE-I to develop them. (Try to incorporate the statement, elaboration, examples, and illustrations into your description in a natural, flowing way, without explicitly labeling them with S, E, E or I.)

3. In your own words, explain the components of a paper.

*4. Suppose X writes a paper that contains *all* the components. Does that show that it is a good paper? Does it show that it is based on critical thinking?

Practice: SEE-I

*5. In James's plan for a paper on "sin taxes," he came up with a thesis statement and four main points. Here is one of his main points:

> **Main point #2.** The money from sin taxes can be used to pay for medical treatment that abusers of those substances [tobacco and alcohol] bring on themselves.

Put yourself into James's point of view and write out an SEE-I for that main point as you think he would.

Practice SEE-I: *state*

The next two questions contain prompts. Prompts are often given as topics to write about, either for courses or as part of a test such as the SAT. For each, write a **statement** in your own words of what it means: a single, clear, concise sentence (maybe two).

*6. A quotation from Aldous Huxley. It is given as a prompt for paraphrase by the Foundation for Critical Thinking:[10]

> The propagandist's purpose is to make one set of people forget that certain other sets of people are human.

7. A prompt given by the SAT for its writing exam in SAT II (reported by the *New York Times*):[11]

> There is always a however.

Practice SEE-I: *elaborate*

*8. How do you elaborate? How do you go about explaining more fully, in a paragraph or more? What if you run out of things to say?

For practice, look back at the elaboration-part you wrote for Question 2. How full was your elaboration there? What are some ways you could have expanded your elaboration and made it fuller and clearer? The real question here is not about elaborating more fully on the specific responses you gave in Question 2. The real question is about reflecting on paths you can follow to give better elaborations in *anything* you write.

Practice SEE-I: *exemplify*

*9. Here again is James's main point about sin taxes:

> **Main point #2.** The money from sin taxes can be used to pay for medical treatment that abusers of those substances [tobacco and alcohol] bring on themselves.

Here are two *examples* James might give in his SEE-I for the same main point as in the previous question.

> For example, if you do something, you have to take responsibility for the consequences of what you do. It's up to you.

> For example, if you drive your car into a pole, you are the one who should have to pay for it.

What do you think?

Practice SEE-I: *illustrate*

*10. Come up with an illustration for the concept of "democracy."

11. In your own words, what is the difference between an *example* and an *illustration*?

Practice: *staircasing*

*12. James decides to staircase his main point #2 (given in question 3). He reads it slowly and carefully, looking for parts or aspects of it he might focus on. He can then use an SEE-I to expand on those and make his paper clearer and more substantial.

   What is a focal point in it that you might choose to staircase? Write out an SEE-I for it.

*13. Suppose you are Sheila and have to expand your paper. Here is one of her main points:

> **Main point #5.** American students leave the university with a huge student debt that burdens them for years to come.

What are some focal points in her main point #5 that you might choose to staircase?

14. James's thesis was that we should raise "sin taxes" on alcohol and tobacco and then use that money to pay for the treatment of people who abuse those substances. But James was uneasy about his position from the beginning. On p. 18, it was noted that James did not consider how other people might disagree with him, and he decides to take some other points of view into consideration. (He can make a decision about whether to include those other points of view in his paper.)

Put yourself in James's mind. What are some other points of view you might consider?

*15. **Write about writing.** You may at this point feel overloaded with using SEE-I. Why is it being emphasized so much?

16. Take *gun control* as a topic. If you were going to write a paper that was primarily argumentative or persuasive about this topic, what would it look like?

If you were going to write a paper that was primarily expository or analytic about this topic, what would it look like?

How might descriptive or narrative writing function in a paper on this topic?

17. Without looking back, what is something you learned in Chapter 1? It might be an idea you hadn't encountered before, or one you hadn't thought about in quite that way before.

18. **Find a topic.** Choose something you are reading, one that interests you. Take as your *topic* either the reading as a whole or an important idea in the reading. Give an SEE-I for it.

19. Choose some topics that you are interested in, ones that you believe you could write about in an informed, interesting way for, say, five pages. Find at least five or six. At this stage they can be topics that are already focused in your mind, or they can be general topics.

For at least some of these, you can probably see that you will need to do some research on them to write a good paper. How would you go about researching them?

In later chapters, you may be asked to think critically about some of these topics (though you may choose alternative topics later) and to write about them using the concepts and processes of critical writing.

CHAPTER 2

Beginning the Paper: The Elements of Reasoning

The box on the right—the "GPS"— shows where you are in the critical writing process. This chapter is on how to "analyze" a topic. Specifically, it is on how to analyze a topic "around the circle." Learning to give a reasoned analysis of a topic puts virtually everything else in your grasp. Analysis around the circle is one of the most powerful tools in critical thinking.

> **GPS**
> - **topic** →
> - **analysis ("around the circle")** →
> - plan: thesis, structure, outline →
> - writing →
> - "the other side" →
> - improvement →
> - flow

Introducing the Elements of Reasoning

Once you choose a topic, the starting point is to develop your thinking about it, and then to move from there to a concrete, articulated plan for your paper. The plan has the thesis statement at its heart as well as the other main points you will use as the structure and outline of your whole paper. The plan is what brings cogency and logical organization to your whole paper. The **elements of reasoning** are the tools both for developing your thinking about the topic and for constructing a strong overall plan.[*]

---

[*]As mentioned in Chapter 1, a good initial source for exploring the elements is Paul and Elder, *The Miniature Guide to Critical Thinking: Concepts and Tools*, and Elder and Paul, *The Thinker's Guide to Analytic Thinking*. The "elements of reasoning" are also called the "elements of thought."

The Elements of Reasoning

The elements of reasoning, eight of them, are displayed in the circle below.[1] These eight identify *the parts* of the reasoning process. To say these are "the parts" of reasoning means this: Whenever you are reasoning about something, thinking about something, trying to figure something out, all eight of these elements are present in your thinking:

- you have a *purpose*; you have *goals*;
- you are addressing some *question at issue*, some *problem*;
- you are making *assumptions*;
- you are using *information*;
- you are employing *concepts*, using key *terms*;
- you are drawing *conclusions*; you are *interpreting* what is going on;
- you are thinking about it from some *point of view*; and
- there are *implications and consequences* of your thinking.

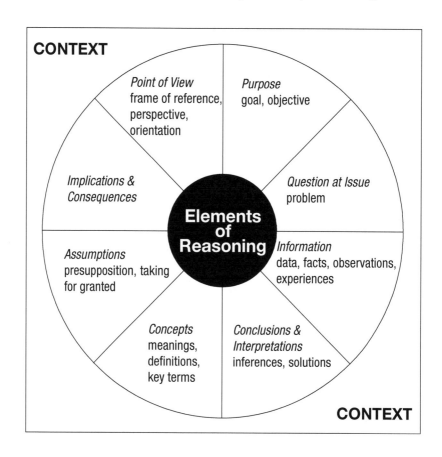

Just ponder for a moment two points that follow from this. One is about how widely the elements apply, and the other is about how useful they are. In the first place, these are the elements of *all* reasoning, *all* thinking. That means that *anything* that involves thinking contains these eight parts. That includes, for a start, decisions, arguments, essays, poems, songs and music, personal relationships, social, political and religious institutions, scientific theories and experiments, mathematical operations, medical procedures, artworks, emotions, historical epochs, and so forth. The list goes on and on, indefinitely.

Second, one of the great advantages of the circle of elements is that if you want to understand something—again, virtually anything—the elements give you the essential tools to do that. They let you carry out a *critical thinking analysis*. The word "analysis" means, roughly, breaking something down into its component parts. *Analyzing something* is a crucial way to understand it. So if you want to understand something—whether a decision, an argument, an essay, or something else—you can analyze it using the elements of reasoning.

Suppose you are concerned about the way we use pesticides and you decide to write a paper on it. How can you do it? A standard way to start is to jump right into unstructured "research" about pesticides. You search for some sources on the Internet or on your library search engine, you find out some things that some authors say, and then you hope that they fit together in some coherent way. Cutting-and-pasting is just an extreme version of this process. Writing this way almost guarantees that the paper will be weak and uninteresting.

By contrast, the elements of reasoning provide a dramatic way of opening up the topic. Instead of just approaching the topic cold, you can ask:

OK. For what *purposes* are pesticides used?
What are the main *questions at issue* with regard to the use of pesticides?
What are main *assumptions* people make about the use of pesticides?
What are the important *points of view* with regard to our use of pesticides?
And so forth.

Answer any of those questions and notice how your thinking automatically becomes more focused. Instead of a vague approach to an overly general topic, you have questions that guide you in thinking through one or more important issues focused on pesticide use. These questions also guide you through your research on the topic. Instead of just finding an article on some random aspect of pesticides, you can look for articles that address the specific questions and issues you yourself have raised. With just this much thinking focused on the elements of your reasoning, you have already taken a major step toward logical organization, both in your thinking and in the paper that will result from it.

Notice also how even one of these questions can sometimes start to give you almost the whole structure of your paper. Take *point of view*, the element keyed in on at the end of Chapter 1. You could easily structure a whole paper around this question: "What are the main points of view with regard to our use of pesticides?" In your paper, you could research and then spell out the main points of view reputable authorities have about the use of pesticides. For each one you would state it clearly and concisely; you would then elaborate on it, explaining not only the main ideas but also the supporting points or reasons given; you would then give examples, ones that capture each point of view you are analyzing; and then you could give an illustration. (This is, of course, SEE-I in action.) *Point of view* is not the only element that can structure an entire paper. The same thing can happen with *any* of the elements.

Without the elements of reasoning to guide you, you have only hit-or-miss ways of approaching the topic. If someone tells you to "Think about the use of pesticides!" you can say "OK"—but you still don't know what actually *to do*. You might start with something you already think: that we shouldn't use pesticides, or that we should use them with moderation, or that they're bad for the environment, or that they are important for agriculture. But these are just hit-or-miss assertions you might make. At this point, you probably haven't thought about the topic enough to come to a justified conclusion. And even if you have, it was probably still in a hit-or-miss way. There was probably nothing systematic in your approach, either in the way you thought about the topic or in the way you might have researched it.

> The focus in this book is on critical writing, so the topics addressed are mostly those that people often write about in papers for classes. But the circle of elements also helps you understand important topics that lie outside the usual subject matter of courses. For example, consider the relationship you have (or maybe don't have) with your parents. What assumptions do you make about your parents? What assumptions do you think they make about you? What are the main questions you have about them or your relationship with them? What is your concept of "being a parent"? Any of those—and others—can open up insights for you.

Doing research is a much more open-minded and effective way to approach a topic than just writing about impressions you may have. Research lays a foundation for giving people a reason to trust the validity of what you say. But research too may have a strong hit-or-miss quality to it. Yes, you are gathering information about pesticides, but you may not be gathering information that fits together in any coherent way. Sources regarding pesticides often go in utterly different directions and address utterly different aspects of pesticide use. Without the focus of the elements, there is a strong chance that you will end up just with a hodgepodge of information that comes from whatever sources you happen to stumble upon. A distinct danger is that your paper will end up merely reporting that X says this, Y says that, and Z says something else. You have nothing to guide your research or your thinking.

The elements of reasoning are that guide.

By using these elements, your paper will still incorporate research, but the research will be used to address questions that you yourself are asking. The paper that emerges will be the product of *your* informed thinking. That means you won't simply be reporting what some author happens to say. Instead, you'll be finding the various points of view yourself, assembling them, and explaining them clearly. Moreover, you can easily use other elements to amplify the paper and make it richer. You could, for example, identify some of the *implications and consequences* of each point of view. Or you could identify the main *assumptions* each is making. All of these are things you can do with the power of your mind, guided by the elements and supported with sound research.

The value of the elements. It is important not to see the elements of reasoning as additional work for you. It's not as if you have to write a paper and now you *also* have to apply the elements. (As an analogy, it's not as if you learn to drive a car and *also* have to learn to use the steering wheel.) If you think of these elements of reasoning as additional burdens, you'll miss most of their power. These elements are *tools to help you reason*. The main goal of using the elements is to make your writing (and thinking) *better*. In the process, they also make your writing *easier*.

It is also important to remember that writing a paper is about more than just writing a paper. In fact, it is about more than writing a paper and getting a good grade on it. Critical writing is a way of learning about a topic that is worth learning about, and of exploring and developing your thinking about it. It's a way of learning to value your own best thinking, acquiring skills and habits of mind that will stay with you in an ongoing way, making your life more fulfilling.

Using the elements conscientiously (and, later, the critical thinking standards as well) will result in a paper that is better reasoned, better organized, clearer, more precise, and more accurate. But, once you are at home with the elements, they will also make virtually every aspect of writing a paper substantially easier. The elements of reasoning, because they function as tools that guide you through the writing process, do a good portion of the work for you.

The end of Chapter 1 laid out seven major tasks involved in writing a paper critically. The elements, we'll see, help with *all* of them. The main task they accomplish is that they help you analyze a topic, so you can write about it with deeper understanding and authority. In a direct way, the elements will enable you to create a *plan* for your paper. It will let you generate your *thesis statement* as well as the *main points* of your paper. With them in front of you, you will have an outline you can follow step-by-step in writing your paper. In addition, you will have the substance of the *introductory section* and *concluding section* of the paper. All of those are direct results of using the elements of reasoning thoughtfully. Less directly, the elements will also focus your research, they will help reveal the weakpoints in your paper, and, finally, they will furnish you with guidelines for revising and improving your paper.

Getting a "Feel" for the Elements: Using the Elements to Understand a Topic

Remember from Chapter 1 that a topic is what you intend to write about, something that, in your best judgment, is important to both you and your audience. Some random examples are global warming, the novel *Pride and Prejudice,* or the importance of social life for college students. In fact, a topic can be almost anything.

But since you are writing a paper, you have only a limited amount of time and a limited number of pages available to you. As they stand, the three topics just listed are far too general and unfocused to guide you in writing even a moderately effective paper. People could write not just papers but whole books about them; they might go in countless directions and address countless different aspects of them. Still, the first topics you come up with may be just as general and unfocused as these.

Topics can, of course, be more specific than these. (An example is "the effects of global warming on the north Alaskan coast from 1990 to 2010.") But even a specific topic is still too general to allow you simply to construct a plan for your paper. Whether your topic is general or specific, a set of inter-related problems confront you when you begin to work on it:

- What do I focus on?
- How do I get myself to focus?
- How can I even begin to approach the topic so that I can get an interesting thesis statement to write about?
- How can I find the main points that will make up the bulk of my paper?
- How can I understand the topic in the time available, at least well enough to write an interesting and well-reasoned paper about it?

The answers to all these questions hinge on the elements of reasoning. Just look at the three random examples from the paragraph before last. Though the topics are radically different from one another, they all contain the elements of reasoning, and thus the elements open up each of them. *Global warming*: When people discuss global warming, they have *goals*, there are *problems* or *questions at issue* that they are addressing, and there are *assumptions* they are making, and so forth around the circle. This is true whether these people are scientists, politicians, wetlands engineers, or just a person walking down the street. Or, switching topics and elements, Elizabeth Bennet, the main character in *Pride and Prejudice*, *interprets* her situation in certain ways; she draws *conclusions* about what to do, and she makes *assumptions* about the people she knows; she carries a distinctive *point of view* with her through all her experiences. Or, again switching topics and elements, "the importance of social life for college students" hinges on the important *implications and consequences* of various patterns of social life, and the way these fit in with different types of students' overall *goals*.

With the elements you are never at a loss about how to explore a topic, a question, an issue, a theory, a situation, virtually anything. With the elements you have a set of questions that open up any topic.

The elements focus you. They focus your thinking and they focus your topic. As a result, they give you a center around which you could write a virtually unlimited number of papers. Consider just one of the elements, selected at random: *purpose*. You can ask a whole series of questions centering on purpose, goals, or objectives. Consider the pesticides example again. There, the question was "For what purposes are pesticides used?" But there are any number of other questions you could pose about *purpose*: What are the goals of companies that manufacture pesticides? What are the goals of the farmers and businesses that use them? What are environmentalists trying to achieve by reducing pesticide use? What are the main objectives of the Environmental Protection Agency with respect to pesticides? For any of those groups, how do we know what their goals are? To what extent are they achieving their goals? How have those goals changed over the past two decades? How and to what extent do those various goals fit together? Any of these questions could easily be the centerpiece of a paper on pesticides, and they all are generated from just a single element: *purpose*.

Something very similar applies to research. Notice how much more focused each of these is than just "doing research about pesticides." Don't let yourself be overwhelmed by how many questions there are. You certainly don't need to answer or even consider all of them. Any *one* of them will give you a definite path to pursue as you think about pesticides, and it will give you a path to pursue in your research about it. As you find sources that give you answers, you'll interpret what they are saying in line with your own questions, and you'll develop these answers using your own SEE-I's. The research will become integrated with your own thinking.

That's what the elements do. They focus you, and they do it in a way that is relevant and often insightful. One single element—purpose—will generate a whole set of focused questions. And the same thing will happen if we choose any other element.

In a preliminary way, take some time to get "the feel" of the elements. Do this without being overly concerned yet with whether you have a clear grasp of them. Take three or four topics, and, with each one, ask yourself questions about it using the elements, and then write down some brief answers to them. At this point, you don't need to give a full answer to the questions. But after you've written a few, step back from your answers and focus on the process you engaged in. Take some time to write down some insights about how the elements opened up the topic for you. Envision how your responses might give you a thesis statement or at least a major part of one. Next, imagine that you had to do some reading on the topic: Contemplate how using the elements of reasoning would help you see what to look for in the research you might do.

Thinking Your Way through a Topic: Analyzing "Around the Circle"

At this point, at the beginning of the critical writing process, what the elements do for you can be transformative: by giving you a focused understanding of your topic, they let you construct the whole logical foundation for your paper. Later on, you'll see, they help your writing in any number of additional ways. They help you make it better, expand it, fill it out, find weakpoints in it, and even help you carry out the construction of individual paragraphs.

But all of these insights are for later, and they're optional. It's right now, when you are starting off with maybe no more than a bare-bones topic, that the elements make the most substantial contribution to your paper.

By "going around the circle," you lay out the logic of the topic, the way its parts fit together as a coherent whole. Going around the circle of elements lets you take an unpromising general topic, focus it, generate a thesis statement, and find the main points you will make about it. More specifically, the circle of elements helps you:

- analyze your topic at the very beginning of the process, focusing it and opening it up so you can begin your paper with direction;
- generate a strong workable thesis statement, one you can build your paper around;
- identify the main points and other supporting points you will be making;
- create the structure and outline of your paper, the parts of it coming together to give you virtually a step-by-step blueprint to follow as you write it;
- see clearly and distinctly what you will need to research;
- construct the introductory section and concluding section of your paper, again virtually step-by-step.

Thus, using the elements will generate virtually the entire plan of the paper, and a good deal of the writing of it. The "step-by-step" is never just mechanical. As with all aspects of critical thinking and critical writing, the "steps" have to be followed mindfully. Nevertheless, again, the focus and direction supplied by the elements do a great deal of the work for you.

How to give a critical thinking analysis: Analyzing around the circle. Understanding a topic, grasping it, thinking your way through the logic of it, involves a process that can be called "going around the circle" or "analyzing around the circle." For many people, the words "analysis" and "analyzing" are not part of their everyday vocabulary, but for critical thinking, they are key words to grasp and internalize. *Analyzing* something (or giving an *analysis* of something) means taking it apart with a view to understanding it. So "analyzing around the circle" means applying each of the elements of reasoning to the topic.

Analyzing a Topic X:

- What is the *purpose* of X? What are its main goals or objectives?
- What are the main *questions* being addressed within X? What are the main problems being addressed?
- What are the main *assumptions* being made about X? What is being taken for granted within X?
- What are the *implications* and consequences of X? What follows from it logically?
- What important *information* or data can I gather about X?
- What are the main *concepts* within X? How are the key terms for those concepts understood or defined within X? What do those terms mean?
- What *conclusions* are being drawn about or within X? What interpretations are being given? What inferences are being made?
- What are the major *points of view* about X? What different frames of reference or different perspectives on X need to be considered?
- What is the context or background of X?

Remember that X, the topic you will be writing on, can be almost anything: a pressing issue you want to clarify in your mind and maybe come to a conclusion about: the content of an important essay or book, a subject or area in a course you are taking; an artifact, such as a painting, an architectural design, or the layout of the cafeteria; a piece of literature. It could be a more personal topic too: a decision you have in front of you; an important relationship you have; a frustrating situation, such as the problem of parking on a campus. (Because of the almost unlimited range of possible topics, the wording of the questions above may have to be changed somewhat to fit. Going around the circle with respect to a character in a novel may require different wording from going around the circle with respect to a scientific theory, a piece of music, or a relationship. Tailoring the questions to fit the topic is itself a part of thinking critically.)

When you "go around the circle," you may be surprised at the thinking power, and the writing power, the elements give you.

Examples in Practice

The three examples that follow are intended to show how someone might analyze a topic "around the circle" in order to write a paper about it. As in Chapter 1, these are extended examples that go on for several pages. They show not just the results of the person's analysis but the *process of reasoning* that the person might actually go through to arrive at these results.

In the first example, Charles starts off with just a general, unfocused idea for a topic he's interested in. The challenge for him is to find a focus within that general topic. He has to narrow it down to something he can write a paper about. He uses the circle of elements to do that. The second example is different. In it, Lucia is writing a research-based paper. She has already done a little research, and she includes her research results in her analysis right from the start. The challenge for her is to come up with a well-thought-out plan both for the further research she needs to do and for the paper she'll write using this research. She tries to be thorough in her analysis so that if some research doesn't work out, she'll have alternatives readily available. The third example is briefer. It details Kara's responses to the elements rather than her thought process in coming up with the responses. But even in this abbreviated example, you can see her thinking taking place and the way her thinking changes as she uses the elements.

A question you may wonder about is: Why does this book have such extended examples? You may even be tempted to just skim over them to get to more of the abstract instructions about how to reason things out. Why does the book show *the process* of reasoning things out? The answer is that these examples are intended as a main way to learn how to analyze a topic critically. It's like learning a sport: abstract instructions only do only one part of the job—you actually have to see someone doing it and you have to practice doing it yourself. That means it is important to put yourself in the minds of these students. You need to work through the analyses, not just read them passively. It works best if you ask yourself, "How is X applying it here?" "When it comes to my own analysis, what can I learn from how X is doing this?" As you plan and write your own papers, you will run into unforeseen difficulties. You can look back at these examples as guides. These students will be working through difficulties that are like the ones you yourself may face.

Note that none of the analyses below is perfect or expert. They show the thinking of individuals at different levels of educational experience, writing abilities, and critical thinking skills. As you read through them, try to put aside whether you agree or disagree with what the writer believes. The responses they give will probably need to be modified and filled out, and they do not necessarily represent the views the writers would have after more reflection, research, or learning, or if they had started their analysis in a different way.

Example #1. Charles is looking for a topic. He knows that a strong paper needs a topic that's important to his readers as well as to him. He comes up with "dieting" as a topic that fits with both of these requirements. It's a topic that's important to him personally. He's gone on diets in the past, but he thinks "they didn't really do me much good at all," and he feels even more overweight than before. And he is pretty sure that a lot of other people have had the same experience.

But he also recognizes that it will be a challenge to write about something as open-ended as *dieting*. It's a topic that could go in a hundred different directions. What he needs is a focus. As you follow Charles in his reasoning, you'll see how the analysis around the circle opens up new aspects of dieting he can write about. As he works his way around the circle, he finds several different focused paths that would make a good foundation for a paper. (In the example, the description of his thinking process is in ordinary print; what he actually writes down is in *italics*. As you follow Charles's analysis, keep the circle of elements in front of you. Refer to it so you can become familiar with how someone can use the elements to work through a topic. That familiarity will help you when you analyze your own topics.)

Charles begins with the element "purpose."

Purpose. *The overall purpose of going on a diet is*
- *to lose weight.*
- *to be healthier overall.*
- *to look better.*

Question at issue, problem. This element highlights either questions or problems (or both). Charles looks for ones related to dieting. He decides just to write them down as they occur to him, in the hope that one or two of them will point him in a direction that might give him a focus:

Questions
- *How can I lose weight?*
- *What kind of diet can I go on in order to lose weight?*
- *How can I do it as quickly and as painlessly as possible?*

Problems
- *A major problem is keeping the weight off once you've lost it.*
He recognizes this as the biggest problem for him personally.

Point of view. He moves to the element "point of view," but the main thing he's doing now is still searching for a focus for his paper. As a result, he's not too bothered by seeing that his responses go in different directions. He is consciously being flexible.

- *the point of view of the Atkins diet (that's the one I personally used),*

Also: the point of view of Weight Watchers or Jenny Craig or other plans.

He realizes that he could describe the differences and similarities in various dieting programs, and he could maybe also compare how effective they are. That by itself is a possible focus for his paper.

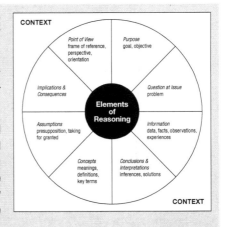

He also tries to use "point of view" in a different way, one that connects to the "problem" he just raised about keeping the weight off:

- *There is the point of view not just of the diet plans, but of the person who wants to lose weight and keep it off. How does that person look at dieting?*

Information. He starts trying to list information about dieting, but he finds that there is way too much of it. He begins by doing a Google search on "diet," then on "losing weight," then on "keeping weight off." The trouble is, everything goes in a dozen different directions. (He finds one website that was actually titled "50 Easy Ways to Lose Weight" and thinks "That's about 49 too many!")[2] Then he starts Googling individual weight-loss plans (like the Atkins Plan), but he realizes that he needs to have a direction to his thinking *before* he can find information that will be helpful. So he decides to put off gathering information until he's narrowed things down. (Information is often an excellent element to explore *after* you have already found a focus.)

He turns to the element "concepts" and asks himself, "What are some of the main concepts related to dieting, and how can I spell them out more clearly?"

Concepts.
- *Dieting*
- *Being overweight*
- *Keeping the weight off*

He stops for a minute and asks himself, "What exactly do I mean by 'dieting'?" To him it means paying close attention to what you eat ("No more McDonald's or Burger King"). He breaks it down into three parts:

- *what can you eat?* • *how much?* • *how often?*

He recognizes that these are questions he'll need to research. He also sees that research will let him be more exact about how much weight is "overweight."

Implications and consequences.

- *getting healthier*
- *looking good*
- *having a positive self-image*
- *being comfortable with yourself*

These are all positive consequences of losing weight, but Charles knows that implications and consequences can be negative as well as positive. This is an important step. Now Charles has several other good angles to help him plan his paper. He can write about the positive consequences of

Focusing explicitly on *concepts* can open up paths to pursue in your paper that both you and your reader might never have seen otherwise. That's because the role played by concepts mostly goes unnoticed. Looking for *key terms* in your analysis helps draw your attention to concepts you might easily overlook.

The element "concepts" includes the *meaning* of key terms or phrases, their everyday meaning, as well as more sophisticated uses. It includes meanings of terms not just in a superficial way (as in a brief dictionary definition, for example) but in a deeper way you can dwell on and explore.

Notice the way Charles dwells on and explores the concept of *dieting*. He might never have thought to explain the concept of dieting if the circle of elements hadn't called his attention to the key terms he was using. Thinking about this concept enriches his paper substantially.

losing weight, such as the ones he's listed, or he can take the angle of writing about the negative consequences. He writes down several of these:

- *the strong desire for food*
- *the feeling of never being full*
- *missing out on the comfort you get from food*

He also now thinks that there are implications and consequences even if you're completely successful in losing weight:

- *Afterward, people may gradually stop paying attention to maintaining a healthy diet.*

He thinks a little more about that last one. He realizes that it gives him another possible focus for his paper: the assumption people often make—that once they lose weight, it will be easy to keep it off.

Charles now has several paths he can take in his paper. He can write about:

- the differences and similarities in several popular diet plans;
- the positive and negative consequences of losing weight;

- assumptions people make about how easy it will be to keep the weight off once they lose it.

Assumptions. With that last plan in mind, he lists two assumptions he thinks a lot of people make:

- *Once they lose weight and see how good they look, they assume it will not be much of a struggle to keep the weight off.*
- *They assume they can keep the weight off and keep looking good without making a major change in how they live their lives.*

Based on what he's done so far, he thinks that both of these assumptions lead people down the wrong path.

Conclusions. Interpretations. He draws a conclusion at this point:

- *Just "dieting to lose weight" will not work.*

He thinks that you may lose the weight, but if your goal is to keep the weight off so you'll be healthier and look better, then losing the weight is only half the battle. So he draws an additional conclusion:

- *You have to think long range right from the beginning: when you commit to losing weight, you have to commit to making a real change in the way you live your life, not just for now, but for the future too.*

He draws another conclusion:

- *There is a lot of misleading information about dieting. There are "plans" for losing weight, but they don't address the problem of keeping the weight off by changing the way people live their lives.*

Charles's conclusions bring a good deal of his plan together. He has identified important implications and consequences of dieting. This gives him a good amount of substance for his paper. (For example, he can give an SEE-I for each of them.) He has also identified common assumptions and key concepts

Terminology: "Conclusion"—the element of reasoning—is quite different from the "concluding section" of a paper. (What makes it confusing is that writing professionals often use the single word "conclusion" for both of them.) *Conclusion*—the element of reasoning—refers to conclusions you arrive at in thinking about your topic. You can bring them into your paper at any point, not just at the end.

By contrast, the *concluding section* is the section at the end of your paper. It is typically where you summarize all the main points you have made in the paper.

as well. This gives him a stronger plan. (He can state, elaborate, exemplify, and illustrate those as well.)

At this point, Charles goes back to the element "information" from before. But now he knows the paths his paper can take. As a result, finding information won't be hit-or-miss anymore. He will be able to tell what's relevant and what isn't. For example, in his research he can find reputable websites that give information related to any of the specific implications and consequences he identified:

Information, again.
- *information about how your body adapts to weight loss*
- *information about the physical causes of why people quickly regain the weight they've lost*

He thinks that describing the science of how people regain weight will be a strong addition to his paper. In addition, he sees that he can gather

- *information about the misleading plans to lose weight that are out there.*

He says, "I can start with those '50 Easy Ways to Lose Weight.'"

Context. Charles thinks about "context" in the box around the circle of elements. It fits in with his ideas for the paper in a major way.

- *Part of the context is the epidemic of obesity in the U.S.*
- *Another is the emphasis in the media on looking good and being thin.*
- *In my own social context, everyone I know has tried to lose weight, or at least they want to be skinnier.*

> **Context.** *Context* is not literally one of the elements of reasoning. It is the background of the reasoning, the environment in which the reasoning takes place. Sometimes focusing on context, and writing about it in your paper, will ground your paper and make it far richer. Sometimes it can just be left out of the analysis. In the examples of student analyses in this book, sometimes the students address context directly. In other examples, they don't. It's a choice.

He decides that in his paper, if he has enough space, he could describe the flood of advertising about diet plans, with all the focus only on losing the weight, not on changing the way we think about our lives.

As you follow the progression of Charles's analysis, you can see that it gives him a much greater understanding of the topic and its ramifications than he had before. Some of the ideas he comes up with are ones that were in his mind already without his realizing it. Others are new thoughts. Still others give him paths for doing good research. Starting off with the vague idea of just losing weight, his thinking becomes deeper, more precise, and more organized.

It may be hard to see fully what Charles has accomplished with his analysis around the circle. Until he gets to implications, his responses go in several different directions. In many cases, that's a natural way to let your thinking develop. In Charles's case, it gives him at least three different paths he could follow in his paper.

But then there is a shift in Charles's thinking. He identifies an implication about what happens *after* people have lost weight:

Implication: *Afterward, people may gradually stop paying attention to maintaining a healthy diet.*

Once he does that, the responses he writes down start to center on this theme: the *assumptions, conclusions* and *interpretations* he identifies all fit with this implication. Then the *information* he identifies develops the same idea. *Context* does so as well. Now he can look back at the earlier parts of his analysis and find responses that fit this new directionality in his thinking. Both his thinking and the foundation of his paper start to come together.

A snapshot of the next chapter. Analyzing the topic around the circle—reasoning your way through it—is an accomplishment in itself. In Charles's case, the follow-up question will be how he can turn his analysis around the circle into a well-defined plan for the paper. (That is the subject of Chapter 3.) Another way of saying this— to go back to the framework for critical writing—is that he needs the thesis statement and the other main points of his paper. Though it is not guaranteed, one of the great benefits of using the elements of reasoning is that he can be pretty sure that his thesis and main points will be there right in front of him, in the responses he wrote down in his critical thinking analysis. What he has to do is *see* them there. He may have to re-state them more clearly, but he can be confident that they are there.

Once he identifies the thesis statement and the main points, he will have the structure of his whole paper, and he'll have an outline he can follow as he writes it out. He may add points to his plan, subtract some, re-state some more clearly, and incorporate any research on them—but he will *have* the plan for his paper.

With this plan in front of him, he can then write the actual paper by using SEE-I: stating, elaborating, exemplifying, illustrating, and "staircasing."

It will be a paper that is built by his own thinking.

Example #2. The second example is different. Lucia plans to major in psychology and perhaps go on to graduate school. She is currently taking an intermediate-level psychology course. A paper is required, one that has a large research component. The paper is a major part of the course. The syllabus describes it as "writing to learn." A topic that caught her attention in the course was a psychology experiment called "Lost in the Mall." In the study, experimenters actually planted a false memory in people. In the experiment, they had family members tell the individual a made-up story about when he or she had been lost in the mall as a child. Then, later, the individuals "remembered" the incident themselves—even though it never happened at all. It wasn't just a fuzzy memory either. Not only did people "remember" being lost, but they also "remembered" very specific details about who found them—even though those details had not been mentioned by the experimenters. The people unconsciously just made them up, and the details became part of their memory. Some of the individuals were completely certain, even though it was a "false memory": it was a "memory" planted in their minds by others. She decides to write her paper on the topic "false memory."

Lucia tries to be thorough in her analysis. When it comes to researching and writing the actual paper, she knows she won't write about everything in her analysis. But a thorough analysis will give her focused points she can choose to include or not. It also gives her fallback alternatives in case some of the research doesn't work out. (This example also shows both her actual written responses (printed in *italics*) and her thinking (in ordinary print). Once again, keep referring to the circle of elements (p. 36) as you follow her analysis.)

Lucia starts with the element "information" because she knows she will be writing down information about the "Lost in the Mall" experiment. She knows she will have to research and write about more than just that one experiment, so a goal she has is in her analysis is to guide her in the research that lies ahead. (In her analysis, she uses an "**R**" to stand for "research" she needs to do.)

Information. **(R)**
- *how the experiment was carried out*
- *the conclusions the experimenters drew*

She turns to the element "question at issue." Since the experiment she is writing about is on "false memory," she writes down questions that the experiment was trying to answer about false memory. But she also includes some questions about how the experiment applies in people's lives.

Question at issue.
- *What produces false memory?*
- *How was the experiment conducted, and what does it show about false memory?*

- What makes memories reliable?
- *How much faith should I put in my own memories?*

As Lucia looks at her first question, she realizes that the "Lost in the Mall" experiment shows only one of the factors that lead to false memory. The false memory there was produced when adults were told a made-up story about what had happened to them as children. This leads her to another question at issue:

- *In addition, what other factors lead to false memory?* **(R)**

This last question about "other factors" gives her a specific direction she can pursue in her research, one that goes beyond the single experiment she began with. She decides that she can look for other experiments that show additional factors leading to false memories. The direction this idea gives her is highly fruitful—indeed, almost too fruitful: the search engine at her college library lists more than half a million entries on "false memory" alone! Even restricting herself to peer-reviewed articles would be over-whelming: there are almost 200,000 of them![3] Even the sub-topics and sub-sub-topics are far too general to give her a focus. Without a specific direction in mind, the research she does will be not only time-consuming but almost certainly unproductive: she will just be wandering through journal articles, with no idea of which of them she can use and which she can't.

With the direction she now has, though, she searches for and finds a number of articles that pinpoint factors leading to false memory. Based on reading the abstracts for these articles, she comes to a conclusion:

Conclusion.

- *There are at least four major ways that false memories can be induced in people (for example, one of them is how you phrase the question that you ask an eyewitness).*

She now selects four key experiments to report on.[4] (One of them is the "Lost in the Mall" experiment she began with.) She chooses experiments that opened up a whole new area of how false memory can be induced. With these, she reads the whole article (not just the abstract), taking notes as she reads. With that, she goes back to the element "information," but now she can be much more specific. Here is the information she lists:

Information.
- *describe each of the four experiments in detail, including*
  - *how the experiment was set up and carried out*
  - *the conclusions the authors drew*

As she reads about them, she takes notes, stating the conclusions, explaining the experiments, and giving examples.*

Her topic has become focused, and she now knows how she will proceed in her paper. The descriptions of these key experiments will form the bulk of it.

She still, however, wants to be sure she has enough for a major research paper. She goes back to the circle of elements to continue her analysis.

When she moves on to the element "purpose," she asks herself, "What is the purpose of these experiments?"

Purpose.
- *to establish scientifically, in controlled, double-blind experiments, factors that make our memories false*

Context. When she first read about the "Lost in the Mall" experiment, she watched a video where the author gave a good overview of the experiment. As she watches it again now, she gets a larger picture of how false memory works and where it fits in with other issues in psychology. Lucia realizes that this is "**context**" (from the square around the circle of elements). At this point, she doesn't write down any specifics under "context," but she makes a note that summarizing the overview would make a good addition to her paper. (She bookmarks the video so she can go back to it later if she needs to.)

She now moves on to one of the elements of reasoning she has not addressed yet:

Concepts.
- *The most important concept in the paper is "false memory." (**R**: I need a good scholarly definition of "false memory" from a reputable source in psychology. But in addition, using an SEE-I, I will write out my own understanding of false memory, based on what I learned about it in my reading.)*

She decides she can also use an SEE-I to describe technical concepts that apply to psychology experiments. These include:

- *control group*
- *double-blind experiment*
- *operational definitions*

Describing these concepts gives her added material she can use in her paper.

---

*You can see that the notes she is taking are in fact parts of SEE-I.

Assumptions.

- *That the findings hold in the real world. That the results will be applicable in real-life situations.*
- *My assumption up until now was that I could rely on my memory.*

Points of view.

- *The point of view of the experimenters is a scientific one. They are using science—clear, careful experiments—to find out how accurate our memories are.*

The last element she addresses is "implications and consequences." She finds that the studies about false memory sometimes have profound implications in the real world, and she lists some of them. These are additional points she can explore and write about if she needs to expand her paper.

Implications and consequences.

- *There are legal implications about not relying on eyewitness testimony. (Because of these experiments, judges now instruct juries not to put too much trust in eyewitness testimony.) (**R**: If I decide to include this, I should get exact information about it.)*
- *People have been convicted of serious crimes based on the mistaken false memory of eyewitnesses (**R**: Find good examples of this, from reputable sources).*
- *An implication that is much more personal is that the feeling of certainty you experience when you "remember something" isn't automatically trustworthy. This is disturbing.*

She writes down two last thoughts before she finishes her analysis. She could classify them as either conclusions or implications. They are extensions of the original topic, and so she may not use them in this paper at all. But she thinks either one of them would make a good topic for another paper she might write, in this class or if she goes on to graduate school:

- *Our whole concept of memory is* wrong*! I always thought memory was just a picture of what happened. But that's not true at all.*

- *You can't simply trust a memory or even an eyewitness account.*

Notice how Lucia is becoming more enlightened about her topic as she uses the circle of elements to guide her. She will be reporting on several experiments, and so she has a lot of information she can include. But her paper will do a good deal more than just report on "information" from the experiments. She analyzes the experiments.

She integrates them. She interprets them. She explains concepts and draws conclusions from them. The "information" from the experiments will be an important part of her paper, but the other elements of reasoning give her a level of understanding that opens up any number of relevant areas she can write about.

Example #3. When you use the circle of elements, it often generates thoughts and possibilities that would probably never have occurred to you without the analysis. It is a major benefit of the elements of reasoning when you write a paper, but also when you are just trying to figure something out.

Kara has been studying *Romeo and Juliet* and wants to write a paper on Juliet. She knows she has to narrow it down. There is no real focus to it at all. As you read through the example, notice the way Kara's mind is working. She uses the elements to focus her topic and to open new ways to think about it. (This example shows mostly her actual written responses, rather than the thinking she goes through. But you will still be able to follow the progress of her thinking. The "→" shows when she sees herself coming to a new thought in the analysis.)

Topic: Juliet (in the play *Romeo and Juliet*)

question at issue. The major question at issue for Juliet, from the moment she meets Romeo, is: How can she be with him?
   Another version: How can they manage to be together and share their love despite the deadly opposition of their families?

concept. The main concept for Juliet is love. This concept shapes everything she does. (It is the main concept for Romeo too.)

conclusion, inference. An inference Juliet makes is that love with Romeo is possible, despite the obstacles.

context. The context is the feud between their two families, the Montagues and the Capulets. The feud makes it impossible for Romeo and Juliet to be in love openly.

purpose. Her all-consuming purpose is love for Romeo. More than anything, she wants to be with him. When they secretly get married, her goal is to be married to him openly.

point of view. Juliet does not try to see the situation from her parents' point of view, much less from the point of view of Romeo's family, the Montagues.

→ Another **question at issue**: *Would she have been better off if she could have seen things from their point of view? Was it even possible for her to do that?*

information. *Juliet takes a sleeping potion that will make her look dead until Romeo can find her. A messenger is sent to Romeo to let him know that Juliet is still alive. He is supposed to tell Romeo that Juliet has taken a drug to make her <u>appear</u> dead, but that she will wake up, and then they can run away together. But the messenger is delayed. When Romeo arrives he thinks she <u>is</u> dead. It affects him so much that he kills himself. When Juliet wakes up, she sees that Romeo is dead. She stabs herself.*

[Kara thinking: "I need to give actual quotations from the play to make my points more vividly. A good one is Romeo saying 'Thus with a kiss I die' (R&J V, iii, 120) and then Juliet saying 'O happy dagger!/This is thy sheath. There rust, and let me die' (V, iii, 168–169)."]

assumptions.
- *Juliet assumes that love will prevail over all the obstacles.*
But she makes another crucial assumption right before the very end: that the messenger will reach Romeo in time.
  - → *Even more than that:*
  - *she assumes that everything about the elaborate plan will all work out perfectly.*

    But a million things could go wrong with the plan → *Such as?*

- *the sleeping potion might not work; or*
- *it might work only for too short a time (Why would she believe that the "distillèd liquor" (IV, i, 94) would last for exactly "two and forty hours" (IV, i, 105)?); or*
- *instead of making her just appear dead, it might actually kill her; or*
- *her family might stay around her "dead" body for too long a time and catch Romeo coming to her; or*
- *her family might prevent Romeo from visiting her crypt.*

  Juliet can't see <u>any</u> of these possibilities due to her assumption that all will turn out according to her plan.

conclusion. *A conclusion I draw is that Juliet was engaged in unrealistic wishful thinking!*

→ *This brings up some further* **questions at issue**: *What could Juliet have done if she saw the possibilities more realistically? How might she have acted so as to be able to make her love for Romeo come true? Wasn't there a less drastic way to come together with Romeo at the end?*

> ***implication.*** *Maybe they really weren't "star-crossed" as lovers. Maybe it wasn't "fate" or "the stars" that doomed their love. Maybe their deaths were the result of making plans that were too risky and drastic and not well thought out. (Romeo also jumped to a fatal conclusion at the end.) There were other things they could have done. Being in love doesn't mean that you stop thinking. It means you should think even harder about how to be with the person you love!*

The Usefulness of the Elements of Reasoning

When you actively employ the elements, your thinking will be sharpened and become deeper. Sometimes your thinking will change, and sometimes it will intensify. These elements yield insight. Take some time to ponder the examples and the different ways the elements changed and deepened the way these three writers thought about their topics. In your mind you can envision the paper they would likely have

You may wonder: Why did the students in the examples start off with that particular element? There is no surefire answer to this question. They look at the elements in the circle, pause to consider them for a few seconds, and then choose ones that they think might open up the topic and give them a good beginning.

written without the analysis, versus the one they can write now. The whole substance has become richer, more developed, better organized—more full of sheer thinking.

Charles's analysis of dieting is a good example. You can see the evolution of his thinking as he explores the topic of dieting. Both his understanding of dieting and the focus of his thinking change in the course of his analysis. They become far more exact and insightful. Notice that much of the exactness and insight is prompted by the engaged way Charles uses the elements.

You can see this evolution of thinking in a different way in Lucia's research-oriented analysis of false memory. As she starts off she is still groping toward a more definite direction to take in her research. She knows she'll report on the "Lost in the Mall" experiment, but that's really the only idea she has at that point. In the beginning she has no real question at issue. And she knows that reporting on a single experiment is far too skimpy for a research paper.

The problems she faces are the same ones almost anyone faces in doing research. Even putting aside unreliable sources, there is such a super-abundance of information, articles and studies about virtually any topic that it can seem impossible to find a way through it. But by writing out her analysis around the circle, Lucia is able to plan and organize the research she will do. The plan is the product of her own thinking, focused by using the elements of reasoning.

The third example, the one about Juliet, shows a more major change in thinking. Kara is analyzing the character of Juliet directly, including Juliet's goals, conclusions, point of view, question at issue, and the concept of love that guides her life. But Kara's thinking changes radically as she works her way through what she sees as Juliet's *assumptions*. You can almost see the rapid progression of her insights, one right after the other. By the end, the whole focus of her thinking—and of the paper she will write—has shifted. She comes to a conclusion that surprises even her: that it wasn't fate or love that led to the death of Romeo and Juliet. It was "unrealistic wishful thinking." You don't have to agree with Kara to see that she will be able to write a highly original and interesting paper.

In each of the three analyses, the writer starts with a very general topic (dieting, false memory, Juliet). It is a major challenge to come up with a crisp, workable thesis statement from within topics as general as these. But notice how the analysis around the circle creates focus and specificity. It brings out important aspects of the topic and gives a solid foundation for finding not only a thesis statement but the other main points of the paper as well.

Using the elements in practice. There are many ways of going around the circle. The process allows for great flexibility and creativity. The goal to keep in mind is that you are trying to gain a deeper understanding of the topic so you can write about it with authority. People need to be able to trust that what you say is reliable. It needs to be the product of your best, informed reasoned judgment. But, in addition, as you analyze a topic around the circle, a major thing you are looking for is insight. You are trying to generate aspects of the topic you may have never thought about before, aspects of the topic worth dwelling on, for both you and your readers. The insights might lie in an assumption you had never considered, an implication you hadn't noticed, a question that goes to the heart of the topic, or a fresh way of interpreting the issue. You won't get insight for every element or for every topic, but it's one of the things to aim for.

With that end in mind—writing a paper out of strong understanding and insightful reasoning—you can use the circle in any number of ways. It is definitely non-linear. For many people, it is helpful to begin with the *question at issue*, or with *purpose*, or with *concepts*, but it's not a requirement. You can actually begin with any of the elements you think might work out well. Similarly, there is no automatic order to the elements. You can proceed through them in any order that, in your best judgment, will be most helpful. Moreover, if you can't see how one or two of the elements fits with your topic, you can just skip them and come back to them later.

How thorough does your analysis of the topic have to be? As thorough as it needs to be for you to become knowledgeable about it, to understand it, to let your mind work its way through the topic, so you can write in an informed, reasoned way. Your thesis statement, main points, and the plan and structure of your paper will grow directly out of the analysis. (That's the topic of the next chapter.) For a simple, short paper (or an essay exam), you may not even need to go through all the elements. Sometimes just three or four of them

Critical reading and critical writing are closely linked to one another. There is a strong sense in which you cannot write well unless you read well. Reading something *carefully*, critically, is also a highly effective way to come up with an excellent idea for a paper. (This point also applies to videos, lectures, speeches.)

There are different ways to understand and convey what an author is saying in a reading.

(a) **Summarizing.** Give a short, condensed explanation of what the author is saying, including a clear, concise statement of the main point the author is making.

(b) **Clarifying.** Give an **SEE-I** for the reading. (Note that (a) contains both the statement and part of the elaboration in SEE-I.)

(c) **Analyzing. Analyze** the reading by going around the circle of elements.

can give you key insights. But even with a short paper, going around the full circle probably won't take an extravagant amount of time, and it can make your paper far better. If, however, you are writing a paper that explores a topic or question in a deep or comprehensive way, going around the circle fully and in depth allows you to explore the topic or issue with a completeness it would be difficult to achieve without the elements.

It is important to remember that the elements are supposed to be *helpful*. They are a set of tools, and they make both your thinking and your writing powerful, clear, and focused. There may be difficulties in getting used to them, but with practice they soon become more natural, more available for you. Going through the process of critical writing can seem laborious, especially at the beginning. Any set of real skills will probably seem that way at first. Think of what it takes to learn to play a sport, or to learn to play a musical instrument—specifically, learning how to do those *well*. It takes time, guidance, and practice. You have to pay attention to multiple factors all at once. The same holds for learning to use your mind—specifically, learning to use your mind *well*.

But it gets easier. In fact, it gets much easier. As you continue, you internalize the processes. Your skills (in sports, music, or thinking) soon seem to flow. You may still frequently have to monitor how well you're doing, but it starts to feel like second nature. You find yourself naturally tracing out implications and consequences, reflecting on the concepts you are using, looking at things from multiple points of view.

At this point, you need to start practicing critical thinking analysis. Take a topic you are interested in and analyze it around the circle. At the beginning, don't hold yourself to too high a standard. Get the feel of identifying purposes, assumptions, conclusions, and so forth.

You need to do this several times, with topics that are very different from one another. Try it with a topic that is far too general, and then see how the elements start to bring focus to it. Try it with a reading you have done and notice how the elements let you understand the reading far better. Try it with a more specific topic for one of your classes—something you might consider writing a paper on.

So What Is Critical Thinking?

It may seem odd that it is only now, at the end of Chapter 2, that this book addresses the question of what critical thinking itself is. Shouldn't this have come at the beginning? Since critical *writing* is built on critical *thinking*, shouldn't it have been defined right from the start?

The trouble with spelling out the concept of critical thinking at the beginning is that none of the specifics were in place yet to make it concrete and usable. A description at that point would only have been vague and unhelpful. In fact, the idea many people have about critical thinking *is* just a vague one: it is just "good thinking,"[*] or "careful

---

[*]But we usually compliment people on their "good thinking" only if the conclusions they come to agree with what we ourselves believe. It often seems that for some people, they just assume that, whatever critical thinking is, it is the kind of thinking that they themselves do.

thinking." But the problem is that vague conceptions like these do not help you know what *to do* to think critically about a topic (or even really to understand what critical thinking *is*): Good thinking about *what*? Thinking carefully or better about *what*? When you think critically about a topic, what should you be focusing *on*?

After seeing the elements of reasoning in action you are now in a better position to recognize much more exactly what critical thinking is. In a nutshell, critical thinking involves two parts. First, it involves explicitly reflecting on your thinking. Specifically, this means that what you think *about* are the elements of reasoning: assumptions, goals, implications and consequences, the questions you should be asking, and so forth around the circle of elements. You do this with your own thinking and with respect to the thinking that is involved in the topic itself.

Second, it means that what you think *about*, again explicitly, is the *quality* of your reasoning, *how well* you are thinking. But the "how well" is not just something vague and directionless. This will be taken up in Chapter 5, but you are already in a position to see some of what it involves. It means you consciously examine the extent to which you are meeting the "standards of critical thinking." At least four of these standards have already come up prominently in the examples: how *clear* the thinking is, how *accurate*, how *relevant* to the topic at hand, and whether it is focused on what is most *important*.

Chapter 2: Practice and Assessment Exercises

Read the "Note on the Exercises" in Chapter 1 (p. 29–30).

*1. In this chapter, what are the main concepts and processes for critical writing?

Practice at analyzing around the circle of elements: Critical reading
*2. In 1955, civil rights protesters, led by Martin Luther King, Jr., boycotted buses in Montgomery, Alabama. They protested the arrest of Rosa Parks and the law that required African Americans to move to the rear of public buses. They knew they would be met with violence by Montgomery citizens and police.
    Here is what Dr. King said:[5]

> *We have discovered a new and powerful weapon—non-violent resistance.* Although law is an important factor in bringing about social change, there are certain conditions in which the very effort to adhere to new legal decisions creates tension

and provokes violence. We had hoped to see demonstrated a method that would enable us to continue our struggle while coping with the violence it aroused. Now we see the answer: face violence if necessary, but refuse to return violence.

Analyze his speech by going around the circle of elements.

*3. Here is an excerpt from a book on traffic laws and lowering accident rates and traffic fatalities:[6] (Vanderbilt, 2008, 237).

> In Finland, which has one of the lowest crash rates in the world, drivers are given fines based on a calculated calculus primarily involving their after-tax income. The law, intended to counter the regressive nature of speeding tickets (they take up a larger part of a poor person's income than a rich person's), has led to some very high-profile speeding tickets, such as Internet entrepreneur Jaako Rytsölä's $71,400 tab for going 43 miles per hour in a 25-mile-per-hour zone. There has been some grumbling, especially among the wealthy, but the law remains popular; in 2001, the legislature overwhelmingly rejected a cap on fines.

Using this description as your basis, analyze the thinking of the legislators who passed the law.

4. Some context: Sayyid Qutb was disgusted with what he saw as the materialism of American culture. He was an Egyptian who spent several years in the United States. (He also condemned the racism, obsession with watching sports and other entertainment, and the violence he said he found in America.)

His views and life form one of the main influences and inspirations behind the jihadists, including Osama bin Laden. In the following passage (quoted in Haddad, 90), he is speaking about Americans and the way he interpreted them as living:[7]

> Their enjoyment is nervous excitement, animal merriment. One gets the image that they are constantly running from ghosts that are pursuing them. They are as machines that move with madness, speed and convulsion that does not cease. Many times I thought it was as though the people were in a grinding machine that does not stop day or night, morning or evening. It grinds them and they are devoured without a moment's rest. They have no faith in themselves or in life around them.

Analyze Qutb's thinking by going around the circle of elements.

*5. As you start to get the feel of the elements, apply a few of them to the issue of *dealing with stress* in your life. At this stage, you can use the elements without necessarily having a paper to write.

- What is your main goal in dealing with stress?
- What is the main question at issue for you?
- What are some of the implications and consequences?
- What information do I have about it?

*6. Look back at Charles's analysis of dieting. When he gets to *implications and consequences* (p. 48), he finds that he has several paths he can pursue in the rest of his plan. Moreover, the path he chooses will strongly influence the paper he ends up writing. Here are the paths he sees. He can write about:

- the differences and similarities in several popular diet plans;
- the positive and negative consequences of losing weight;
- assumptions people make about how easy it will be to keep the weight off once they lose it.

He chooses the last one. Write a brief account of why you think he chose that path? What were the thoughts that led him to that choice? Can you see why he thinks that third path is insightful?

7. Look back at the examples of "False Memory" and "Juliet." As in Question 6, write about why you think the student gave this or that response in her analysis. Immerse yourself and exercise intellectual empathy: What was she thinking as she worked through her analysis? What move would you have made?

Getting more skillful at using the elements. Keeping on track and being flexible.

*8. In thinking about a paper, Anthony starts off with a question: "Can money buy happiness?" He answers, "Of course not!" But he decides to analyze it around the circle. His problem is that he doesn't know exactly how to apply the elements to a question.

He could begin with *purpose* and ask, "What's *my* purpose in trying to answer the question?" but he realizes that would throw his analysis off-track. He wants to analyze whether money can buy happiness, not why he is asking the question.

How should he do it?

9. A student is taking a course in American history. There are a large number of facts in the course. One of them is that the Civil War started when South Carolina bombarded Fort Sumter in 1861. A course requirement is to write a research paper, but the student is puzzled about how to write a paper about a bare-bones fact.

Facts often seem to bring our thinking to a stop. They feel like an endpoint rather than something to think about critically.

But that impression is misleading. Though it doesn't seem so at first, facts are often very rich topics to analyze. The elements of reasoning open paths by which to think about the facts in deeper and more probing ways. With the single fact about Fort Sumter, virtually all the elements yield rich areas to research and then write about:

- What *assumptions* did the soldiers who attacked Fort Sumter make about the bombardment?
- What did they think the *consequences* would be? (Did they realize they might be starting something that could result in hundreds of thousands of people being killed?)
- What were their *goals*? Were their goals realistic?
- How did they *interpret* the situation when they started the bombardment?
- And so forth.

All of these are focused research questions, and the answers the student could find to those questions (maybe even just to *one* of those questions) could well be the heart of a strong research paper.

What are some important facts in a course you are taking? Choose one and analyze it using the circle of elements.

10. **Critical reading and critical writing.** As noted in the box in Chapter 2 on p. 60, reading something carefully, with focus, is one of the best ways to come up with an excellent topic to write about. Your topic can be what the writer is saying as a whole, or it can be one or more of the ideas that the author is advancing.

    Take something you are reading and analyze it in each of the three ways mentioned:

    a) Give a concise summary of what is being said in the reading.
    b) SEE-I the reading.
    c) Analyze the reading around the circle of elements.

11. Sheila is the student who wrote a paper arguing that American universities should be as inexpensive as European universities are (p. 11–13). As she did research on European universities, she found that they are ranked just as highly as American universities and much less expensive. In addition, she found that many of them are more highly ranked than the American university she currently attends, that the cost of their tuition plus room and board would be only a fraction of what she is paying now, and that a number of them let you take all your classes in English.

    So now she starts to think that maybe she should transfer to a European university. She decides that at least she should consider it.

So put yourself in Sheila's mind. Her topic is *transferring to a European university*. Analyze it as Sheila would.

*12. As Sheila herself analyzes her possible decision, she realizes that going to school in Europe would mean leaving her boyfriend for a long time. She wonders about whether she should include that as one of the negative *consequences* of moving to another country for her schooling. She thinks, "I'm supposed to be thinking about this decision rationally. That's why I'm analyzing it by going around the circle. Leaving my boyfriend is just an emotional part of the decision and so it doesn't belong in my analysis."

13. As noted earlier, you can use the circle of elements to analyze very general topics as well as topics that are already more focused. Analyzing a focused topic usually gives you a more readily usable plan for a paper. Starting with a general topic often leaves you more vulnerable to saying only empty generalities, but by analyzing it around the circle, it can also lead to new and unexpected insights. It can sometimes open up new ways of thinking about the topic.

Compare how you would analyze:

- *reducing our reliance on fossil fuels* (a general topic) versus
- *the environmental impact of converting from coal-produced energy to solar energy* (a more focused topic)

   or:

- *Barack Obama's presidency* versus
- *Barack Obama's use of drones* versus
- *changes in the use of lethal drone strikes after 2016 when Barack Obama made public the legal framework for conducting such strikes against suspected terrorists*

*14. **Thinking about writing.** The starred response to question 1 listed three main concepts and processes in Chapter 2:

- the elements of reasoning (as a whole)
- each of the individual elements of reasoning (plus *context*)
- analyzing, or "analyzing around the circle"

   Write out an SEE-I for each of them.

15. For one of the main concepts or processes in the previous question, analyze it around the circle.

   For example, suppose you choose *the elements of reasoning (as a whole)* as your topic.

   You would write out answers to questions such as:

- What is the purpose of the circle of elements as a whole?
- What is meant by the term (the concept) *elements of reasoning*?
- From what point of view is it presented?
- What are some main assumptions that underlie it?
- And so forth.

16. **Write about your own experience.** Take as your topic something that's important to you personally—such as a relationship you have, a decision you need to make, a dream you have for the future, the way you were brought up, your image of yourself—and go around the circle with respect to it. As you do so, consciously make yourself open to thoughts and ideas that never occurred to you before.

    It helps to be already familiar enough with the elements in the circle so that you are not fixing all your attention on the names for them. (It's like playing an instrument. When you are first learning guitar, you focus all your attention on getting your fingers right. But when that becomes more familiar, your playing can help you express the music itself.)

*17. **Think about writing.** Take on the point of view of the author of this book: What are the main outcomes for the book so far? Explain them.

18. **Reflect on your experience.** Which important terms or concepts in this chapter do you believe you grasp pretty well? Which don't you understand so well?

    Which terms or concepts are new for you. What aspects of the terminology of writing are giving you trouble?

*19. Analyzing by going "around the circle" is a deeper and more systematic way of *understanding* something. How do you ordinarily go about understanding something? Take a concrete example such as understanding what a book is saying, or understanding the kind of friendship you have with someone or how well a particular sports figure plays, or understanding something in a course you are studying such as classical conditioning, Hamlet's motivations, or office management. How do you do it?

20. There is a sense in which this is the main question in the exercises to this chapter. At the end of the Exercises to Chapter 1, you were asked to choose some topics that you are interested in, ones that you believe you could write about in an informed, interesting way for, say, five pages. For this question you may continue with those or choose alternatives.

    Take several of the topics—at least three—and analyze them by going around the circle.

Self-Assessment: Test It Out #1

How Can You Tell How Well You Did?

Test It Out #1: Being clear about the main thing you will say in a paper. How can you tell how well you did? (Actually, it's hard to test out something like this at the beginning. You don't know what you don't know, and that means if you write something, it's difficult to tell how good a job you've done without getting feedback from someone who already knows a lot about writing. Still, you can give it a try.)

One frequent response to encountering this self-test is not actually to do it. For example, people sometimes go directly to this section without having written out any thesis statements of their own. Sometimes people do that as a conscious choice, but more often they do it only semi-consciously: they turn to this section in the hope that reading the comments here will be enough to let them write their own thesis statements.

It's *possible* that this method will work for you, but it's not likely. A good comparison is that critical thinking is like playing a sport. Someone can *tell* you how to play soccer, and they can show you how *they* do it—but unless you actually do it yourself, you haven't learned how to do it. Coming up with a thesis statement is something you have to *do*, not just read about.

Another frequent response to the self-test is to sidestep writing a thesis statement and do something else instead. For example, people sometimes say things like:

- I'd look at some websites or articles and find a thesis statement there.
- I'd do research on the topic and then I'd come up with a thesis statement based on what I found out.

To a certain extent, the second one is a hopeful path to take, but it sidesteps the point of the self-test. After you do research, you still have to come up with a single specific, focused statement that expresses the main thing you will say about your topic. That's where the challenge of it is. A suggestion is that you take self-test #1 again, but this time choose a topic that you already know a lot about (such as a personal issue in your life).

The comments that follow assume that you have actually written out a statement that expresses the main thing you would say in a paper about the topics you chose.

Assessing the thesis statements you came up with. Here are some criteria you can use to tell how well you did. Your thesis statement needs to be:

- a single statement (not just rambling sentences that go on and on),
- one that is focused and specific,
- one you could build your whole paper around without going off into side issues,
- one that you could write about in an informed, interesting way for, say, five pages.

It will probably still be hard to tell if your thesis statement meets those criteria. A comparison that might help is to look at the three pairs of sample thesis statements that follow. Each is from a highly reputed writing center at a major university. In each pair, (i) is not nearly specific and focused enough to make an effective thesis statement; in each pair, (ii) is stronger.

i. There are serious objections to today's horror movies.
ii. Because modern cinematic techniques have allowed filmmakers to get more graphic, horror flicks have desensitized young American viewers to violence.[1]

i. There are some negative and positive aspects to the Banana Herb Tea Supplement.
ii. Because Banana Herb Tea Supplement promotes rapid weight loss that results in the loss of muscle and lean body mass, it poses a potential danger to customers.[2]

i. Drug use is detrimental to society.
ii. Illegal drug use is detrimental because it encourages gang violence.[3]

Now look at the thesis statements you yourself came up with, and see if your own are closer to (i) or (ii).

Here is a last question, one that goes to the heart of critical thinking. It's a question about strategy for the future. If you did not come up with a thesis statement that, in your best judgment, really works, the question confronting you is:

> *How* will you come up with one? What is your *plan* or *strategy* for coming up with a rich, substantive thesis statement?

That is exactly one of the main questions this book is designed to help with.

[At this point, go back to "To the Student: Test It Out #2, (p. xxxi–xxxii)."]

CHAPTER 3

Constructing the Paper: Planning, Researching, Writing

The GPS on the right locates where you are in the process. In the first stages, you started off with a topic (perhaps one that was general and unfocused); then you analyzed it around the circle. This chapter centers on two more stages of the GPS: *planning* out the paper, and then *writing* it. The lower box on the right again lists aspects of critical writing that run through everything. Among those aspects, the focus of this chapter is on *research*.

> **GPS**
> • topic
> • analysis →
>
> • **plan: thesis, structure, outline** →
> • **writing** →
>
> • "the other side" →
> • improvement →
> • flow

Constructing the Paper Out of the Analysis: Thesis, Main Points, Structure, Outline

By analyzing around the circle, your knowledge and understanding of the topic has both focused and deepened. The next stage is to come up with a logical plan—the thesis statement and main points that together constitute the outline of the paper as a whole.

The question now is: How do you come up with a thesis statement? And how do you then come up with the main points (and any further supporting points) to back it up? And how do you then assemble those parts into a coherent whole, one that maps out the structure of your whole paper and guides you, step by step, through writing it?

And the answer to those questions is that, to a large degree, *you have already done it.*

> **Pervasive** aspects
>
> • **research**
>
> • critical thinking standards
> • revision
> • fundamental & powerful concepts
> • giving credit

Or at least you probably have. If you have analyzed your topic using your best thinking and research, your thesis and main points (and even additional supporting points) are almost certainly there in the responses you have given, waiting to be extracted.

You may already see the way that will work. One of the main things the analysis around the circle gives you is a stronger, deeper ownership of your topic. As you look at your analysis, your responses will show aspects of the topic that you see as important, that fit together, and that are, in your judgment, insightful.

So, from your analysis, how do you construct your paper? Your analysis straightforwardly lets you discover or construct your thesis statement—the idea your entire paper is built around. In much the same way, it lets you see the main points of your paper—and thus an outline of the whole thing.

There are two paths you can take to find the plan of your paper.

Path #1. Letting it emerge. This path begins by realizing that there is a good chance your thesis statement is already stated in your analysis, right there in front of you. What you have to do is *see* it there. If you look, your thesis statement may jump out at you from your analysis. It may be in your response to *any* of the elements. Look for it: it is the most central and significant statement in your analysis. It may be something you wrote down as an implication or a conclusion. It may be one of the assumptions you found or a concept you explicated. Or it may be a combination of more than one of the elements. Wherever it appears in your analysis, the thesis statement is the one that stands out for you. It is the one that, in your best judgment, contains the most central thing you want to say about your topic.

In addition, and almost as valuable, your analysis very likely also contains the main ideas you will use to back up or explain the thesis statement. You may have to state them more clearly and fit them together in a more coherent way, and you may decide to add to them, but most of the full logical plan of your paper is probably already there in your responses to the elements. The essence of "letting it emerge" is *seeing* the plan of your paper in your analysis.

Path #2. Constructing it. This second path is the one you follow when the plan of your paper does not emerge for you, when there is no response that stands out as *the* central thing you are saying in the paper. This path is your Plan B. In this second path, you *construct* your plan out of the responses you gave as you analyzed the topic around the circle. You do it in a straightforward way.

Here's how. You read your responses carefully. As you do this, you pick out the most important points you raise in your analysis. These are the responses that, in your best judgment, carry the most weight and insight. You construct the plan of your paper straightforwardly by joining them together.

You will still have to do the work of making them fit together to form a coherent whole. You may also have to re-state some of these points in different words, and, down the road, there may be other points you choose to add, or points you decide to subtract, or other adjustments you may make. But this is the foundation.

Suppose you read your analysis around the circle, and you pick out four of your responses. Call them A, B, C and D. These are the points that, in your best judgment, are most important, the ones that carry the most weight for the topic you are writing about. Those four statements, then, constitute the plan of your paper:

A
B
C
D

The reason this process works so straightforwardly is that you have already put in a good deal of reasoning (including knowledge you may have acquired through research) into the analysis around the circle. The elements of reasoning then work by sorting out your understanding of the topic into separate statements in the responses you've written down. That is what lets the logic of the topic emerge so you can *see* it there. From those responses you can then select the ones that are most important. Seeing them as a whole in front of you (and perhaps adjusting them so they fit together better), you will be expressing the main points of your paper, the main things you want to say about the topic. When you think of the process this way, it seems only natural that a critical thinking analysis would reveal the plan of your paper.

It is important to notice what has just happened. The one path is "letting it emerge." The other path is "constructing it." Either way, what you have at this point, very near the beginning, is a well-defined, specific overall outline of your paper—or at the very least a major portion of it. Moreover, your plan for the paper has been vastly improved by applying critical thinking concepts.

In addition, some of the responses you include in your paper may be based on research you have already done. For others, you can mark an **R** next to any of them you still need to research. What this means is that your research will not be haphazard. Instead, you'll be guided in it by the well-organized plan you have built.

A frequently recommended way to write a paper is to read or view something, then summarize it, and finally identify your response to it. (Sometimes your response will be how you disagree, or see the issue from a different angle, or apply what is said in an important, different way.) This is often an excellent way to generate a thesis statement.

But analysis "around the circle" gives you more choices. In your analysis around the circle, your response will usually show up as a *conclusion* you draw about the article, or your way of *interpreting* it differently, or as an *assumption* you make about it.

In some approaches to argumentative writing, your response to an article is assumed to be the thesis of your paper. But notice that it doesn't have to be. Giving the analysis "around the circle" will often put your reaction to it in a different light, and you may end up choosing your thesis statement from among your other responses. Using the circle of elements makes you less limited.

Additional benefits of the analysis. The central benefit, then, of a critical thinking analysis is that it gives you a logical organization for your paper. Moreover, when you are actually writing the paper, you may find that you need additional supporting points to amplify or back up the thesis and main points: these too are likely to be in the responses you have already given in your analysis. But there are unlooked-for benefits as well, and some of them are substantial. A major one that will be explored more deeply in a few pages is that the analysis also gives you a guide for your research. In addition, though, with a well-thought-out analysis and plan in front of you, you should in fact have a substantial portion of the paper pre-written.

Introductory section and concluding section. The goal of an *introductory section* is to tell the reader the thesis of your paper and the main points you will be making—this is precisely what your plan spells out. You may have to re-phrase some of them, but they are essentially there in front of you. Something similar applies to the *concluding section*. There, the goal is to summarize what you've been saying in the paper—in essence, these are again the thesis and other main points—plus any insights you gained during the writing.

Giving credit. An essential part of writing a paper is giving credit. This usually involves giving citations in your text to sources you have used and giving full reference information for these sources on a page at the end titled "Works Cited," "References," or

"Bibliography" (see p. 198–199). Many times, writers will hold these off to the end, even though this is the most burdensome approach. Alternatively, if you cut-and-paste reference information about sources as soon as you come across them (and maybe bookmark them as well), giving credit will be much easier. You can then simply ignore sources you ended up not using.

Taking notes. As you analyze around the circle and then build your plan, you will be mentally processing your responses and the points you are choosing from those responses. You'll be thinking about what you mean by a given main point or why it's important. Examples may come into mind, or you may find yourself wondering if this or that is the best way to say it. Usually, that kind of processing is something that people are only slightly aware of, and it's something they often do only in their heads. But you can do at least some of that processing at the keyboard as well. In a way, it's just taking notes on what is going on in your mind.

This is a place where SEE-I can be particularly helpful. If you take written notes as part of the planning process, you can use SEE-I as a way of making the notes more productive. As you process, you try to *state* what you are saying more clearly, you *elaborate* on what you mean by this or that. You can prompt yourself to write down *examples* or find good *illustrations*.

You probably won't do it for all your points, but any written notes you take—even if they are only partial SEE-I's—will be there on your computer for you to incorporate into the paper when you are writing out the actual sentences and paragraphs. Often, people can't get themselves to take notes as they write, but if you can, it will make it substantially easier to write the body of the paper (see "Writing Before You Write," p. 100–102).

Going through the Process, Step-by-Step: An Example, with Commentary

Michelle is writing a paper for a class. The instructor suggests some possible topics but also lets students choose their own. Michelle has had some rough experiences where she has been the victim of stereotyping, and she decides to choose that as her topic. In addition, she decides she is already familiar enough with stereotyping to write the paper based in part on her own knowledge and experience. But, even though her instructor has not called this a "research paper," she knows her paper will be a lot more reliable if she researches some of the main points she will be making.

She also knows that as it stands "stereotyping" is far too general to yield a focused paper by itself. It is certainly not a "thesis statement": it's not even a statement, just a single word. (At this point, recognize how easy it is to find yourself in Michelle's position. You have a topic you're interested in, and you want to write about it, but it's far too general and too open-ended even to begin.)

Michelle begins by giving a critical thinking analysis "around the circle." Her analysis is a brief one, but her responses are the result of some intense thinking. There is a lot more thinking going on than appears in her written words. With each element, she doesn't just apply it mechanically. She consciously calls on her best judgment as she applies it to stereotyping. She recognizes that her answers may not be perfect and they may change later, but they are the genuine products of her thinking, at this moment in time. (She places an **R** next to responses where research is needed or would be helpful.)

Michelle's Analysis

Topic for paper: **Stereotyping.**

question at issue:
- *What is stereotyping and what harm does it do?*

information:
- *Stereotypes of groups are often inaccurate.*
- *People who are being stereotyped are not all the same.*

assumptions:
- *It is unfair to treat people as if they are all the same.*
- *The amount of stereotyping is increasing in our society.*

points of view:
- *the point of view of the people who are using stereotypes: People just use stereotypes without even thinking about how they affect other people.*
- *the point of view of the person being stereotyped: It's negative. That person feels unfairly treated and not given a chance to show what he or she can do.*

implications and consequences *(of stereotyping):*
- *Individuals are classified and judged not by who they are or what they do, but by their race or gender or some other classification.*
- *Sometimes people are denied jobs or housing or other opportunities because they have been stereotyped.* **R** *[She thinks research will probably give her some actual data about this point.]*

purpose:

- *to judge individuals on the basis of what they themselves do, not on the basis of assumptions society has about the groups they belong to.*

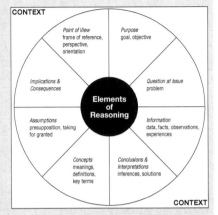

conclusion, interpretation:

- *Stereotyping is unfair.*
- *It does harm to people.*
- *Stereotyping makes us interpret people's behavior by using unfounded cultural generalizations. (R: Find some actual examples of people being judged by a stereotype.)*

concept, key terms:

- *An important concept is* <u>stereotyping</u> *itself. A stereotype is an over-simplified idea or image people use to classify members of a group. (R: Get a more exact definition.)*
- *Another key term in my analysis is* <u>harm</u>*: The harm caused by stereo-typing can be*
  - *emotional (for example, the feeling of being unfairly treated),*
  - *economic (for example, being denied a job or a promotion),*
  - *even physical (for example, people have actually been beaten and killed for being gay).*

context: Stereotyping is a major issue in America today, and maybe in other countries too. You find it everywhere—in news stories, in things people say to you, on social media.

Below, Michelle is using the response in her analysis to come up with a strong thesis and main points. To get a feel for how this might work in your own case, it will help if you immerse yourself in her thought process.

The path of "letting it emerge."

Michelle is strongly opposed to stereotyping people, and she thinks that many of her responses are important. If she had to choose only one as her thesis statement, it would be one of her responses under point of view:

- *The person who is stereotyped feels put in a box and not given a chance to show what he or she can do.*

She could simply take this as her thesis statement and then search through her responses for her other main points. But she thinks that several of the responses she gave are equally important. Because of that, she decides to use path #2—"constructing it"—to find the main points she will build her paper around. These will constitute her logical plan for the paper.

The path of "constructing it."

She re-reads her analysis several times and sees any number of possibilities. Out of those, she chooses five as the most important things she wants to say in her paper. Two of them are <u>conclusions</u> she wrote down, one is a <u>consequence</u> she thought was extremely important, and two of them are from <u>point of view</u>:

Outline

1. *Stereotyping is unfair.*
2. *It does harm to people.*
3. *A consequence of stereotyping is that sometimes people are denied jobs or housing or other opportunities because they have been stereotyped.*
4. *People just use stereotypes without even thinking about how they affect other people.*
5. *The person who is stereotyped feels unfairly treated and not given a chance to show what he or she can do.*

Take a moment to reflect on Michelle's process so far. At the beginning, she has a choice about whether to use Path #1 or Path #2. She can choose one of her responses as her thesis statement. She would then take other responses as the main points of her paper. She will choose to have a single thesis statement if she thinks it is the best way to look at the issue. In this instance, she doesn't do that. Instead, she sees her paper as centering on all five of the points in her outline, giving her a well-defined plan for writing her paper.

It is important to pause here to appreciate how this process applies to your own writing. Coming up with a specific, articulated plan is a major achievement in itself. Moreover, it is an achievement that many people find extremely difficult, and it's one that many people never master. With it you have a logical plan for writing virtually your whole paper.

Moving into the Writing: SEE-I

Michelle will write her paper using SEE-I all the way through. One at a time, she will take each of her main points and *state* it (maybe re-phrasing it to be clearer and more precise); then she will *elaborate* on it, explaining it in detail, in a paragraph or more; she'll give some well-chosen *examples*;

and, wherever it is helpful, she'll come up with a powerful *illustration*—a comparison, analogy, simile or metaphor—to bring it home to the reader.

She will also *staircase* her SEE-I's (p. 25–26). That is, she'll look closely at each of the main points in her paper. She won't just read them—she'll look *closely* at them and search for ideas, words, or phrases within them that could be clarified further. By drawing a circle around them, and then giving an SEE-I for them, she will generate fresh new ways of developing her paper.

Introductory section. There is a sense in which Michelle already "has" the introductory section of her paper, or at least the essence of it. It consists of the five main points of her paper, the outline of it, this time written out in a cogent paragraph. It's a chance for her to say these points clearly and with enough detail for the reader to understand the main emphasis of her paper and why it is worth reading.

The body of the paper. Michelle will write—or "develop"—the body of her paper all the way through using SEE-I. She'll begin by stating her first main point:

Stereotyping is unfair.

It may seem that this simple statement is perfectly clear all by itself, but that impression is deceptive. There is a good deal about the statement that needs to be explained more fully. How might Michelle elaborate?

She can start by explaining just *how* stereotyping is unfair. What exactly about stereotyping makes it unfair?

She might explain some differences between fair and unfair treatments, and maybe also explain exactly what she means by "fairness." She might explore the difference between just *feeling* you were treated unfairly and actually *being* treated unfairly. It will take several paragraphs to spell out fully what is involved in the unfairness of stereotyping.

> This stage, the bulk of the actual writing, is usually called "development." This is a good word for the process you go through as you write a paper because you are *developing* the main points in your outline. That is, you are explaining those points, expanding on them, giving examples and illustrations, showing the reader what is involved in those points.

Next she'll move on to *examples*. Here she'll try to give examples of different kinds so she can show the wide range of stereotypes that people use. For instance, she might give one example having to do with race and another having to do with gender. To broaden the point beyond race and gender, she might give examples of other kinds of stereotypes, maybe about age groups (perhaps including a personal example of a stereotype often applied to her own age group) or about people in different professions (students, politicians, rock stars…).

She will then work to come up with an *illustration*: an analogy or a metaphor, something she can compare with stereotyping. Here she's looking for situations other than stereotyping where people are treated unfairly because of inaccurate assumptions made about them, maybe an innocent person being convicted of a crime, or even having people repeatedly calling you by a nickname you hate. In any case, this is an opportunity for her to be creative and clear at the same time.

Then she will move on to give an SEE-I for her next main point:

Stereotyping does harm to people.

Again, it might seem as if this point is clear enough all by itself, but there is a good deal Michelle can develop about it. She might describe the frustration, sometimes even the rage, that comes from being stereotyped. She might describe how when someone treats you badly, you might never even know if it was because they were stereotyping you, but you'll suspect it just the same. So when you're a victim of stereotyping, the harm continues into the future. She might bring in emotional, economic, and even physical harm. (She thought of these in her analysis around the circle under *concepts*.) These different kinds of harm will give her a range of *examples* as well. Her illustration would focus on things that can harm you in a way analogous to the way stereotypes harm you. (She says it is like *getting a virus on your computer*.)

There is a good deal of creativity in her paper already, and it comes out further in what she decides to "staircase." For instance, her third main point is:

> *A consequence of stereotyping is that sometimes people are denied jobs or housing or other opportunities because they have been stereotyped.*

In her SEE-I she describes how people are often rejected for jobs and how they are denied access to housing. She researches (**R**) this point as well, finding actual information about the effect of discrimination on jobs and housing.

She could now move on to her next main point, but instead she considers the idea of *staircasing*. Inside the main point she's just written about, she focuses on one part of it:

> A consequence of stereotyping is that sometimes people are denied jobs or housing or other opportunities because they have been stereotyped.

The circle tells her that she can use an SEE-I to explore the "other opportunities" people miss out on by being stereotyped. These would include opportunities that people never even know about. Michelle writes, "You could be held back in elementary school because you were stereotyped, and as a result you might later miss out on a college education or a career—and you would never even know it." She wonders about opportunities she herself has missed out on without even realizing it.

Exploring these "other opportunities" opens up a rich additional area Michelle can write about. But it's a *choice*. She isn't *obligated* to SEE-I the "other opportunities." She can decide about that now or later, based on whether she wants to use it to expand or deepen her paper.

You may have noticed that a major part of the way staircasing works is through *focus*. It draws your attention to aspects of a statement or paragraph you ordinarily would just glide over, without giving them a second thought. This focus is a good deal of what makes staircasing such a powerful tool. In Michelle's case, you should recognize how easy it would have been for her *not* to have noticed the phrase "other opportunities" at all. Staircasing draws her attention to it.

As she continues writing her paper, she develops each of her main points, and also thinks about her topic as a whole. As she does, her creativity continues to play an important role. It comes out in the way she elaborates, in the wording she uses, in her choice of evocative examples that hit home with the reader, in rich illustrations that help the reader feel the seriousness of being stereotyped.

She works to try and come up with a really good illustration for what it is like to be stereotyped. She wants people who haven't thought about it much to envision what it's like. She has already compared it to a computer virus, but she is dissatisfied with that illustration. For her, that comparison doesn't capture the feeling of it at all.

It takes her some time, but she finally comes up with an illustration that she thinks conveys it better:

> Being stereotyped is like carrying a load of bricks on your back. It weighs you down. Things around you look fair—equal opportunity for jobs, education, housing—but you are carrying a weight that other people aren't.

One of the reasons this illustration works well for her is that it is *structural*: it helps structure her thinking about other aspects of stereotyping in a more unified way. It generates a whole range of further ideas about stereotyping. For instance, she considers the idea that each of the bricks you carry is a time when you have been stereotyped and have missed out on something because of it. You fall further and further behind. You may not even notice the weight increasing—you may think it's your own fault that you're further behind. Or you may think, "It's just one little brick. Why am I making such a big deal about it?"

The ideas based on that illustration develop further. She thinks that when people look at you, they may not see *you* at all. They may just see the bricks that you are carrying. People may do that without even meaning to—in a way it seems almost automatic: "When a person is carrying a load of bricks, what you notice is not the *person*, but the bricks on the person's back!" But no matter how automatic that reaction is, she thinks, they are still adding more bricks to the ones you are already carrying.

Her illustration is powerful enough for her to consider making it part of the title of her paper: "Carrying the Weight of Stereotyping."

Concluding section. In her concluding section, she may choose to re-state her main points. She can do so in different words this time, partly to avoid uninteresting repetition, but also because her thoughts about stereotyping will have evolved over the course of writing the paper. (She may also use the changes that have emerged in her thinking to revise the introductory section.)

Making your points more unified. You may have noticed how well Michelle's points flow together. They all interconnect, and as a result she has no trouble writing them out in a way that seems unified and natural. That may not always be true for you. In the purest case, the main points you select will fit together smoothly, and the reader's attention will follow along just as smoothly. But sometimes, when you assemble the main points together, they may seem choppy or disjointed. They may not fit together so naturally.

When that happens you may have to do some work to make them more unified. Sometimes you may end up dropping a point you've chosen or adding another one. More usually, you may have to work to re-phrase them, combining them so that they form an organic whole. The goal is to convey their underlying coherence. You want the reader to feel the smooth logical flow.

Enhanced SEE-I: Developing Your Paper

There are many ways to develop your paper. So far, the suggested ways have been based on SEE-I. But SEE-I is more flexible than may at first appear, and it can be expanded and refined to give you more choices about how to write the content of your paper.

Elaboration. A great variety of further ways to elaborate and explain a point will be spelled out with Socratic questioning in Chapter 5 (see p. 164–166). Socratic questioning in fact gives you virtually unlimited means for developing your paper.

Examples and contrasting examples. It has already been mentioned that you can give several examples, not just one, so that you can depict different aspects of the point you are making. Doing so will give your paper significantly greater breadth.

> Notice that the description of SEE-I is somewhat different from the one in Chapter 1. The differences should remind you that "clarifying with SEE-I" is not a cut-and-dried procedure. The same holds for the other processes of critical writing: There is more than one reasonable way to go about doing them.

But, in addition to giving examples, you can also give *contrasting examples* to make your point not just clearer but also more precise. While an *example* shows what is *included* in a concept, a *contrasting example* shows what is *excluded*. In Michelle's case, as we have seen, her examples of stereotyping include illegitimately denying someone a job because of the person's race or gender. For a contrasting example, she would describe something that is *not* stereotyping, some reasons why, in her view, a person might legitimately be denied a job. Here is what she comes up with:

> *Suppose a job requires you to be able to speak to clients in Spanish. In that case it makes sense for applicants to be denied that job if they can't speak Spanish. An inability to speak Spanish is not a stereotype. Why? Because it's directly related to the job requirement. However, denying applicants a job because of their race or gender is stereotyping them.*

Notice how giving a contrasting example not only helps you understand what she means by stereotyping but also pinpoints it. That's greater precision.[*]

Illustrations. Finding a good illustration can dramatically increase the clarity of the ideas you are trying to communicate. But they can also easily be over-used. That is particularly true when the illustration is hackneyed or a cliché. When someone writes something trite such

---

[*] A few more contrasting examples in this book: on p. 22, the elaboration-part of the SEE-I for criticality gives four examples of what criticality is *not*; there are several contrasting examples in the section "So What Is Critical Thinking?" (p. 61–62).

as "It was like pulling teeth" or "It was like watching paint dry," it's hardly an illustration at all. It merely *says* that the thing was very difficult or very boring—but you don't actually get an image of someone pulling teeth or of laboriously sitting for hours watching paint dry. As a writer, the goal is to come up with an illustration that strongly *conveys* your point to the reader. Though illustrations in general are very helpful, if you can't come up with a good one, it may sometimes be better just to stick with examples. (Again, it is "SEE and sometimes I.")

Illustrations can be:
- quiet
- vivid

- overdone
- forced
- too flowery
- hackneyed
- cliché

- structural

Sometimes illustrations can be quiet or understated and still play an important role in clarifying. Michelle might begin a paragraph in her paper by saying:

Stereotyping, like other forms of discriminatory behavior, ...

It is an illustration, but a quiet one. It is a comparison of stereotyping to other similar kinds of behavior. Though it is understated, it nevertheless helps to clarify the writer's approach to stereotyping.

The most powerful illustrations are **structural**, such as Michelle's comparison between being stereotyped and carrying a load of bricks on your back. A structural illustration communicates your ideas clearly to the reader. But, almost as important, it also tends to unify your paper overall, and it clarifies and develops ideas in your own mind, generating aspects of the topic that you haven't thought of. Notice how Michelle's analogy illustrates so many of her points about stereotyping: its unfairness, the harm it does, and the practical consequences it has. It even gives readers a way to picture how people can use stereotypes "automatically," without even thinking about it. As Michelle says:

> When a person is carrying a load of bricks, what you notice is not the person, but the bricks on the person's back!

Her illustration also brings her some new thoughts about

Choices. An important aim of this book is to show the wealth of choices critical thinking opens up for you as you write a paper. You have *options* everywhere: about how to focus your topic, generate ideas, find main points you want to emphasize, organize your paper, develop it, staircase it, and expand it (maybe to meet length requirements). Later, the book will introduce you to other choices critical thinking offers you as well.

stereotyping: how the harm can build up over time, and how people might think they are falling behind through their own fault, without realizing it might be because they are carrying a heavier weight. Again, you don't have to agree with the points Michelle is making to see how powerful her structural illustration is.

Staircasing. Staircasing too applies more widely than might at first appear, and it gives you far-ranging opportunities to expand and strengthen your paper. Staircasing isn't confined only to the main points of your analysis "around the circle." You can also decide to staircase concepts and ideas that come up in your elaboration (or sometimes even in examples and illustrations you give). Thus, in one of her elaborations, Michelle says, "You could be held back in elementary school because you were stereotyped, and because of that you might later miss out on a college education or a career—and you would never even know it." She could circle the phrase "never even know it" and give an SEE-I for it, elaborating on how that might happen in a person's life, giving examples of it, or stories about it, and maybe an illustration as well.

The key is that staircasing allows you to focus on concepts and ideas that are important for your paper, and then to develop them, regardless of where those concepts and ideas occur.

> **Rhetoric.** Rhetoric has to do with *how* you say (or present) something. An essential part of effective rhetorical writing is keeping in mind your intended audience as well as the circumstances in which you are writing. Enhanced SEE-I, though it's not the whole story, straightforwardly helps with this. Other aspects of rhetoric will come up in Chapter 6, on paying attention to how your paper flows.

Researching the Paper

Doing a critical thinking analysis focuses you. The circle of elements gives you the tools that let you concentrate on what is most relevant and important about a topic. That is what makes it so useful for planning out your paper, for coming up with both a significant thesis statement and a structure of well-thought-out points to back it up.

But analyzing around the circle also helps dramatically with *research*. It focuses you there too. It guides you in seeing what you have to research to make your paper substantive and compelling. It also, more optionally, suggests other specific aspects of the topic you can research to make your paper fuller and more authoritative.

Conversely, doing research in an ill-defined, un-thought-out way can be one of the most frustrating aspects of writing a paper. Many times, when students are assigned a research paper on a particular topic, they go about the research haphazardly, in a way that seems to rely on hoping they will just stumble across what they need by sheer luck. They start looking for sources on a topic guided simply by a search engine that highlights key terms. Typically, thousands of possible sources come up: some are reliable, some are not; some are relevant, some are not, and some you can't tell about; some are available online, some are not; and many of them plunge you into the most intricate, specialized, and advanced aspects of the topic, aspects that are extremely unlikely to be usable in your paper. This way of doing things can sentence you to a huge amount of fruitless and discouraging work. By relying on the elements of reasoning as your guide, your research will be focused and lead you to a substantive approach to your topic.

Two Roles of Research in Planning and Writing a Paper

What is the goal of research? And what roles does it play in writing a paper? The goal of a paper is not just to report what people say in their publications, and the goal certainly is not to cut-and-paste what various sources say. (What would be the point of that?) Moreover, it's not as if "doing research" solves your problems in writing—not even if what you're writing is a "research paper." When you are engaged in critical writing, research will play two strikingly different roles for you. Before you begin, you use it to become familiar enough with the topic to write about it with understanding. Then, when you analyze the topic around the circle, you target research in a more focused way. One of the most helpful consequences of using the circle of elements is that your analysis often displays for you what specifically you need to research.

"Research" is another word for "finding out," but the goal of research itself is not just to amass facts about a topic. It's not a passive activity. The goal is to learn about a topic and *understand* it. Researching is a critical thinking activity. Similarly, the main goal of a critical writing paper is for you to learn about and think your way through a topic, using reliable research to make your thinking more accurate, clear, relevant, and more attuned to what is important, and then to communicate your well-informed thinking to an audience.

Writing a substantive paper requires knowledge of the topic. You can't write effectively about a topic unless you know and understand enough about it. You can't engage in critical writing (or critical thinking of any sort) just off the top of your head. Occasionally (as with topics about your personal life, for example), this knowledge can come directly from you: You may already know the topic in enough depth to analyze it around the circle and then write the paper out of your own understanding and background knowledge. More usually, though, writing a paper requires active research. Even when knowledge comes directly from your own experience, it usually enriches the paper if you corroborate your experience with research into the experiences of others. (Research is also a key part of most of the writing you will have to do when you are out of school.)

In a larger sense, though, your research is a reflection of who you are and of what you stand for. You will be saying many things in your paper. Some of what you say may come from your personal experience, some from your own thinking about the topic, and some from the sources you consult. But no matter where they come from, by writing them in your paper, you are vouching for them. In effect, you are giving your word that people can rely on what you say. You obviously can't *guarantee* that what you are saying is absolutely true, but you *can* guarantee that you've made a good-faith effort to find out what's true, that you've exercised your best judgment, and that you have used sources that you have every reason to believe are reliable. Again, doing good research is part of being a trustworthy person.

Though research plays many roles in writing a paper, two of them can be highlighted. Part of the difficulty with doing research comes from mixing up these two kinds of research and what can be accomplished by each.

Background research. Often, you may write a paper about a topic that initially you know very little about. For example, an instructor may assign you a paper on "democracy in Singapore" or "college life at Oxford." Or you may choose a topic yourself: maybe you have just read Jane Austen's *Pride and Prejudice*, and you'd like to write a paper on Jane Austen as a writer. Unless you already know a great deal about democracy in Singapore or Oxford or Jane Austen, you will have to do research even to *begin* giving a logical analysis of it. (The same thing comes up when you are out of school: employers often require people to write reports on new projects they initially know very little about.) One of the traits of a critical thinker is intellectual humility: even when you already know about a topic, you may have to realize that there is a lot of background knowledge you lack about it. Besides, it hardly seems reasonable to assume that all your background knowledge is automatically accurate. Background research will help in those cases too.

Focused research. Focused research has a different goal. This is the kind of research you do when you have fairly specific questions about a topic you are exploring or a point you are making. What focuses the research is *the circle of elements*. Using them to analyze a topic displays for you, and calls your attention to, those points that you need to do research on.

For example, if a main point in a paper you're writing is about whether capital punishment is a deterrent, you almost certainly have to research that claim. You can't support a claim like this simply by having an impression that it's true. Seeing the point singled out in your analysis helps you see that you need research that focuses on that specific question.

Doing Background Research

Background research is what gives you the knowledge about your topic, the familiarity with it, to let you begin. It is a starting point, not an end point. It lays a foundation, but it may still be necessary to do further (more focused) research to adequately support individual points in your paper. The goal in doing background research is to gain the insight and understanding you need so that you can analyze the topic around the circle—and then write the paper—in an informed way.

For some topics, you may be able to analyze them with a fair degree of confidence without doing a good deal of background research. If you're an American, depending on the specific issue you are focused on, "democracy in the U.S." may be an example of that for you. So may be "college life at your school." (As an aside: Note that it would make sense not to be over-confident of your background knowledge of either of these areas.) Contrast those topics with "democracy in Singapore" or "college life at Oxford." With topics like these last two, you may lack the background understandings to do an analysis of them around the circle. You probably don't have any idea of the main *points of view* about democracy

The problem is not just that topics such as "democracy in Singapore" or "college life at Oxford" are too general to serve as a topic. They *are* very general. But you can go around the circle even with respect to general topics, provided you have enough knowledge for the analysis. Excessive generality is a problem, but using the circle of elements often allows you to take even a general topic and extract from it a thesis statement and the main points.

in Singapore, or what *assumptions* Singaporeans make about their democracy, or what are main *questions at issue* facing students at Oxford. Without such background familiarity, you can't even begin to do an analysis around the circle. The point of background research, then, is to give you enough *familiarity* with a topic to engage productively in an analysis. You have to use your own best critical judgment to decide at what point your "familiarity" with a topic is "enough."

What kinds of sources can you use for background research? There are many. You may get a good deal of background knowledge from a class you are taking, if the topic has been covered in some depth, or by reading books or the introductions to scholarly books where the topic has been covered as a whole. Many people use Wikipedia for a first stab at background research, both for a brief overview and for a list of further sources that can be consulted. Your instructor may require you to turn in a preliminary list of references you will use to get general background knowledge of a topic.

> **Wikipedia**. Many instructors have reservations about Wikipedia and caution students to exercise considerable critical judgment when using it. It is difficult to tell, for example, about the reliability of a particular entry (those who run Wikipedia try to address this problem). You generally can't use Wikipedia itself as a reference, but you can often use it to direct you to sources that are reputable.

Go back for a moment to when Michelle was just thinking about writing a paper on stereotyping, before she began even planning it. Notice that she *decided* that she could write the paper based on her own familiarity with it. She recognized, right from the beginning, that she would have to do some *focused* research, but she decided she did not need to do *background* research. Contrast that with Lucia, who analyzed "false memory" in Chapter 2. Lucia already had *some* familiarity with her topic. It came from her course and from seeing a TED talk on it. But though she had some background knowledge, she soon decided that she didn't have enough. So she consulted some general books by reputable authorities to give her a fuller understanding. Notice that she knew she still had focused research to do: Background research is almost never enough by itself.

In both cases, though, it was a *decision*. That's important. Neither writer just drifted into writing the paper. They both made explicit, conscious, critical thinking decisions.

The critical thinking approach to background research requires self-awareness. *You decide* whether to engage in background research, and how much of it you need to do given the time available. The decisions you make may still be misguided, and you may have to live with the consequences of that, but at least it was your choice.

Doing Focused Research

The goal of focused research, by contrast, is fundamentally different from that of background research. It is not aimed at giving you an overall background familiarity. If anything, it relies on the idea that you already have enough familiarity with the topic to analyze it around the circle, and to do that pretty well. By contrast, then, it is the kind of research you do when there are unknowns you need to have answered so that you can write a paper that people can trust, or if there are parts you need to check on or confirm with more reputable information. It's the kind of research that is focused on the individual important points you singled out in your critical thinking analysis.

You do focused research when you need more information, or more exact or more reliable information about points you will make in your paper. For example, look back at Michelle's analysis of stereotyping. She marked three specific areas with an **R**, places where research would enhance her paper. One of her points was a *consequence* she recognized: that sometimes people are denied jobs or housing or other opportunities because they have been stereotyped. She marked this with an **R** because she realized that having reputable quantitative data on job discrimination and housing discrimination would make her paper far more substantive and powerful. Without reputable data her point might simply be an empty assertion. After thinking about it for a moment or two, she sees no reason why anyone would rely on an uncorroborated opinion, just because she happens to believe it strongly. In addition, she marked an **R** next to the *concept* of stereotyping, recognizing that it might be helpful to have a more exact definition, and also next to one of her *conclusions*, to focus her on finding some actual examples of people being judged on the basis of stereotypes.

You also engage in focused research when you check to see whether a point you are making is indeed accurate. Could it just be hearsay, or something you acquired from unreliable sources? Could your belief about X be biased? Focused research helps you check. For example, in her analysis of stereotyping Michelle identifies the assumption that the amount of stereotyping is increasing in our society. If she decided to make this one of the main points in her paper, she would *need* to check by researching it: it could well be that the amount of stereotyping in our society is staying the same over time, or even decreasing. It may just be that we are now more aware of stereotyping than before. Her original point may be just an impression she has, rather than something that has been confirmed with objective data. Again, she knows people need to be able to trust what she says in the paper, and she wonders, "Why would anyone trust my point here, if even I don't really know it's true?" Only research using reputable authorities will give you answers you can count on, and even then reputable authorities do not always agree.

The main way to engage in focused research for a paper is by using reliable sources, such as scholarly books and articles and reliable websites. Peer-reviewed, scholarly articles are often a necessary part of writing a paper that is based on research. A standard way to do focused research on a topic is to use a library's scholarly search engine. And there are many search engines that are reliable guides to research in specific disciplines or groups of disciplines. Many other sources, though, are not reputable enough to rely on them: random websites or blogs, magazine articles, programs on TV, editorials in newspapers, and many others. You can use them sometimes as examples, or as a topic to analyze, or as representatives of a point of view, but you can't simply trust that the information they give is accurate, relevant, precise, or clear enough to be relied on.

A key difference between background research and focused research. There is a serious pitfall involved in mixing up the roles played by the two different kinds of research, and it is easy to fall into. The pitfall is that the sources you use for background research will seldom give you the focused information you need, and the sources you use for focused research will seldom give you the overall familiarity you need for background knowledge.

You can think of the role of research this way:

▶ background research → analysis around the circle
▶ analysis around the circle → focused research

- Background research is necessary for acquiring the knowledge and understanding to analyze the topic in the first place.
- Focused research is then needed both to substantiate and to fill in the points you have chosen from your analysis around the circle.

Thus, if you are focused on understanding the democratic process in Singapore, the introductions or opening chapters to scholarly books and scholarly history-based encyclopedias on the recent history of Singapore may be good sources for acquiring the background knowledge and the "familiarity" you need to start analyzing the topic. But they wouldn't give you the more precise information you need to back up or authenticate specific points you make in your paper.

Similarly, peer-reviewed, focused, scholarly articles will not usually give you background knowledge of a topic you are unfamiliar with. They are usually not best used as an initial foundation from which to start your paper. You can easily sidetrack your whole topic by engaging in focused research at too early a stage. Scholarly articles are usually too restricted in scope to give you the overview you need. This is not a defect in the articles themselves. Rather, part of the point in writing peer-reviewed articles is to do original investigation on a focused, specific topic. Research using peer-reviewed, scholarly articles works best by giving you specific information in response to your analysis around the circle and focused on the specific points you have chosen. As an example, look at the following text box.

An example: I did a Google search on "democracy in Singapore." The first two sites were Wikipedia articles, but right after these two sites, both of the next two were political pieces criticizing this or that aspect of Singaporean democracy (one of them was written by a politician running for office). Neither of these articles would help someone get an overall understanding of the background of democracy in Singapore. They might even be seriously misleading.

Searching a more scholarly database may also bring too much focus too quickly. I did a search of "Scholarly & Peer-Reviewed" articles at a university library on "Jane Austen as a writer." The first was somebody's review of an obscure book that mentioned Jane Austen; the second was on Austen's view of animals, and the third was on her relationship with literary tourism. No help. In fact, the same was true when I looked at the entire first page of 70 scholarly articles: not one of them would give me the helpful background knowledge I needed to write about Jane Austen as a writer. Moreover, I got roughly the same results when I used library databases more specifically attuned to literature (such as the *Literature Resource Center* or *JSTOR Arts & Sciences*). Again, these peer-reviewed and scholarly articles were far too specialized to give an overview of Jane Austen as a writer.

The point, then, has two parts. The first part is that using peer-reviewed and scholarly articles is *essential* for doing reputable research for a paper. They are the most reputable source for the focused research you need to do. But the second part is that they are not meant to supply you with background knowledge or an overview.

Research and Critical Thinking

As you engage in research, whether it is focused or background research, remember that you can't leave your critical thinking behind. Thinking is important all the way through. You need to use your best critical thinking as you approach content from reputable sources. Getting accurate facts and data doesn't end the thinking process. Rather, facts and data furnish information that you have to think *about.*

Notice how analyzing around the circle and research combine two different dimensions. On the one hand, there is the dimension of what reputable sources say, the content of what you have found through your research. On the other hand, there is the dimension of your own best critical judgment. It is the combination of these two dimensions—the knowledge you have gained from reputable sources plus your own best judgment—that makes the resulting paper both informed and critical. If you leave out either of those dimensions, there will be serious flaws in the paper.

Here's an example. Tasha is a student in a business course. As part of the course, she is required to write a research-based paper. She is reading an article on a website called businessinsider.com and comes across an article about Amtrak, the national passenger rail system in the U.S. The title of the article is "Why the Heck Is Amtrak Still in Business after Losing Money 43 Years Straight?" In it, the author says, "For 43 years, Amtrak has operated at a loss. It stays in business thanks to a healthy annual government subsidy of around $1b a year." Tasha knows she can't simply rely on the information the author gives, but if it's true, it's an impressive fact. So she checks it out on Amtrak's official website. She knows that that is a reliable source.

Amtrak reports that in the previous year it earned a little more than $3 billion in revenue but had over $4 billion in expenses, thus corroborating the claim in the article. She looks through other years and sees that they check out as well. (You can see the way she gives credit to her sources in the endnote.[1]) As part of her research, she checks out some other reputable sources, and they all confirm what she read at businessinsider.com. With these facts in hand, she concludes that we should stop subsidizing Amtrak and let it go out of business.

Before reading on, check out your own response to Tasha's reasoning. You should feel the solidity of it. It is based on facts given by a reliable source. That's a good place to begin.

But Tasha still has the job of thinking through the issue. Using the circle of elements, she asks, "What are the *consequences* of terminating Amtrak?" She realizes this is a serious question, one that isn't answered simply by the result that it loses money. It's a question she sees she has to investigate. Her research into consequences isn't over: What are the consequences if there is *no* national passenger rail service in the U.S.?

This reasoning leads her to a broader *question at issue*: What is the role of a passenger rail service in the larger picture of America? Again, she doesn't know the answer, but it leads her to think that maybe there is more at stake than just whether Amtrak makes money.

She asks about *purpose*: Is the purpose of a national rail service to make money? Or are there other important goals as well? Then she asks about other services that are paid for out of taxes. Do they make money? Do interstate highways make more money than they cost? That seems extremely doubtful to her. How about police forces or the military? They certainly don't "make money"! For that matter, doesn't Congress "operate at a loss"? Doesn't Congress receive "a healthy annual government subsidy"? She is hit by this thought and says, "If we let them all 'go out of business,' there wouldn't be any country left." As she thinks about it still more, she realizes that she can't think of even a single thing the government pays for that "makes money"! She concludes that that isn't the purpose of government: it doesn't pay for services in order to "make money from them"!

Thus the result that Amtrak operates at a loss doesn't settle the issue. It is one relevant fact, but there are many other aspects of the issue that need to be addressed. Tasha still has to think about how that one fact fits into an overall analysis of Amtrak's role.

The same is true when *you* do research. Information from reliable sources has to be integrated into an overall analysis with a focus that *you* give it, and the information you have researched is only one part of the analysis.

Links between research and creating a plan for your paper. An interlinking quality exists between research and planning out your paper. Each influences the other, not just at the beginning, but all the way through. You can't just come up with a worthwhile outline in a vacuum, but you also can't expect that your research will somehow just "give you" a thesis statement and main points.

There is a distinction you always have to keep in mind, and it's one that people often mix up. It's the distinction between the order in which you proceed in your thinking and the order in which you present your thinking to the audience. Research brings out the distinction strongly. Your goal in doing research is often *to find* a solution to a problem, or *to figure out* a strategy or *come to* a well-reasoned conclusion about an issue. In these cases, the solution, strategy, or conclusion typically comes at or near the end of your thinking process. But when you write a paper on it, there is a very different logic at work. Your goal when you write the paper, by contrast, is *to convey* your thinking to your audience, and the paper you build could easily *begin* with the solution, strategy, or conclusion that was at the end of your thinking process. It could easily be your thesis statement.

Thus, in many papers, you come up with a well-reasoned thesis statement only *after* doing a fair amount of research. It makes sense. It is part of being open-minded. Sometimes you have to immerse yourself fully in a topic or area without the preconceptions that an already-formulated thesis statement might bring. It helps you avoid the "confirmation bias" that unconsciously leads people to corroborate the views they already hold (see p. 114).

Notice that no matter what, the research doesn't "give you" the plan or the thesis of your paper. Both your plan for the paper and the paper itself result from your best research *plus* your own best thinking.

Using reliable sources. In researching and writing a paper, it's essential to use only sources that are *reliable*. That's true not just in a paper but also in writing you do later as part of your job or profession. It comes in whenever you are writing something that someone will rely on.

In a way, using reliable sources can be more difficult than it sounds. The difficult part is not just *finding* sources that are reliable. You can readily find a wealth of available peer-reviewed articles, scholarly books and reputable websites. What is often more difficult is learning to use *only* reliable sources. One of the reasons it's difficult is that when we read something or watch something, we often just take it in. Unless we already happen to have some strong reasons to disagree, what we read or hear just registers with us as if it is true.

> Instructors are often distressed that students are so willing to use unreliable sources in their papers, often without even wondering about it. It's not just instructors: employers and professionals in any career area are seriously distressed at the bizarre beliefs people acquire from unreliable sources. (Imagine your dentist or lawyer learning their professions by looking casually at some random website.)

But this sort of passive acceptance can be disastrous in writing a paper. Your audience expects you to take responsibility for what you write, to stand behind it, and when you use unreliable sources you pass along unreliable information to your reader.

Sources are, of course, not labeled as "unreliable." It is important to realize that writers often just write, and, discouragingly, under many ordinary circumstances they can say almost anything. They can pick data out of context; they can report only a single unrepresentative sentence from a scientific report; they can treat rumor or hearsay as if it were fact; they can distort in order to push a political or personal agenda on you. Think of it: Any doctor can write a book advocating any diet! And unless the diet makes people seriously ill, they can't even be sued for it! For that matter, any non-doctor can do the same thing.

> **"Fact vs. fiction."** People sometimes have the impression that just because a written piece is "non-fiction," it must have some link to the truth. (They sometimes have a similar impression about "documentaries" or podcasts.)
>
> But this reasoning is completely off-track. What makes something fiction is that it contains *fictionalized characters* (as in novels, stories and plays) or intentionally *fictionalized situations*. A book, article, or video in which an author tells outright lies is as much a work of "non-fiction" as a completely factual report.

Instructors recommend scholarly books and articles that have been *peer-reviewed*. That means those publications have gone through a screening process by professionals in the discipline. It means that the authors have credentials in the field they are writing in, and that their writing has been screened by others who also have credentials. (Very few of the diet books written by actual MDs are peer-reviewed or endorsed by the American Medical Association.) Being peer-reviewed, of course, doesn't mean that such articles are always "right," but it does mean that the sources have weight and authority. (An illustration: It's like the difference between being taught basketball by someone who has coached professionally *versus* being coached by the guy on the corner who just has some strong views about playing.)

Writing and Pre-writing

Students are often concerned about time and effort. If you're writing a paper for a course (or, for that matter, writing something as part of your professional work after you graduate), you typically have only a limited time to complete it. Not only that, but you also have a lot of other things in your life that take up your time and attention: other courses, personal life, employment, family, friends, a need for recreation and fun, and a hundred others. Crises and emergencies come up. You may habitually procrastinate, and that's a problem in itself.

You may not always prioritize accurately. Maybe not all of this is legitimate as a drain on your time and effort, but much of it is.

The concepts and skills of critical writing help with this. If you work on them, they can help almost immediately, and the amount of help they give increases as you work at it. They make your paper better. And when you become skilled in them, they can also make writing a good paper substantially less time-consuming.

Writing Better *and* Saving Time

The way people often write their papers is almost a sure-fire way not to do well on them: either they just cut-and-paste or they just start writing. They begin at some starting point and then keep on going to the end. They read an article, feel a strong response to it, and then simply defend the response they have. They often arrange their paper around points that come into their mind as they write or that they happen to find in a source. Usually there is no explicit focus on choosing points precisely *because* they are the important ones. If the paper involves research, it is the research the writer just happens to come across, or that some random search engine presents to them. Often the sources used are unreliable ones. Usually, there is no explicit focus on being either clear or well organized.

Writing a paper in haphazard ways like these not only makes for a weak paper but also uses up a lot of valuable time. It is time spent going in unproductive directions, in frustration, in being at a loss about what to do at almost every point in the writing, in worry about how to fill the pages, and in the hollow feeling that, after all the time and effort you've put into it, you may still not get a good grade on the paper. In the end, the way people often write is not only full of discouragement, it also squanders their time.

A main outcome of the critical writing process is that—in addition to making your paper better—it results in saving time. How does it do that?

- The relatively short time it takes to analyze a topic and construct a logical plan means that you have an outline to guide you step-by-step in writing the paragraphs of the paper.
- SEE-I gives you a smooth and efficient process for creating those paragraphs.
- Staircasing helps you focus on additional important aspects you can choose to develop.

Thus, the main outcome of the critical writing process is that it makes your papers significantly better: clearer, more planned out, more logically organized, full of your best thinking, trustworthy. But a secondary outcome is that the process can end up actually taking less time. It does this in a way that may seem paradoxical but really isn't. It asks you to make an initial investment of your time—that's the time you spend on planning things out with critical thinking—and after that, the remaining parts of writing the paper flow more smoothly and efficiently. The focus in the remainder of this chapter is on how the process of critical writing saves you time.

Planning, and then writing. The initial-investment part is the time you spend on analyzing and understanding your topic. It is true that using the circle of elements takes time, but not nearly as much as you might think. Once you get more familiar with the elements themselves, the time it takes to apply them to your topic gets much shorter.

But then, out of this, you extract a thesis statement and a definite set of main points that constitutes the organized plan for your paper. Having that clear plan in front of you vastly reduces the amount of time and frustration you experience in writing the paper. Instead of worrying about what to do or how to go about it, you now just proceed.

Similarly, having SEE-I as a tool also allows you to reduce the time you spend. With SEE-I you now have a process for writing paragraph after paragraph, creating the paper as you move through it. You state, elaborate, exemplify, and often illustrate, again and again. It still takes work to write the paragraphs, but now you know exactly how to proceed through that work.

Moreover, with process of "staircasing" SEE-I's (and the refinements on p. 84–87), you now have possibilities—definite, focused possibilities— for expanding your paper almost at will. (Another such tool is Socratic questioning in Chapter 5.) So if you are stuck and need to have "more pages," you have a straightforward way to accomplish that. And it's not just *a* way; it's a way that is clear, relevant, and logical. The techniques of critical writing put abundant resources at your fingertips.

"Writing before you write." There is a further dimension of critical writing that also makes writing your paper more time-efficient. It too involves an initial investment on your part, and it too results in making your work easier later on. You can think of it as "writing before you write."

The suggestion is one that was mentioned earlier in this chapter. It's that the best way to "get ready" to write the paper is to write out your analysis—your thesis and main points—as well as SEE-I's for as many of them as you can manage. The suggestion is that you don't just do these "in your head," or put it off until later when you are in the middle of the paper. Instead, you write these out *ahead* of time, before you start writing the actual paper. Here's how it works.

With the thesis and other main points of your paper, the suggestion is that you write them out as clearly and as carefully as you can, making any changes or corrections as early as possible. These main points will then largely be ready to go directly into your paper. (They will be the statement part of the SEE-I.) You won't have to start from scratch all over again when you get to the writing.

The further suggestion is that you move into the rest of the SEE-I as soon as possible. You do this maybe only as notes, as soon as the ideas come up for you, while they are still fresh in your mind—but in writing.

Many people have a hard time accepting that "writing before you write" will actually save them time. And even if it does work for them, people sometimes just can't get themselves to do it. It's like taking the time to stretch before you play tennis. It's a tough psychological sticking point. If you feel that kind of resistance, you're not alone.

Still, the suggestion is that you write several things that seem to be only *preliminary* to writing the paper itself, and that you do it as part of the *planning* process. That might seem too laborious to you. And in a way it could be too laborious if all you were doing was planning the paper, and you still had to do all the work of actually writing it. But "writing before you write" is designed so that by the time you have completed the plan for your paper, a great deal of the paper will in fact already be written.

What follows from this is a kind of ideal process of critical writing:

1. As part of your planning, you write out your analysis, going around the circle of elements, and incorporating your research into it. From this analysis, you write out the thesis statement and the main points that explain or back up your thesis. Those points, again, constitute the overall plan for your paper.*

---

*People sometimes recommend *brainstorming* (or similar associational techniques) as a way to come up with a thesis statement (and maybe main points as well). How well does that work?

There is nothing intrinsically wrong with brainstorming. There is a sense in which both James's and Sheila's outlines in Chapter 1 were the product of something like brainstorming.

The problem is that brainstorming does not give you an actual usable way to find a thesis statement and main points. It relies on the points of your paper just "coming to you."

By contrast, analysis "around the circle" gives you a definite procedure to find or construct a thesis statement and main points. It's not infallible, and it relies on your thought processes and creativity, but it gives you a concrete way to proceed.

Moreover, in a broader context, critical writing (in contrast to brainstorming) provides the concepts that you can use to tell whether the ideas you come up with are "good" or "bad." More precisely, the standards of critical thinking (a main topic of Chapter 5) give you guidance in deciding whether your ideas are accurate, relevant, fair, precise, important enough to emphasize, precise, and deep and broad enough to build a paper on. A distinct danger in brainstorming is that the ideas that just come to you are merely interesting, or catchy, or just *seem* to capture something. While all of those are important, they are not the same as being clear, accurate, relevant, and so forth.

2. As part of your planning, as you sit at your keyboard, you take written notes in the form of SEE-I's: statements, elaborations, examples, and illustrations of the thesis and main points you have chosen (and maybe doing some staircasing as well). You do this also for articles you have found in your research.

At this point you have completed your planning, and it seems as if you're finally ready to begin the actual writing. But in fact, again, the paper is, to a large degree, virtually written.

All along, you seem to be just planning: just taking notes, just carrying out your analysis around the circle, just writing down SEE-I's. By the time you are finished planning, though, a good deal of the paper is there in front of you. Except for taking account of "Other Minds, Other Views" (next chapter), the main work now will mostly be assembling the parts you have already written, polishing the sentences, maybe adding some additional aspects of SEE-I here and there. You may decide to enrich or expand your paper using Socratic questioning (Chapter 5), but that's your choice.

Where Are You in the Process?

The GPS that begins this chapter lays out the process of critical writing up to this point: analysis "around the circle," planning the paper out by choosing a thesis statement and main points, researching it, and then writing it using SEE-I. But this specialized terminology can sometimes distract you from what you are really doing. The terminology is intended to make the parts of writing more exact, but it can also make you miss how down-to-earth the whole process is.

So here is a more down-to-earth way of describing the process of writing a paper. You start with something that matters to you and that you believe will matter to your audience as well. *[That's your "topic."]* What do you have to do then?

▶ Find out about it. *[That's "research."]*
▶ Think it through, understand it. *[That's "analysis around the circle."]*
▶ Decide what you're going to say about it. *[This is the "thesis and main points."]*
▶ Then say it *[using "SEE-I"].*

This is the fundamental process for writing a paper, not just a relatively short one but a paper of any length. (At the end of Chapter 5 there is a section on "Writing Longer Papers.") But beyond papers, the process is something you can use throughout your life in many contexts. You find out about something you're interested in, you think it through, you decide on what position you will take, and then you carry that position through in actions. You may not do all these parts explicitly or consciously, but you can use this process when you think about jobs, classes, decisions, sports, shows you watch, or relationships you are in.

One of the main things the tools of critical thinking bring to the process is that they lay out *what* exactly you need to find out, *how* you can think things through more accurately and deeply, *how* to make better decisions about what to accept, and *how* to carry it through into action.

Chapter 3: Practice and Assessment Exercises

*1. The process of critical writing is partially highlighted in the GPS that begins this chapter. So far, the process runs this way:

   GPS
   * topic →
   * analysis →
   * plan (thesis, structure, outline) →
   * writing

   The process also highlights *research* as a "pervasive aspect."

   Re-state the critical writing process concisely in your own words.

2. What does it mean to call *research* a "pervasive aspect" of writing a paper? Explain how it is "pervasive."

*3. **Think about writing.** What are the main outcomes for this chapter?

   At the end of this chapter, students should be able to:

   a.
   b.
   c.
   ...

*4. Here is a critical thinking question about your understanding of some of the main concepts and processes in this chapter, such as "thesis statement," "letting it emerge," "constructing it," and "writing before you write":

   How can you tell how firm your understanding is of these?

   It's a reflective question that people almost never ask themselves. That is, how can people tell when they understand something pretty well versus when they merely have the impression that they understand it?

Constructing the plan of the paper: Thesis statement, main points, structure, outline.

*5. Look back at Charles's analysis of dieting in Chapter 2. As much as you can, immerse yourself in his thinking: *Be* Charles.

   Letting it emerge. Which of the responses in his analysis do you think is the best choice for a thesis statement?

   Constructing it. Now switch: Act as if no single thesis statement emerged for you. Instead, construct one: Choose the most important responses and blend them together into a unified thesis statement.

*6. As in the previous question, immerse yourself this time in Lucia's research paper on false memory.

   Again, try, first, to see a thesis statement as it *emerges* in the responses she gives in her analysis.

   Then, second, construct a thesis statement out of the most important responses in her analysis.

   Finally, also select the main points for the paper, the ones you would choose if you were Lucia.

7. Carefully read Kara's analysis of Juliet and follow the way her thinking evolves. Make a full plan for her paper. That is, from her analysis, pick out a reasonable *thesis statement* (by using either path: letting it emerge or constructing it) and a set of *main points*.

*8. Kevin is considering going to law school after he graduates, and he considers writing a paper on some aspect of the way the law works. He tries various topics, but when he gets to *implications and consequences* he gets an insight that he hadn't really considered before. The insight began with a piece of *information*:

   > When you bring a lawsuit against a large corporation, a very common thing that happens is that the corporation will have a team of very expensive and extremely competent attorneys on their side, while the only attorney you can afford may be far less competent and overloaded with cases.

   An *implication or consequence* of that, he thinks, is:

   > The person suing the corporation has very little chance of getting a fair trial!

   As much as you can, *be* Kevin: Think of yourself as getting ready to write a paper, and that insight is your starting point. How would you go about making a plan for the paper?

*9. **Making a thesis statement more unified.** In question 7 you analyzed Kara's topic of Juliet. But independently of what you did,
suppose that when Kara reads her analysis, no thesis statement
emerges for her. She doesn't clearly see one already there. So she
constructs one by putting together the responses she sees as most
important. Here is the thesis she constructs:

> There were so many things that could go wrong with such a risky
> decision (like: the messenger might not reach Romeo in time; the
> sleeping potion might not work; it might not work for exactly the
> "two and forty hours" she plans for; it might kill her; her family
> could stay too long at the tomb or prevent Romeo from coming
> back). Romeo and Juliet were not star-crossed lovers. Instead, they
> were victims of unrealistic wishful thinking.

Re-state Kara's thesis statement in a more polished, unified way.

Writing. Questions 10–12 all relate to Michelle's analysis of stereotyping (p. 77–84).

*10. The chapter gave only a partial description of an SEE-I Michelle
might have given for her main point 3:

> A consequence of stereotyping is that sometimes people are denied
> jobs or housing or other opportunities because they have been
> stereotyped.

Carry out more of the SEE-I by giving some examples and an
illustration she might have given for it.

*11. Here are Michelle's last two main points:

> 4. *People use stereotypes usually without examining the way
> they affect people.*
> 5. *The person who is being stereotyped feels unfairly treated and
> not given a chance to show what he or she can do.*

Put aside whether you agree or disagree with Michelle. Write out
a full SEE-I for each of her main points.

12. Look back over Michelle's main points (the full plan is on p. 80).
This time, search through her responses for important words,
phrases or ideas that she could staircase.

Critical reading and critical writing.

13. Question 10 in the exercises to Chapter 2 asked you to read
something critically, carefully. As part of that, it asked you to
(a) summarize what the author is saying, (b) give an SEE-I for it,
and/or (c) analyze the reading around the circle of elements. (See
the box on p. 60.)

With that done, now select a topic to write a paper on. Analyze your topic around the circle of elements, and from that create a plan for your paper as a whole.

14. Question 2 in the exercises to Chapter 2 contained part of a speech by Martin Luther King. You were asked there to analyze it around the circle. (It was a starred exercise, so there is a possible analysis of the excerpt in the Starred Responses section at the end of the book.)

    Suppose you were going to write about what Martin Luther King said. Do you see something there that you could take as the topic of your paper? Some possibilities:

    - Do you see any of the issues he is dealing with from a different point of view?
    - Do you want to investigate how successful or unsuccessful non-violent resistance was in those circumstances?
    - Do you disagree with an important part of what he said?
    - Do you want to write about how you think non-violent resistance would work with a present-day issue?

Expanded SEE-I.

*15. **Structural illustration.** In Chapter 1, Sheila was constructing a paper arguing that American universities should be as inexpensive as European universities are. (That was her thesis statement.) One of her main points was that when people receive a university education, it benefits the society as a whole, so society should pay for at least a large part of it. She didn't give a structural illustration, but she could have. What could she have given as a structural illustration?

*16. Give both an example and a contrasting example for Sheila's thesis statement in the previous question.

17. Illustrations are powerful, and that means they can sometimes overwhelm the content of the point you are making. Sometimes they are vivid. Here is one from a book on the Sahara:[2]

    > The western Desert ... is one of the driest parts of the Sahara, though even here, in ancient days, there was apparently some water, for satellite photos show a skein of erosional channels, as faint and elusive as Martian canals.

    Is it too flamboyant for your taste? Does the comparison to Martian canals help you become clearer?

*18. In Chapter 2, Charles was writing a paper on dieting and came to the conclusion that just "dieting to lose weight" will not work, that if you want to look good, you have to continue dieting on into the future. Write out and explain an illustration for Charles's conclusion.

Research.

*19. Without looking back at the chapter, explain the difference between background and focused research, including where one is needed and where the other is needed.

Background versus focused research.

20. For the possible topics listed below, how much background research would you need to do in order to analyze your topic effectively? Rank them on a scale of 1–5, where 1 means "I have enough background knowledge already" and 5 means "I don't know enough about the topic to write out an effective analysis. I'll have to start out with a good deal of background research."

- dealing with depression
- body image
- the civil rights movement in the United States
- tipping in restaurants and coffee shops
- the importance of grades
- planning a paper
- a relationship you have with someone
- the way you get along with your friends
- a value that's important in your life (such as responsibility, freedom, being respected...)
- aspects of you (such as your gender, ethnicity, upbringing, personality...)

*21. In the example on p. 95–96, Tasha found information (from an article on a business website and from Amtrak.com) that Amtrak has lost money for the last 43 years straight! Based on that information, she concluded that Congress should stop subsidizing Amtrak.

When she thought about it, though, she questioned the reasoning that brought her to that conclusion: she realized many government services (such as the police, the military, and Congress itself) do not "make money." For her, that considerably weakened the force of the facts about Amtrak.

Suppose that Tasha raised a different objection: Suppose she said that the information about Amtrak losing money may not be true, that it may not be a "fact" at all!

Is this a good critical thinking response?

*22. On page 93 in the section on doing research, the text says that you should use only reliable sources, but "even then reputable authorities do not always agree."

　　What should you do if you find reputable sources on an important point in your paper, but the sources do not agree?

Writing before you write.

23. A suggestion in this chapter is that instead of just writing, you take notes as you do the planning, so that you can then incorporate those notes into your paper—especially if you take notes using SEE-I.

　　Why do you think that's difficult for many people? Would it be difficult for you to get yourself to do it? Would there be advantages for you if you were able to do it?

24. **Write about your own experience.** In the view of the author of this book, *revising* a paper is very important. (*Revising* will come up strongly in Chapter 5, but for now take some time to reflect on it.) Temporarily, put yourself in the point of view of the author: Why does he think it's so important.

　　Now how about you? What in your view are the benefits of revising your paper? What are the costs or negative consequences of doing so?

25. **Putting it together in practice.** In the last question in the Exercises to Chapter 2, you were asked to choose at least three topics that you already know about and that you could write about in an informed, interesting way for, say, five pages. You were asked to analyze each of them by going around the circle.

　　At this point, build on what you did there:

　　For each one, plan out a paper by choosing a thesis statement and the other main points that will constitute the structure and the outline for it.

　　For each, write an introductory section to a paper you would write. In that section, your goal is to convey your thesis and main points to the reader in a clear, well-written, coherent paragraph or two.

26. Of those topics you worked on in the previous question, choose one of them to work on further. Based on the responses you gave there, write the bulk of the paper:

　　Write out an enhanced SEE-I for the thesis and each of the main points in your plan. Take your time about doing this. You are *developing* your paper. Try to make the paragraphs you write interesting by explaining well, giving good examples, perhaps a striking analogy, and so forth. Try to come up with a structural illustration (p. 83) for the thesis of your paper. (Remember that when you write out one of your main points and take the trouble to say it really well, it will often seem as if there is no need to say any more about it. But it's almost never true. There are many aspects that can be developed, and without that development, the point will not really be clear to the reader.)

As you write out SEE-I's, search for focal points you can staircase. Incorporate them into the paper as you proceed.

Mark an **R** next to any important parts of the paper that would benefit from research.

As well as you can—given that you haven't actually done the research—write a concluding section.

When you've done that for that one topic, realize that—except for actually doing the research and incorporating what you've found there—you have the bulk of your paper written.

Self-Assessment: Test It Out #2

How Can You Tell How Well You Did?

Test It Out #2: Organizing the main points in the paper. This test may also be hard to evaluate on your own, but here are some critical thinking standards that the main points need to meet:

- each of them should be clear and accurate,
- each of them should be directly relevant to the thesis statement you chose,
- each of them needs to be specific and focused,
- each of them should be important enough to write about,
- each of them needs to be something you could write about for at least several paragraphs (certainly not just a sentence or two), and
- ideally, all of them together should form a coherent whole.

Taking it a little further, you can look at the main points you've written and ask:

- Are they just scattered and unrelated to one another?
- If you've written more than one, do they really just say the same thing, but in different words?
- Do they convey to the reader the fullness of what you are trying to say about the topic?

Shifting to the process. In addition to assessing the main points you came up with, you can ask yourself some questions about *the process* you just went through to come up with them:

- Did the main points for your paper come readily to your mind?
- Did you draw a blank?
- Did only one come to mind?

- When you came up with your main points, did you consider—*consciously* consider—whether they were clear, accurate, relevant, specific, and important (the critical thinking standards just mentioned)?
- Did you invest all your hope in finding your main points later, maybe in research you might do?

If the main points did not come to mind, it's an indication that you're not ready to write the paper, but it's not automatically negative. After all, you may need more time to think about it. In addition, you may well need to do some research on the topic. But here, as with the first self-test, is the crucial ongoing critical thinking question:

> *How* will you come up with your main points? What is your *plan* or *strategy* for coming up with a rich, substantive set of main points?

Having a strategy for coming up with main points is actually

> **Main points and research.** For many topics you obviously have to do research to come up with main points for your paper. If that's true for the topics you chose, the suggestion here is to try it again, but this time with a few topics where you don't need research (for example, a personal issue). The point of self-test #2 is to test your skill at coming up with main points that meet the critical thinking criteria listed.

more important than the main points themselves. The main points are indeed important for this individual paper, but an effective process—having a strategy in mind—will help you come up with strong main points again and again, in everything you write.

Having a *strategy*—for coming up with either a thesis statement or the main points of a paper, or anything else—goes to the heart of critical thinking. It is a major part of what this book is designed to provide. It lays out actual strategies you can use. Those strategies will also open for you, in a way nothing else can, the whole endeavor of writing. And, since it's based in critical thinking, it can also open up better ways of thinking about other aspects of your life.

At this point, go back to "To the Student: Test It Out #3" (p. xxxii–xxxiii).

CHAPTER 4

Other Minds, Other Views: Addressing "the Other Side" and Cultivating Critical Thinking Traits of Mind

"The Other Side"

There is still one factor missing from the plan for your paper. It is that people's minds are different from one another and the views they have about substantive topics may differ. Though this seems obvious, what follows from it is one of the most profound and far-reaching factors in critical thinking and critical writing: A critical thinker seeks to see and understand "the other side." People who are thinking critically search out and address the points of view of those who might disagree with them, or those who might doubt or question their account. As part of this process, they look for the flaws or gaps in their own position. They see not only the positive aspects of what they are saying but also the downsides to their arguments.

> **GPS**
> • topic →
> • analysis →
> • plan →
> • writing →
>
> • **"the other side"** →
>
> • improvement →
> • flow

Many things make this a profound and essential part of the writing. For one thing, it runs in the face of the ways we humans seem to work. Research shows that, usually, if we believe X, we tend to see and feel the force of reasons that support X, but we don't naturally tend to look for the reasons that oppose X. We don't see the aspects of X that we've left out. If we desire Y, we will tend to see in vivid detail the advantages of having Y, but not the disadvantages. And even if we do see some of the disadvantages, we will tend to underplay them. The same holds if we are against something, or fear it, or hate it. Without knowing it, we will tend to find more and stronger reasons to continue our opposition or fear or hatred.

There is a large body of research that dramatically documents this bias,[1] but even without the research, you can see it from your own experience. You already know how easy it is for people to overlook the shortcomings of their own viewpoints. You know people who are prejudiced, biased, entrenched in their own ideologies, opinionated, narrow-minded and unable to see any shortcomings at all in their own views. We tend to see these shortcomings in *other* people's viewpoints, but far more rarely in our own, even when we are attempting to engage in critical thinking.

This tendency applies not just to what people believe but to the choices they make as well. If we have already chosen X over Y, we will have a strong tendency to continue noticing the benefits and underplaying the disadvantages of that choice. If we buy product X and then later see reviews both for and against X, we will strongly tend to remember the positive reviews and actually forget the negative ones.[2]

This is not true for all people, at all times, but it is true for most people, much of the time. (And, interestingly, most of us think that we ourselves are the exception.)[*]

It is a tendency that is part of what is called "cognitive dissonance," and it runs very deep in us. We can sum up the part of it that applies here by saying that we have a strong bias against changing our beliefs and against feeling that our beliefs, actions and choices may not be justified.[3] It is important to note that this is a *cognitive* bias. It is a bias that is not based on people's political, religious or social beliefs; rather, it is built into

It is sometimes astonishing how we can miss even obvious weaknesses in our own arguments. A very common phenomenon is to object to someone else's position without even considering that the objection applies to one's own position as well. For example, people sometimes object to the death penalty by saying, "Executing the criminal won't bring the victim back." That's true, of course. But *imprisonment* won't bring the victim back either. Neither will forgiveness. *Nothing* will bring the victim back. There are strong objections to the death penalty, but that's clearly not one of them.

---

[*]In research fields, this is linked to what is called "confirmation bias" or "researcher's bias" (see p. 15). The idea is that no matter how carefully scientists conduct their research and observe the results, their unconscious beliefs and expectations may cause them to overlook some crucial factor or to observe a result that is not in fact there. Scientists realize this danger. Careful experimenters use explicit strategies (such as double-blind experiments) to help counteract this tendency.

the way we *think*—about anything. It is also important to note that is an *unconscious* bias. That means it is *in addition to* biases we have that we may be aware of.

Applying this to writing your paper, then, it means you have to take account of other minds and other views. It means you have to look for, and then take seriously, "the other side":

- *objections* people might have to your account, and
- *gaps* people might see in your account.

With both objections and gaps, the ones you need to identify are not the minor or incidental ones. Rather, the objections you are seeking out are those that are most reasonable, the ones that have the most substance to them. Similarly, the gaps you are looking for in your account are the ones people on the other side would rightfully view as crucial. (They might say, "But you've left out the most important aspect of the issue....")

"Weakpoints"

As you construct your paper, then, a helpful way to conceptualize the problem is to think in terms of "weakpoints" or "potential weakpoints" in your paper. A "weakpoint" is an aspect of your paper that falls into one of these two categories: *objections* or *gaps*. It is an aspect of your paper that someone with a different point of view would most likely either disagree with or find incomplete.

Why call them "weakpoints"? Since you are committed to your own position, you might think of them as possible objections that "other people" might give against your view or as possible gaps "other people" might find in it. Phrasing it this way emphasizes "other people" and puts a distance between their position and your own.

But there is a virtue in thinking of them as "weakpoints" in your own position, rather than as coming from outside. Conceptualizing them as weakpoints (or "potential weakpoints") in your own position partakes of both intellectual humility and intellectual courage—two essential traits of a critical thinker. It owns up to the idea that virtually any substantive position on a complex issue *does* in fact have weakpoints. It is not just that

> Calling them "weakpoints" does not imply that they are in any sense "wrong." An illustration/analogy: If you build a bridge over a river, it will have weakpoints. That doesn't mean the bridge will break; it means that *if* the bridge breaks, the weakpoints are the likeliest places where it will break.

other people can raise objections to what you or I believe—it is that other people can raise objections that often have merit, that (though we may not initially see it that way) are often reasonable.

The same holds for *gaps* in your account. Again, virtually any explication of a substantive complex issue will in fact have gaps. There will, almost inevitably, be aspects of the issue—important, maybe crucial aspects—that are not addressed.

Why should this be so? The answer is in the word "substantive." When you say something substantive, something that is important, that carries weight, it is something that almost automatically can be looked at in many ways. People carry very different points of view around with them. They have different goals and different values; they have different fears and desires; they come from different cultures and backgrounds; they have different kinds of upbringing and social relationships. All of these affect the way people—reasonable people—conceptualize things. These differences virtually guarantee that any single view of an issue that is substantive, one that people think of as important, will have weakpoints in it.

It is worth reflecting on how bringing out the weakpoints of your position can give you insights into *criticality*. The central idea is this: Part of being a critical thinker is actively searching for the weakpoints in one's own position. It means not covering up those weakpoints, not trying to sidestep them and hope that other person just won't notice, but facing them honestly and openly. It means choosing to answer not just the easiest objections but also the strongest ones. It means taking the risk to examine issues from new perspectives.

Addressing the potential weakpoints in your paper brings in another rich dimension of critical thinking: the intellectual traits of a critical thinker. Three of the traits in particular—intellectual humility, intellectual empathy and fairmindedness—are intrinsically helpful in identifying weakpoints in your paper. But the value of the traits of mind goes well beyond just addressing the other side of an issue. They play a key role in all aspects of critical writing and of critical thinking in general, and it is worth cultivating them in yourself for the way they make your thinking, your writing and your life richer, more skillful and more fulfilling.

Critical Thinking Traits of Mind

There are certain traits of mind essential to being a critical thinker. They are sometimes called "intellectual virtues" or "critical thinking character traits."[4] You can also conceptualize them as critical thinking "habits of mind." No one, of course, embodies all of them perfectly, but we all may have some of them to some degree. Some of these traits will come out more strongly in one area of our lives, and more weakly in other areas of our lives. We can cultivate these traits in our lives and develop them within ourselves. All of them are intrinsically important to critical writing, and to being a critical thinker and reasonable person in general.

Traits of Mind

intellectual humility	intellectual courage
intellectual empathy	intellectual autonomy
intellectual perseverance	confidence in reason
intellectual integrity	fairmindedness
intellectual engagement	

Intellectual humility. At the center of intellectual humility is your relationship with what you don't know. It involves recognizing and facing up to the limitations of your knowledge and abilities. It involves owning up to what you don't know and clearly distinguishing between what you know for certain, and what you just think is true.

Intellectual courage. At its heart, intellectual courage is facing up to the dangers, risks, and fears involved in examining your own thinking and writing.

Intellectual empathy. Intellectual empathy is putting yourself into someone else's thinking. It involves thinking an issue through the way that person would so that you will be in the best position to understand it fully.

Intellectual autonomy. Intellectual autonomy is thinking for yourself, using the discipline of mind that comes through actively using critical thinking concepts and principles. When you hear what people say, or read what they write, you use your own best judgment to decide whether you think it makes sense.

Intellectual perseverance. Intellectual perseverance is sticking with an intellectual task all the way through, not giving up on it unless it is reasonable to do so.

Confidence in reason. At its most basic level, confidence in reason is the habit of trusting the validity and power of reasoning over other ways of deciding an issue.

Intellectual integrity. Intellectual integrity means being guided by principles in how you think and what you write. To a strong degree, it involves being honorable, and thus trustworthy, in both. It means applying the same standards of reasonability to yourself that you expect in others.

Fairmindedness. Fairmindedness is at heart a drive to be honest, fair, and above-board in your thinking and writing.

Intellectual engagement. Intellectual engagement means committing yourself to the task you are working on. It means taking it seriously, being present for it.

The traits of mind come into play at all stages of the writing process: as you think your way through the topic by analyzing it around the circle, as you research it, as you make the choices about what to say in your paper, as you develop the paragraphs (using SEE-I, perhaps in an enhanced form (p. 84–87)), in the carefulness in how you proceed, and in your commitment to being clear, accurate, and relevant in what you say, think, or write. In a global way, the traits show themselves in your whole concept of what it is to write a paper and the meaning it carries for you.

It is important to realize that these are *character* traits—critical thinking character traits. They are more than skills. To the extent that you develop them in yourself, they become part of who you are as a person. Because they are traits, exercising them in this or that particular instance is not something you do only because it's required by someone else. Rather, you exercise them because they are a part of who you are and who you aspire to be.

All of the traits have multiple aspects, and they extend well beyond the abbreviated descriptions above. Though they are basically distinct from one another, there is often a good deal of overlap among them. They are also interlocking: when you engage in one of the traits, you will often find that you are also engaging in several of the others.

Intellectual humility and *intellectual courage*, for example, often work hand-in-hand. Intellectual humility involves facing up to the realization that, even in your very best thinking, there will still be mistakes, shortcomings and unknowns. But, for most people, it takes great courage to own their mistakes and shortcomings in what they do and what they write. And it takes intellectual courage, maybe even to a greater degree, to accept justified criticism about those mistakes and shortcomings. It comes out on an internal level when you resist the demands of your own ego telling you that you are always in the right, that criticism of your views or ways of writing is always unjustified.

Intellectual empathy comes into a paper in many ways. One of the most prominent is when you are doing research or considering the views of other people. There is a real sense in which understanding what someone says means thinking it through the way that person does. This holds as much for empirical research as it does for controversial positions. You can't, for example, understand what Darwin or Curie or Newton thought unless you see their reasoning: what reasons they had for coming to their conclusions, what assumptions they were making, what information they had at their disposal, what they thought the implications were. *Fairmindedness* comes in strongly here as well, in the way you think and the way you describe what other people say, particularly when you disagree with them, when they see things in a very different way from you.

Intellectual autonomy also enters in many ways, both in the content of what you say in your paper and in how you go about saying it. With intellectual autonomy, you recognize that *you* are the one making the choices about what to say and about how to say it. It means you take on the responsibility of making the choices yourself, rather than letting your decisions be dictated by external factors such as group pressure to believe a certain set of ideas, or pressure to achieve something in a given amount of time.

Time pressure, in fact, makes for a good example of how the traits interweave. *Intellectual autonomy, fairmindedness, intellectual courage, and intellectual perseverance* can all play an important role. People often justify waiting until the last minute by saying they have other important things to do, and sometimes it's true. But it's seldom the whole story. They usually do exactly the same thing even when there isn't anything else pressing them. With intellectual autonomy, though, if you have X days to write the paper, you take responsibility for starting early enough so the choices you make result from your own best judgment, rather than from a constricted time frame you may have saddled yourself with.

There is a measure of fairmindedness in giving yourself time to do your best, especially if the paper or the grade is important to you. Though people don't usually look at it this way, it involves being fair to yourself. Intellectual courage can come in as well. Many people find it *hard* to get themselves to start early enough to make their own best choices in the paper: instead, they let time pressure make the choices for them. As you sit down to write a paper, your intellectual perseverance will also be on the line. It comes out in your willingness to work through the essential parts of writing a paper, planning it out (with analysis around the circle), developing the paragraphs (with strong SEE-I's), doing the necessary research, and revising. Without allowing for adequate time to explore significant ideas, you may never learn what it means to be intellectually perseverant because you never give yourself the time to actually persevere through a complex problem.

Developing the traits in yourself helps guide you through many aspects of writing a critical thinking paper, aspects that go well beyond managing your time. As you write a paper, *intellectual integrity* comes in in many ways. It emerges strongly when you take seriously the idea that when you write something, you are giving your word about what you say, you are vouching for it, you stand behind it. And you stand behind your words not just because they express something you happen to believe but because, in your best judgment, they are the clearest, most accurate, most important thing you can say about the issue. Those are *your* words on the page.

Intellectual integrity and *fairmindedness* often interweave in writing a paper. They both are involved in giving credit to others for ideas and words of theirs that you use in your paper. As you work to embody these two critical thinking character traits, you cite your sources not just because a teacher requires it but because it's the right thing to do. And this process can affect the way you live your life.

Both traits play a prominent role in developing the content of your paper as well. They help guide you not to use flimsy arguments even if you think those arguments will persuade readers. They remind you not to spin or distort things to make them sound more reasonable than they are. In the process you give readers a fair chance to draw their own conclusions. You do not manipulate or try to control them by slanting what you write in the service of some agenda. In a more global sense, though, intellectual integrity and fairmindedness come out in the way you think about your work as a whole. You write without bias, without prejudice, without favoritism or spin, and you do so, again, because it's the right thing to do. You do it because that's the kind of person you are, one who has intellectual integrity and who values being fair.

Confidence in reason is also closely related to intellectual integrity and fairmindedness. Confidence in reason drives you to ensure that your conclusions are based on the best reasoning available to you. This includes what you learn from your research, your own experience, and your own best independent thinking. You pay attention to your gut responses and to your intuitions about an issue, but you give them only the weight that is due. You factor in your gut response, but you recognize it as only one factor among several, and that it may be flat wrong. Evidence plays a more direct role in conclusions you come to. You factor in responses based on your past experiences, but you also realize (with intellectual humility) how limited your past experience is, and how much of it is filtered through your own biases.

There is a sense in which *intellectual engagement* underlies all the other traits. Intellectual engagement means taking your writing seriously, putting yourself into it fully. In the process of engaging with critical writing, you will also be putting yourself fully into intellectual humility, intellectual courage, intellectual empathy and the other traits. As you write the paper, your intellectual engagement may come out in the realization that you are spending some small but real portion of your life on this paper, and that therefore you might as well do your best on it. These are *your* words you are putting on the paper: You should make them count.

The traits and "the other side" of an issue. The traits apply to thinking critically in a great many situations and to all aspects of the writing process. But they play an especially central role in taking account of other minds and other views, in seeing "the other side" of an issue, and in finding and dealing with the weakpoints in your paper. Consider intellectual humility, intellectual empathy, and fairmindedness.

In coming to terms with an issue, you have to begin with the realization that there *may be* legitimate objections to your own position; there *may be* aspects of the issue you have not thought about, gaps you may not have noticed. This realization is part of intellectual humility.

The need for intellectual humility comes up vividly when people are writing an argumentative or persuasive paper and giving reasons for a point of view they hold strongly. It is often extremely difficult to see how someone could possibly disagree with substantive points that you find obviously true. The temptation is to think of the people who hold opposing viewpoints as self-serving and dishonest, or as irrational or stupid.

> With intellectual humility, it sometimes helps to think about your own past. There were times in the past, sometimes only a few years ago, when you held beliefs you now realize were seriously misguided, even though you then held them with the deepest conviction.

It also, though, comes up in writing an expository paper (for example, a typical research paper). If you've "covered" the topic thoroughly, it is sometimes hard to see how someone could say that you've missed an essential part, a part that your thesis (and maybe everything else) depends on.

With intellectual humility, as you analyze a topic, you recognize that you are bringing your own unconscious assumptions along with you, and that there are probably implications of your position that you are not aware of; you realize that there are questions at issue that are still un-addressed and problems someone might have with your account.

With intellectual empathy, you work to put yourself into the thinking of other people. Thinking empathetically involves trying to understand how those people are figuring things out, and how people with other minds and other points of view are coming to the conclusions they come to. Tapping into intellectual empathy is probably always beneficial, but it is especially important when other people's views are radically at odds with your own.

Intellectually empathizing with someone's view does not, of course, mean that you agree with them. You may in the end continue thinking of their view as wrong—even as dead wrong. But it does mean that you will be able to see and understand (and sometimes even appreciate) how they reason their way to positions that may directly oppose your own.

> Intellectual empathy can apply even to a position that is off the charts, such as abduction by aliens. If you are writing a paper "debunking" abduction by aliens, your paper will be far stronger if you reason out (and probably do research on) how seemingly reasonable people could come to believe that they have been abducted by aliens. Without doing this, you fail to face a major part of the issue.

Fairmindedness comes in both when recognizing other people's points of view and when trying to find the right words to describe what other people believe. Fairmindedness requires that you report people's positions in a way that they themselves would agree with. You don't have to use their own actual words, but you do have to describe their views in a way that they themselves would see as accurate. If you are describing fascism or communism, fundamentalism or atheism, Chinese, European, Iranian, or American policies and actions, fairmindedness requires that you describe them *neutrally*. As with intellectual empathy, fairmindedness obviously does not require that you are in fact neutral about all points of view: it requires that you *describe* them neutrally. After the neutral description, you are, of course, free to evaluate them negatively, positively, or somewhere in between, depending on the evidence you have been able to uncover in the context of the issues you are addressing.

The "feeling component" in the traits. It is important to realize that there is also a "feeling component" to the traits of mind. They are not something you process just in your head. Thinking about something important is not divorced from passions or emotions (otherwise, it probably wouldn't seem important). With intellectual empathy, for example, you are not just *thinking* through an issue in the way another person does. You are also, in a sense, feeling your way through it: you are, to some extent at least, feeling the force of those reasons, from that point of view. With intellectual humility, there can be a feeling of actual pleasure, for instance, at finding out that you were mistaken, especially about something you always just took for granted. There can be a feeling of awe at the sheer number of unknowns there are, not just in yourself as an individual but in human knowledge as a whole. Fairmindedness does not mean adhering to the letter of fairness, but rather *to the spirit of it*. It doesn't mean merely saying the words in a way that seems fair; rather, it embodies a *desire* to be fair.

Example. Take *terrorism* as an example. If you are writing about terrorism

Addressing the "other side," and doing so fairmindedly, is often dramatically beneficial outside of classes. Try it out for yourself. For example, the next time you find yourself in a heated disagreement with someone you care about, step back from your own view. Instead of amping up your own side or justifying your own views, take some time to mirror back to them what you understand them to be saying. You can ask them, "Is this what you're saying? Am I getting what you mean?" and then say what you heard them as saying, maybe with an SEE-I. In a respectful relationship, both people should be able to hear and express the other person's point of view, even about an issue where they strongly and emotionally disagree—probably *especially* with an issue on which they strongly and emotionally disagree.

and trying to develop your intellectual humility, intellectual empathy, and fairmindedness, how would you approach the topic? Well, right from the beginning, intellectual humility comes in: You recognize that there is a great deal you don't know about people who engage in such mass killing of civilians. You probably don't know the assumptions that led them to their actions, or the way they assess the implications and consequences of their actions, or what questions at issue they were attempting to solve, or many other aspects as well. Of course, you didn't know those before you began your analysis, but with intellectual humility you now explicitly realize that you don't know them. Increasing your knowledge-of-what-you-don't-know is a major part of clear thinking.[5] You may hear commentators confidently stating why such individuals do what they do, but if you pause for just a moment, you'll recognize that the commentators usually don't actually know why. It's usually just speculation. With intellectual humility coming to the fore, you are in a much more reasonable place than they are.

   Developing your intellectual empathy, you would almost certainly do research, using reliable sources that are not one-sided (including perhaps some of their own accounts), on why a given set of individuals targets civilians for mass killing. With this background information you would try to reconstruct how they were seeing the situation, how they were reasoning it out, and why—from their point of view—they did what they did. (There are major challenges in doing this, not just in finding reliable information but also in generating the intellectual courage to immerse yourself in thinking that is threatening.)

Working on your fairmindedness, then, you would describe their goals, motives, assumptions, interpretations, and so forth around the circle, in neutral, unbiased language. You would almost certainly not call them "terrorists" or "freedom fighters" (though you might report that they see themselves as people trying to make the world a better place).

Doing just this much might actually make for an excellent paper on its own. The topic might be "how people who are described as 'terrorists' see their own actions." It would be a refreshing paper in its honesty, its integrity, and its accuracy in describing a point of view that is challenging to come to terms with. (Of course, you could also go on to evaluate that point of view, using your best judgment to decide whether it is itself accurate, relevant, logical, and fair.)

Three Problems in Thinking about "the Other Side"

Three major problems come up when you try to address the "weak-points" in your paper. The first is just *recognizing* the weakpoints in your own position. It's *seeing* how someone might object, or what someone might find missing in your account. Again, this is often surprisingly difficult to do. In an argumentative paper on a controversial issue, the more your own position seems clearly and obviously right, the greater the difficulty of seeing what someone might say on the other side. In an expository paper, the more strongly you feel that you have covered all the bases, that you've explained everything that needs explaining, the more difficult it is to see that someone else might find glaring holes in your presentation.

A second problem is *describing* "the other side"—and doing so in a fairminded way. This involves spelling out the other side clearly, accurately, without bias, and in its strongest version.

The third problem is *incorporating* those other points of view into your paper, developing them there in writing, and maybe answering them there as well.

The first two problems are much more difficult than the third. (As is true for almost everything in this book, the hard part is figuring things out—clearly, accurately, and in a logical way. After that, the actual writing is often the easier part.) The three problems are also closely related to one another.

Seeing "the Other Side"

Some people can readily identify weakpoints in their own thinking and writing. That's particularly true of individuals who have worked over a long period of time to develop a strong sense of intellectual empathy. For most people, though, it does not come easily. They have to *confront* the problem explicitly and directly: How would people with other minds, with other views, see the issue?

Probably the best way to find "the other side" (and the corresponding weakpoints of your own side) is with questions. You can think of them as "self-confrontational questions"—because you are not confronting someone on the other side. Instead, you are confronting yourself: You are confronting the built-in challenge of seeing possible weakpoints in *your own* point of view. And usually the best questions to ask are ones that are direct, hard-hitting, and explicit. The first five of these "Self-Confrontational Questions" center essentially on how someone might *disagree*, while the last three center on what might be *missing*.

Self-Confrontational Questions

- What are some strong objections to my position?
- What is the downside of my position? What are the trade-offs? (For example, money spent for X means money *not* available for Y.)
- What alternatives are there?
- What problems would people see in my account?
- How could I research other points of view?

- What important aspects of the issue have I not addressed?
- Is what I'm saying the whole truth, or is it only part of the truth?
- Is there anything else I should be addressing?

That's a lot of questions, maybe in a sense too many. But the large number is intended to be helpful rather than overwhelming. Of those eight, just one may give you a sudden insight. The questions are most effective when you work in a group with others. Having other people ask you the question tends to bring on a much more engaged response.

If you just say it in the abstract—"Find the weakpoints in your own position"—it may not seem so difficult, but in actual practice it is often extremely difficult. That is one of the reasons why cultivating the habits of intellectual humility and empathy is so important. These habits *prepare* you for the difficulty. The most usual experience is this:

> This is a view I feel very strongly about. I have really good reasons to support my view. As I examine them, all of them seem clearly true and directly relevant. What are the weakpoints? Where would someone disagree? I can't see any valid objections.

What usually happens at this point is that you come up against a blank wall. Nothing comes to you, nothing at all. You just can't see how anyone could reasonably object.

If the position you hold is at all controversial, this idea is almost certainly a delusion. It results from your own feeling of certainty. Your mind fixates on the reasons *for* your position, and this intrinsically blocks out reasons *against* your position.

What helps at these times is to create an intellectual distance from your own point of view. Intellectual empathy is one of the main ways, first, to create that distance and, second, to step across it (temporarily) into that other point of view.

Walking through Examples

Earlier chapters in this book contain a number of examples of students doing the work of writing substantive papers. How might those students now move on to take account of other minds and other views?

As you follow their reasoning below, notice how they really have to push their thinking to find "the other side" of an issue. They use the Self-Confrontational Questions to guide them, but they have to explore in different directions, and some of these directions will almost certainly not work out. Why is that? It's because it's often *hard* to find the other side. They are actually using the questions to generate new insights within themselves.

> As happens many times in this book, seeing a large number of choices can make it seem harder rather than easier. But the intention here is to make it easier.
>
> You're looking for "the other side." Finding it is often an "Aha!" moment. Sometimes, one of the questions will just click for you. At another time, or for another person, a different question may click. Once that happens and you think "Oh! I see it now!" you may decide just to stop there. You are still free to ask additional self-confrontational questions if you want to, but you don't have to. It's your own choice.

Each example centers on different Self-Confrontational Questions: Example #1 is on finding *objections* or *trade-offs*; example #2 is on what aspects *have not been addressed*; and example #3 is on whether the account is *the whole truth*.

Example #1. Objections and trade-offs: Stereotyping. Go back to the example about stereotyping in Chapter 3. In that example Michelle gave an analysis around the circle of the issue of stereotyping. Out of her analysis, she constructed an outline for her whole paper in five major points.

Michelle's Outline

1. *Stereotyping is unfair.*
2. *It does harm to people.*
3. *A consequence of stereotyping is that sometimes people are denied jobs or housing or other opportunities because they have been stereotyped.*
4. *People just use stereotypes without even thinking about how they affect other people.*
5. *The person who is stereotyped feels unfairly treated and not given a chance to show what he or she can do.*

Before you read on, immerse yourself in Michelle's analysis. Those five points constitute the thesis of her paper (as well as the structure and outline of it). Pause for a moment to feel the force of those points, and of the reasons behind them, the harm and the unfairness of stereotyping. You need to feel it, as much as possible, as your own. By immersing yourself in it, you can maybe get some of the sense of how Michelle sees it as being exactly correct. Envision how you could straightforwardly use her outline to write the paper yourself, using SEE-I all the way through. Notice that this is a strong, solid structure for a paper. Identifying weakpoints in it will not nullify that. Rather, it will be doing justice to "the other side," and it will likely make her paper even stronger.

It is important to see that Michelle is convinced of her point of view: it makes sense. Stereotyping *is* unfair. It *does* cause harm, and it *does* prevent people from being given the chance to show what they can do. For people who have been seriously harmed by stereotyping, it *is* like carrying a load of bricks on your back.

So how can Michelle find weakpoints in her paper?

She starts with one of the Self-Confrontational Questions and asks herself:

*   "What are some strong objections to my position?"

But she honestly can't see reasons someone might raise against her position. She thinks, "Any objections like that would have to be *in favor of* harming people." She rejects that as being unreasonable: She says, "If there is another side to this, that can't be what they are advocating!"

But then she changes the question a little, putting the emphasis in a different place. She asks herself:

*   "What would someone *say* in opposition?"

That question then leads her to ask who that "someone" is: "Which people *do* say anything in opposition?"

She remembers that she has heard people who actually advocate stereotyping in certain circumstances. They do it in the form of "profiling." She has heard something like that from people responsible for airport security. She realizes that, whether she agrees with them or not, when they advocate profiling, they *don't* do it because they are in favor of harming people. She spells it out:

> Police and other law enforcement officials sometimes say that stereotyping—profiling—helps them prevent crime. I'm not saying I agree with this, but that's what they say. At an airport, for example, the nationality or accent of individuals, or the way they are dressed, might alert an airport security official that an individual should be screened more carefully than others. My own view is that this is biased and even clearly unfair, but officials often believe that it makes airplane flights safer.

To Michelle (or to you), what these officials say may or may not be a valid objection to her position on stereotyping, but that misses the point here. The point is that it *is* an opposing point of view, one that is widely held and acted upon. And those people are actually doing it because they believe it is in the interest of *not* harming people, of keeping people safe.

Seeing her words in front of her, Michelle pauses to reconsider a couple of things she wrote down. She notices that she voiced her own disagreement not just once but twice! She decides that though *she* thinks the officials' position may be biased and even clearly unfair, that's not the way the officials themselves conceptualize it. To capture their point of view, she deletes the parts that are about *her* response rather than about what *they* believe:

> ~~I'm not saying I agree…. My own view is that this is biased and even clearly unfair, but~~ officials often believe that it makes airplane flights safer.

Though Michelle is still strongly opposed to stereotyping, she works to exercise intellectual empathy as she considers it. As a result, she finds that she can't simply ignore the other point of view. She may end up thinking it is misguided or wrong, but she still has to grapple with this other position. What the objection adds to her paper, though, is a frank, honest position against her own. Including it in her paper will make her position far more realistic. It will enrich her paper substantially.

To reinforce her sense of the weakpoints in her paper, Michelle decides to ask herself another one of the Self-Confrontational Questions:

- "What is the trade-off?"

She now realizes that airport security's point of view is built on a trade-off with respect to stereotyping: According to at least some officials, stereotyping is an important tool they use to pick out individuals most likely to try to destroy an airplane. They believe that by profiling people, they are making society safer, that they are *preventing* harm to others. She also realizes something else—that some police officials say the same thing as airport security, and they probably even give the same reason: that stereotyping people who are more likely to commit a crime makes people safer. So the trade-off is presented as one between stereotyping and safety.

Her first reaction to the "trade-off" is to dismiss it out of hand. She starts to get angry just thinking about it: "What about the harm to people who are constantly targeted by stereotyping?" She finds herself saying, "The whole thing is ridiculous! As if stereotyping somebody actually makes anything safer! That's crazy!" She finds that she really dislikes the whole idea of a "trade-off" between something as unfair as stereotyping and some vague idea of safety. It takes her several minutes of sitting with the discomfort, but she holds off on the impulse to dismiss it out of hand. It's a stretch for her to get back into intellectual empathy and continue with describing this other point of view.

If this were you rather than Michelle writing the paper, remember that reasoning this idea out empathetically does not imply that you agree with this use of stereotyping, or with this rationale for it. You might agree or disagree (or be somewhere in the middle), and you would probably make your position clear in your paper. But take a moment to envision how the paper would be far richer because you included a section on this opposing point of view. With this addition, the resulting paper is more than just an idealistic vision of why we should avoid stereotyping. Rather, it also addresses aspects of how stereotyping is in fact used and defended in the real world.

Example #2. Aspects not addressed: False memory. "Weakpoints" are not always based on objections or trade-offs. Often they point to new areas that can be explored. In addition to making your paper stronger, they can enlarge your thinking and your future choices.

Go back in your mind to Lucia in Chapter 2. If you remember, she is the prospective psychology major who so carefully planned out an important research paper on the topic of *false memory*. Now, though, she is confronting the problem of "finding the other side," and her problem is different from Michelle's. Lucia is not arguing for a thesis the way Michelle was. Instead, almost the whole of her paper is a detailed exposition and analysis of experiments on false memory. She wonders, "What is 'the other side' of an issue when basically you are *describing* something?" Here is how Lucia thinks about it:

> Lucia: *I'm having trouble finding "weakpoints" in my paper. My whole paper is dealing with well-confirmed, repeated experiments. The experiments show that a statistically significant number of people could be induced to "remember" events in their lives, or things they "saw" as a direct eyewitness. In the experiments, it was "suggested" to them that they'd been lost in the mall, or that they'd seen Bugs Bunny at Disneyland! Then, later, the people actually "remembered" those events, even though they <u>never happened</u>! Some of the people were absolutely certain. But they never saw what they swear they saw!*

Notice that the thoroughness of Lucia's analysis doesn't mean that there is no "other side." It's not that she has left something out of her analysis. (That could have been the case, but it wasn't.) It's that there was something she hadn't noticed about the topic itself (and perhaps others haven't noticed as well).

The difficulty Lucia faces is a psychological one. It's one you may share with her, and it comes from being deeply immersed in a topic. The more deeply immersed you are in a topic or a point of view, the more difficult you may find it to step outside your approach and see what you have not addressed. It's a difficulty faced by even the most accomplished experts in a field. A good guideline to take to heart is that in *any* substantive topic that *anyone* addresses, there will be aspects that are seen, and there will be aspects that are not seen.

Again, she faces the question: What could be "the other side"?

Lucia consults the list of Self-Confrontational Questions and starts off by looking for *objections*. But since she is describing scientifically conducted experiments, she can't see that there are objections that would carry any real weight. So she moves down the list of Self-Confrontational Questions to two that focus on what might be *missing*:

- What important aspects of the issue have I not addressed?
- Is there anything else I should be addressing?

At first, these questions don't help her much either. For her, the problem seems more difficult because she was so thorough in her analysis around the circle. She is proud of that, and she likes the confidence it gives her. But since she gave such a thorough analysis, it makes it harder to see what aspect of the issue she has not addressed.

It takes considerable intellectual perseverance to keep working at it and living with the frustration it gives her. She likes psychology, so there is a sense in which she does actually enjoy the mental exploration. Still, it's also frustrating to keep looking for what might be missing.

She thinks she could describe more experiments, but she decides that this isn't the point of "the other side." The point instead is to find aspects *of these experiments* that she has not addressed. As she continues thinking about it, her attention starts to focus on one aspect of the experiments she hasn't paid much attention to. Here's the way she works through it now.

> Lucia: *In all the experiments, false memories were induced in a statistically significant percentage of people. That makes it solid evidence. But now I wonder about the percentage of people where the experimenters were <u>not</u> able to induce false memories. What's going on with them? What made those individuals immune? I'm still impressed that experimenters could make people remember things that never happened! But what about those people where it didn't work? What accounts for the result that those people had memories that "stayed true" despite what the experimenters did? What is different about the people who continued to remember that they never were lost in the mall?*

Lucia decides that this is an important aspect of the experiments she hasn't addressed, and so it qualifies as "the other side" in the

Giving space to "the other side." When it comes time for Lucia to incorporate writing about "the other side" in her paper, she won't just write the two short italicized sentences on page 132. Though they carry an important insight, she has to *convey* the insight to the reader. She'll do that with an SEE-I, and those two short sentences will be the statement-part of her SEE-I. She'll then elaborate on how it has been left out, and she'll give examples and illustrations of this point.

It is important to see that she will almost certainly not try to answer the question she's raised. That would be an entirely different project. Her paper centers on the false-memory experiments, but she has made her paper better by raising such a significant question that has not been addressed.

truest sense of the term. Not only is it a good addition to her paper, but it seems as though it might lead to a deep insight, one with much larger significance. As she ponders it, she realizes that, as far as she can tell, it holds for all the experiments in false memory. Here is what she writes down:

> *None of the experiments works for a hundred percent of cases. What is going on in the cases where it doesn't work?*

She has been considering going to graduate school in psychology, and her goal is maybe to become a professional psychologist. She now thinks that this might be an area for her own experimentation when she gets there. It is solidly embedded within the point of view of experimental psychology. It seems to her that this is an area where important new research and experimentation can be done.

Both Michelle and Lucia are impressed that they were completely unaware of the "weakpoints" while they were planning out their papers. Both of them now have choices about the extent to which they will give attention to these weakpoints in their papers and how much space to devote to them. They will describe them with at least a brief SEE-I, and they might also decide to try to answer them from their own perspective. (They might use an SEE-I for that as well.) Either course of action would make their papers deeper and more thorough.

Example #3. The whole truth: The life of a typical college student. Sometimes finding the weakpoints in your point of view comes out not by facing the issue head-on, but rather from an angle. It can help to look at what you are saying in the paper and asking yourself the Self-Confrontational Question: "OK. What I'm saying seems clearly true, but is it the whole truth?"

An example comes from the Purdue Online Writing Lab.[6] This is a highly respected and very helpful website. One of its main goals is to help students find a viable thesis statement for a paper. It gives an example of an expository thesis statement:

> The life of the typical college student is characterized by time spent studying, attending class, and socializing with peers.

You can probably see right away how it is an excellent thesis statement, one that is clear, accurate, and important enough to write about. (Those are three of the standards of critical thinking—see p. 150–151.) Further, this single statement in effect lays out the plan for a whole paper. You can see how it would work: Imagine yourself in the writer's position and picture how you could write the whole paper by following those three points step-by-step. Before going on, take a minute to feel how *"true"* the statement is: that *is* how typical college students spend their time.

Now imagine yourself plotting out the paper and then looking for weak-points. A Self-Confrontational Question you could ask would be:

- Is that the whole truth? Or is it only part of the truth?

Asking that question can make you wonder, "What *other* ways of spending time have I not looked at?" And that question in turn can make ideas and answers arise. For example, sleeping is an obvious exception. It is an exception that probably misses the writer's point. Still, sleeping is a way people do spend a lot of time, one that's frequently overlooked. But considering that example can bring to mind other ways students spend their time, ways they may not even recognize. How much of a student's time is spent on just getting from one place to another, or on just waiting around, or on thinking about things like relationships and one's future? Even the time spent "studying" is often spent more on being distracted, or worrying about tests and grades, than on actual studying. There is a lot of pressure in being a student, and dealing with it takes up a lot of time and may lead to considerable stress. Elaborating on these other ways of spending time would make an excellent "other side" in the paper.

Adding this as "the other side" could well make your paper more comprehensive, deeper, and more striking. As before, you would describe the main features that characterize the life of a college student. This would still make up the bulk of your paper as you state, elaborate, exemplify, and illustrate each of the three.

But now you would also mention that students may spend more actual time on the incidentals of college life. Even more important, you would also note that stress and pressure are often a part of college life, and dealing with them is another characteristic way students spend their time, one that is often overlooked.

Take a moment to reflect on how the process worked in this example, and think about the difference between this case and Michelle's. Michelle has strong convictions about stereotyping, so you can easily see why she might have difficulty finding the other side of the issue. But a peculiarity of humans is that we can have difficulty seeing the other side even when it's not controversial, even when we don't have previous strong commitments.

(If you're like me, this is the way the process goes: I saw the statement about how college students spend their time. It was crisp and well stated, and as I envisioned that thesis statement in my mind, I was taken up by how true it seemed. When I first encountered the thesis statement about typical college students, I found myself saying "Yes. Of course." The question "What are some *other* ways students spend time?" just did not arise in my mind. Seeing the "truth" of a statement can blind you to the possibility that there may be "false" in it as well. I myself am surprised at how often this happens.)

Looking for "the other side" works not just in writing a paper but for almost anything that has complexity to it. It gives depth and comprehensiveness to your thinking in a way that is often dramatic. Even to other people, you begin to be recognized as someone who can look at an issue from multiple sides. Once you get used to it, you can use just the key terms in the Self-Confrontational Questions to open up a position for you. When you're looking for "the other side" of almost anything, here is what you're looking for:

- objections
- downside, trade-offs
- alternatives
- problems
- other points of view
- unaddressed aspects
- partial truths

Describing "the Other Side" Fairmindedly

Seeing how other minds, with other views, might disagree, or what they may find missing, is the first problem. The second is *describing* their objections in a fairminded way. But the two problems are almost inseparable. If you describe the other person's position in a biased or slanted way, there is a strong sense in which you are not actually "seeing" it. What you are seeing is a parody or distortion of the other side, not its actuality.

A good guideline for telling whether you have described another person's position fairmindedly is that an observer who reads your description of the "other side," one who doesn't know your position on the issue, should not be able to tell which side you are on. Another guideline is that someone who actually *is* on "the other side" should be able to read your description and say, "Yes, that is exactly my position."

One thing to notice about writing a paper and seeing its weak-points is how many of the intellectual traits are involved. This chapter so far has been focusing primarily on three of them—intellectual

Other Minds, Other Views **135**

humility, intellectual empathy, and fairmindedness. But the other traits are involved as well, maybe in fact all of them. For someone as strongly against stereotyping as Michelle is, for example, it takes great *intellectual courage* to reason out the case on the other side and describe it fairmindedly. It takes *intellectual integrity* and *confidence in reason* for Michelle to work her way through objections to a position she holds so strongly. The temptation we all feel is simply to dismiss objections, sometimes even to ridicule them, so we don't have to face up to the possibility that there may be some truth in them. Michelle has to maintain the confidence that the most reasonable view will succeed. When you address the other side of an issue, you are attempting to hold yourself to the same standards you hold others to. You commit yourself to the idea that views and positions are to be reasoned out, not answered just by a gut reaction or by simply dismissing the other person.

Incorporating "the Other Side" into Your Paper

Once you identify the other side, you can incorporate it into the structure of your paper. Often, even when writers have succeeded in identifying a point of view opposed to their own, they still have difficulty empathizing with it, and the description of it they give in the paper ends up sounding hollow or biased or lukewarm. Constructing an SEE-I for a point of view you disagree with is a useful way to get more deeply in touch with the thinking behind it, and it increases the power of your paper substantially.

Notice the stretch it involves toward intellectual empathy, confidence in reason, and fairmindedness. You have to elaborate, give an example, and maybe an illustration—but all from the other side's point of view. This means not just reporting on an example and an illustration that someone else in fact gives; it means constructing your own, finding an example that fits the other person's point of view, and an illustration that expresses it well. Thus, if you are arguing in favor of reducing taxes, you have to elaborate on the strongest position *against* reducing taxes, explaining why (from that point of view) it seems reasonable to keep taxes in place, or to increase them. Then you have to give an example, one that those who are against reducing taxes might give. It has to be a good example, one that *they*

A deeper but far more challenging way to understand an opposing point of view empathetically is to go around the circle of elements with respect to it. Doing this makes you thoroughly immerse yourself in "the other side." It is extremely difficult to be that empathetic.

would find convincing. You can also give an illustration—but it too has to be from the point of view of those who think taxes should not be reduced. Giving an SEE-I requires that you richly imagine the other side's thinking process. There is a sense in which you, for the time being, immerse yourself in the other side.

Go back once again to Michelle's paper on stereotyping. At this point she recognizes that she has found more than one objection to her position. She decides that, contrary to her first reaction, the strongest objection she has found is the one about the trade-off between stereotyping and ensuring safety. She realizes that she has a good foundation for constructing an SEE-I for that point of view, so that she can later put it directly into her paper.

As the statement-part of the SEE-I, the "S," she formulates the objection about trade-offs as carefully and concisely as she can:

S: A trade-off with stereotyping is that if it is given up, a certain level of security might have to be given up also.

(Michelle finds that it's still a stretch for her to say this so neutrally. It *feels* to her as though she is actually agreeing with the trade-off idea. She knows she is describing the *other side's* point of view, but she still feels the dissonance of it.)

E: She now *elaborates*. She explains both the trade-off and how it occurs. She further elaborates on the kind of *security* that is at stake and on how important that security sometimes is. She adds that in a certain sense there may be benefits to stereotyping people (at least in certain situations). As a further part of her elaboration, she decides that she will do some research (**R**) on how stereotyping has in fact been used in airport security (maybe in other countries). For the law-enforcement point, maybe she can find legal experts who argue in favor of it. She hopes she will even find a good quotation about this.

E: She already has an *example*, about airport screening. She decides to try to find an additional example, one that is different from airport security. (She also staircases her statement by focusing on "a certain level of security." She knows we can never be completely secure, so she could explore just how much security we would be giving up if we quit stereotyping people.)

She thinks of a *contrasting example* as well (see p. 85). She pictures a group of older women standing on a corner in the clothes they wore to church. No one considers them a threat. She thinks, "They could stand there talking for an hour and nobody would accuse them of loitering. Law enforcement officers would not stop to check their IDs." She thinks *they* have been stereotyped too—but, because it is not harmful or unfair, that is *not* the kind of stereotyping she is talking about.

I: The *illustration* part gives her difficulty. She realizes that it has to be an illustration of the *opposing* point of view, not of her own view. She looks for a situation where we *do* make judgments based on a category, rather than on the specific thing within that category. The illustration she finally comes up with is an analogy: that stereotyping might be like bombing another country in a time of war. It is true that innocent civilians will be killed, but many people would say it still has to be done to protect your country.

In the end, Michelle decides that she still holds her position on the unfairness of stereotyping. She finds, though, that she can now appreciate the other point of view, and she can actually empathize with those who think it is justified. But she makes the judgment that the unfairness and harm significantly outweigh the increase in security. She reasons that, in stereotyping, the harm and unfairness is done to huge numbers of people to catch the very tiny number of people who might threaten security.

Notice that incorporating "the other side" into your paper does a good deal more than simply increasing your paper's length. More important, it adds richness and authenticity to your paper. This happened not only in Michelle's case but in the other two examples as well. Lucia discovered a whole new aspect of the experiments on false memory, one she sees as something she might pursue in graduate school and beyond. In the thesis about *college life*, "the other side" opened up new areas to think about, particularly the stress and pressure of being a student and how dealing with them eats into students' time. At the very least, addressing "the other side" makes the paper into a genuine attempt to reason through an issue, one where other points of view are fairly and accurately considered and described.

A capsule: How to incorporate weakpoints into your paper:

- Develop them using SEE-I and staircasing.
- Spell out all aspects of the SEE-I in a fairminded way.
- Admit any important strengths in the other side.
- Answer them, to the extent you can; sometimes you may actually have to say you are unable to answer them.

The Order of the Writing Process

A question you might be asking yourself is, at what point in the writing process should you start looking for "the other side" of a paper you are writing? That is, when you're writing a paper, at what point do you start looking for other points of view on the issue?

There are really two answers to this. Here is *one* answer: For many people, the best time to find the weakpoints in their paper is after they've constructed the logical plan for it. It's at that point that they have the outline of their paper. They know their thesis; they know many of the main points and further sub-points they plan to use. They can envision the paper as a whole. They may also have at least partial SEE-I's for all or many of the main points in their paper. The overall structure of their paper is there in front of them, and much of it may already be "pre-written." And with this well-constructed outline, they can follow it step-by-step to write the paper. Knowing this overall structure often gives writers the best vantage point from which to see the weakpoints of their paper, what someone might say as an objection, or what someone might say was missing.

But there is another way to answer the question, one that brings up questions about the sequence of the writing process as a whole. The answer comes from understanding that critical writing is not really a linear process at all. It may seem linear because presentations in books and in classes try to be orderly. But in fact, in writing you often go forward and then back, changing, modifying, anticipating, jumping ahead, re-thinking the beginning, and changing the order as you need to.

It may be helpful to see a solid, usable sequence to follow in writing a substantive paper. Here is an effective one:

A Sequence for Writing a Paper

- do background research to understand your topic overall, to become "familiar" with it →
- analyze your topic around the circle →
- from your analysis around the circle, find or construct
  - your thesis statement
  - the main points you need in order to back up or explain your thesis statement, pre-writing as much as you can using SEE-I
  - the content of the introductory and concluding sections of your paper →
- identify "the other side" (the weakpoints) →
- do the focused research you need to get reliable information about the points in your paper (and maybe about "the other side" as well) →
- write the body of the paper by using SEE-I and staircasing throughout:
  - for every major point in your paper
  - for every important part of every major point in your paper

o to clarify and report on the research you are using in your paper
o to explain other points of view

The sequence leaves out essential parts such as giving credit and revising, but it offers a general-purpose sequence you can follow. Even so, it's not a rigid sequence. Skilled writing and reasonable thinking both require flexibility, sometimes large-scale flexibility. You can probably see that already. There are far more variations than can be mentioned here. As Chapter 3 recommends, for example, you could easily decide to write out some SEE-I's before you do anything else.

- Or: you might find that you need to do more research at any point in the process.
- Or: you might change your mind about a point you're making, or at least modify it.
- Or: you might decide to deepen or expand your paper by addressing additional parts of your analysis around the circle.
- Or: you could *begin* your paper by being confronted with an opposing point of view right at the start.

There are dozens of other possibilities, and almost any of them can occur at virtually any stage in the writing process.

Chapter 4: Practice and Assessment Exercises

*1. Identify and briefly explain the main outcomes for Chapter 4. (The suggestion is to answer this question without looking back on the chapter.)

Extended examples
*2. In Chapter 2, Kara gave an analysis "around the circle" of Juliet in Shakespeare's play. The example didn't show her getting to the point of actually coming up with a thesis statement or constructing an outline. What she said there was that Juliet was making the unrealistic assumption that everything in her elaborate plan would work out perfectly. She lists seven different ways the plan was almost certain to go wrong. Kara ends by saying that Romeo and Juliet weren't "star-crossed" lovers at all, that they died because they made plans that were "too risky, drastic and not well thought out."

What might be some weakpoints in the paper Kara plans to write?

3. If Kara does find a weakpoint in her paper (perhaps a possible objection to it), should she include a section describing that weakpoint or should she just write the paper laying out her own point of view? What are the advantages and disadvantages of each choice?

Questions 4 and 5 have to with the paper James intended to write about "sin taxes" (p. 8–11). He didn't think that he (and people like him) should have to pay for people who have medical problems because they made the *choice* to abuse substances like tobacco and alcohol. Here is the outline of his paper:

Thesis statement. We should raise "sin taxes" on alcohol and tobacco and then use the money raised through these taxes to pay for the treatment of people who abuse those substances.

Main point #1. People who don't smoke or drink excessively should not have to pay for medical care for the people who do.

Main point #2. The money from sin taxes can be used to pay for medical treatment that abusers of those substances bring on themselves.

Main point #3. People choose to smoke and drink. It is voluntary.

Main point #4. The healthcare costs of tobacco and alcohol in the U.S. is $121 billion per year.

Exercise intellectual empathy and, as much as you can, put yourself into James's mind.

*4. In one of the questions in the Exercises to Chapter 1, it was noted that James was uneasy about the argument he was giving in the paper. Even at the beginning, it seemed pretty harsh to him. When he was nearly finished. He looked for "the other side."

If you were James, what would you see as the major weakpoint in the paper?

*5. Finding "the other side" is more wide ranging than you might at first realize. In addition to finding the major weakpoint in James's paper overall, look for weakpoints in each of the points in his outline:

a. Identify some weakpoints specifically related to James's thesis statement.

b. Identify some weakpoints specifically related to his main point #1.

c. Identify some weakpoints specifically related to his main point #2.

d. Identify some weakpoints specifically related to his main point #4.

*6. Look back at the extended example of Charles as he thought about dieting (p. 46–50). Again, immerse yourself in his thinking. Put yourself in Charles's shoes, and follow along as he reasons through the issue. He hasn't analyzed his topic around the circle and he hasn't constructed an outline of his paper, but you can see the general direction his thinking is headed. His thesis will revolve around the idea that losing weight quickly isn't the way to be healthy and look good in a long-term way. Instead, he says, you have to change your whole approach to life.

Again, that is a strong thesis. It might well make a good basis for a paper. Nevertheless, there are "other sides" to the issue, ones that Charles could identify, describe, develop (using SEE-I), and maybe answer.

What are some weakpoints you might find if you were Charles?

7. In Chapter 1, Shelia planned to write a paper arguing that:

American public universities should be as inexpensive as European universities are.

What do you see as "the other side" in Sheila's planned paper?

*8. Recall some of what happened with Lucia's paper on "false memory." In Chapter 2, she planned a research paper on this topic, and in Chapter 4 she came up with a weakpoint—a gap— in relation to the issue of false memory. The weakpoint she found was that the experiments do not account for those people who were *not* susceptible to having false memories implanted.

One of the things that makes this such a rich point is that it opens up an area that she hopes to pursue in graduate school, perhaps with original research of her own.

Can you come up with any other weakpoints in Lucia's projected paper?

*9. Here are two possible objections to Lucia's paper on false memory:

• We can't know for sure that the experimenters were able to im-plant false memories in people. How do we know for sure that they there wasn't another time when they *were* lost in the mall and they were merely remembering it?
• Maybe the experimenters just happened to find a few people who had false memories. We can't know for sure that this is true for a lot of people.

What do you think of them as weakpoints?

10. In Michelle's extended example, the weakpoint she found cen-tered on safety: that the "other side" would hold that there was

a trade-off between stereotyping and safety. The weakpoints she found centered on the first group of Self-Confrontational Questions (p. 125). Here are the last three Self-Confrontational Questions:

- What important aspects of the issue have I not addressed?
- Is what I'm saying the whole truth, or is it only part of the truth?
- Is there anything else I should be addressing?

Apply these last three to Michelle's paper and come up with some weakpoints based in them.

*11. In Chapter 3 (p. 95–96), Tasha thought critically about an article that criticized the government for supporting Amtrak because the passenger service has lost money for 43 years straight. She did research to verify that data, but then she thought critically about it and realized that she couldn't think of a single government program that "made money": not the police, not schools, not the military, not even Congress. She concluded that government's purpose in supporting services was not to make money from them.

Did she find a weakpoint in the article?

Critical thinking traits of mind

12. A sentence on p. 121 of this chapter says:

> It is often extremely difficult to see how someone could possibly disagree with substantive points that you find obviously true.

Write down some views that you hold very strongly. They might be views you have about political, religious or social issues, about people from other countries, about music you like, the range of body images you consider attractive or unattractive... about anything, really, as long as you hold your views very strongly. The views you hold might be positive or negative.

The activity here is not to identify what people on the other side might say. It's not, at least here, to state objections they might raise to your views or gaps they might find in them. Instead, it is to exercise intellectual empathy, intellectual humility, and intellectual engagement. The activity is, first, to recognize that there are people who have very different views from yours about those issues; second, to take seriously the idea that many of those people are honest, reasonable, sincere, responsible individuals; and, third, to write an account of how such individuals could hold views that seem (from your point of view) so clearly and obviously *wrong*.

13. Complete the sentence by filling in XYZ in a way that works for you.

    - People who believe XYZ are really stupid [unreasonable, dishonest, selfish...].
    - People who do XYZ are really stupid [unreasonable, dishonest, selfish...].

    Now put yourself in a different frame of mind. Let your intellectual empathy come to the forefront. Sit for a while with the idea in the first half of the following sentences, and then fill in the blank in a way that makes sense:

    - Though some people who believe XYZ may be stupid (unreasonable, dishonest, selfish...), many of them are not. They believe XYZ because _____.

    Do the same not just for beliefs but for *actions*:

    - Though some people who do XYZ may be stupid (unreasonable, dishonest, selfish...), many of them are not. They do XYZ because _____.

    This will not work for every single way of filling in the blank, but it is true for a surprising number of ways you can fill it in.

14. Write about the traits of mind. Which of the traits do you think would be important to develop in order

    - to write better?
    - to be more successful in your professional life after you graduate?
    - to find more fulfillment in your personal life?

*15. What are some things you could do to help develop the traits in yourself?

Write about your own experience

*16. A box in the chapter (p. 121) asks you to remember beliefs that you once held that "you now realize were seriously misguided, even though you then held them with the deepest conviction."
    What are some examples of that for you?

17. What are some controversial topics that matter to you? What are two or three widely held points of view about those topics that differ substantially from the views you hold? At this point, just identify those other points of view, and then describe them without bias.

Write about writing

18. Why is it important to address the weakpoints in what you write?

19. Write a **summary** of Chapter 4 in the form of an SEE-I.

Self-Confrontational Questions

20. Look at issues and ideas that you encounter. They can be political, personal, student-oriented, almost anything. Practice using the Self-Confrontational Questions to find "the other side" in relation to these issues and ideas. Then take the ones you disagree with and describe them neutrally, non-judgmentally, fairmindedly. Try it with issues or beliefs that you hold very strongly. That is when it's most difficult.

*21. In this book, the Self-Confrontational Questions are intended to help you recognize the "other side" of what you are saying in a paper. But their value extends well beyond that use. Independently of papers you may write, the questions give you ways to find the other side of views you hold in your life. They sometimes reveal things to you that you never thought of before. They are ways of helping you find the truth of things. Consider the following:

*Everything happens for a reason.
A person is considered innocent until proven guilty.
Karma: The good or bad deeds you do will result in good or bad deeds being done to you in return.
Possession is nine-tenths of the law.
*You can't trust people who lie.
People catch colds from being out in cold, damp weather.
*You can't know the future.

22. The last questions in the exercises to the previous chapters asked you to choose topics to write about (Chapter 1), to analyze several of them "around the circle" of elements (Chapter 2), and to construct a full outline and then write the paper on one of them (Chapter 3). For this chapter, take what you have planned and written, and now find the "other side," describe it fairmindedly, and incorporate it into your paper.

Self-Assessment: Test It Out #3

How Can You Tell How Well You Did?

Test It Out #3. Being trustworthy. You can check to see how similar your response is to two of the most usual paths people take:

Path 1. Get some articles on the Internet that talk about Lincoln's presidency and the Emancipation Proclamation and report on what they say about the stages he went through.

Path 2. Find a reputable source that directly explains the stages Lincoln went through on his way to issuing the Proclamation. Then use that source as a guide and describe Lincoln's process step-by-step.

Actually, neither of those two paths is a very promising one, though there are some positives and negatives about each of them. For example, a positive in Path 2 is that it mentions "reputable" sources. That is more trustworthy than just looking for "some articles," reputable or not (as in Path 1). The sources you happen to find might be highly inaccurate, misleading, or one-sided.

A positive about Path 1, on the other hand, is that it mentions seeking out several sources, rather than just one, as in Path 2. Using multiple sources lets you encounter different points of view about the topic. A downside of that, though, is that those different points of view were not designed to fit together—they may even be in conflict with one another—and reporting on what they say is likely to end up giving you a hodgepodge. Path 2 might thus seem more promising. At least it is *organized*. The problem is that *you* are not the one who has organized it. You've taken the *author's* organization. Even if you supplement what the author is saying by adding in some other sources, it's still pretty far from writing a legitimate research paper.

You could try combining the positives from the two paths and correcting for other difficulties they contain. That might make them better, but the problem is actually deeper than that. Any paths like the two mentioned will still be seriously off-target. They do not give you a model that fits with *the point* of writing a genuine paper, and there is a still deeper reason behind that.

The deeper reason is that both of them indicate that you don't really "get" the topic you are writing on. Maybe you do, but probably you don't, at least not very much. Moreover, both of them indicate that you don't "get" what it is for *you* to write a research paper. Writing a research paper is not just turning in a book report. It involves learning about the topic and thinking it through in an informed way. What is missing from Path 1 and Path 2 is that they both leave out the *thinking* part.

How *would* you write a research paper on the stages Lincoln went through, a paper that's the product of your own thinking but based solidly on reputable sources?

Well, first, since you're writing on the stages Lincoln went through, you have to understand what he actually went through on the way to issuing the Emancipation Proclamation. Notice that it's an *understanding* of Lincoln's process that you need. Moreover, it's *your* understanding of it. A major part of coming to understand a topic like this is consulting reputable sources and taking what they say seriously. But it doesn't mean merely repeating what someone else says about it.

Understanding it doesn't mean understanding it perfectly or understanding *everything* about it, or somehow becoming an expert. It means understanding it to a reasonable degree, a degree that's appropriate for someone in a course at this level. It means you could explain it to someone; you could talk about it, and do so knowledgeably. It means that when it comes to the stages Lincoln went through, you know what you're talking about.

The "research" is the path you take in order to understand the topic.

It is important not to be thrown off by the word "research." Instructors call it that—and it *is* research—but what that means is that you are trying to find out about X so that you can understand it. The goal of doing research is to help you understand your topic in a way that is as clear and accurate as you can make it. In fact, you engage in "research" all the time in your life. You find out about electronic equipment you may want to buy, about games, careers, schools to attend, friends, fashion, anything that matters to you. (The hope is that you use reliable sources to find out about these, but whether you do or not, it's still "research.")

So, for the topic in this self-test, you have to do the reading, viewing, and listening that will allow you to construct an understanding of the stages that Lincoln went through. That almost certainly means looking at different sources, reliable ones, evaluating what they say, selecting what is most relevant and important, fitting their points together until you have a clear, coherent account in your own mind. Some of this will be background research so that you can start to get an overview of the way Lincoln evolved in relation to the Emancipation Proclamation, and some of it will be focused research to give clarity and accuracy to your understanding of specific points.

You will then be in a strong position to write the paper out of your best understanding. It's based solidly on sources—and you would certainly give credit to those sources—but it's *your* understanding that is now the foundation. How would you continue? You might choose what, in your best judgment, were the most important stages in Lincoln's process. Those would probably be the main points of your paper (the subject of self-test #2). You might sum up those phases, or Lincoln's process overall as you see it, in a single, clear sentence or two—a thesis statement (the subject of self-test #1).

CHAPTER 5

Making the Paper Better: Critical Thinking Standards and Socratic Questioning

Revising the Paper: Making It Better

The GPS box on the right locates the focus of this chapter at *improvement*. In the critical writing process, it is the stage of making the paper better. The "Pervasive" box below the GPS again lays out aspects of critical writing that run through everything. These pervasive aspects have been present all along, even if you haven't been consciously aware of them. A goal of this chapter is to bring two of them more fully in front of you. The *critical thinking standards* give you tools for improving and expanding your paper in an almost unlimited way; they make *revision* an organic and empowering part of your writing.

But don't be misled by the order of the GPS, or by the word "revision," or by this being Chapter 5. It doesn't mean that, after four chapters, and after you've planned out and written your paper, now is the time to start revising and making your paper better. In reality, you have been revising and making your paper better all along. The whole

GPS
• topic →
• analysis →
• plan →
• writing →
• "the other side" →
• improvement →
• flow

Pervasive aspects
• research
• critical thinking standards
• revision
• fundamental & powerful concepts
• giving credit

critical writing process is designed to make your paper better, and you have been doing so even if you weren't completely aware of it. The mere process of focusing on your thinking almost automatically makes your paper better.

Think of what you've already done. Every time you gave an analysis around the circle, you were improving your paper in a major way. Instead of just a vague, general topic or idea, you now have a *clear*, *relevant* and *precise* analysis of the topic. This is a major improvement all by itself. When you chose the points that you would build your paper around—the outline of your paper—you chose the *main* points, the ones you judged to be most important and most relevant: not the points that just happened to jump into your head. The result gave an organization to your paper that carried the *logic* of your thinking with it. Moreover, one dramatic way of making a paper better is to make it clearer. And you have focused on becoming clearer: every time you've given an SEE-I, you have targeted clarity directly. You have, in effect, revised your paper while you were writing it. Then, when you researched reliable sources to make your paper better informed, you were directing yourself toward the critical thinking standards of *accuracy* and *relevance*. When you addressed "Other Minds, Other Views" and identified "weakpoints" in your paper, you were making your paper *deeper*, giving it greater *breadth* as well as *fairness*, and making it more *sufficient*. All of those are major ways of making your paper better. In fact, every aspect of critically planning and writing a paper is designed to make your paper better, to improve it over what it would have been.

So maybe the title of this chapter should be "Making the Paper *Even* Better."

Two of the main tools for making your paper better are closely intertwined. They are the *standards of critical thinking* and making interventions using *Socratic questioning*.

The Standards of Critical Thinking

You have already used the *elements of reasoning* in constructing your paper, but you may be less familiar with using the *standards of critical thinking*. The contrast between the two is central. The elements are the parts of reasoning. (They are like the parts of anything else—of your body, your car, or your computer.) The elements are there in a person's thinking whether the person is aware of them or not. They are the parts of all reasoning, whether that reasoning is accurate or inaccurate, clear or unclear, relevant or irrelevant. When people are reasoning about anything, they have a *purpose*, they are addressing a *question at issue*, they are drawing *conclusions*, and so forth around the wheel of elements. But that doesn't necessarily mean that they are reasoning *well*. Their purpose may be logical or illogical; their question at issue may be important or trivial; their conclusions may be deep or superficial.

The critical thinking standards are different. (Just because your car, say, has all its parts, it doesn't mean it meets the standards of being a "good" car: it doesn't mean that it's reliable, or safe, or even that it runs.) The standards of critical thinking are the quality control in thinking. They are the standards that turn a person's reasoning into *good* reasoning. Again, the contrast between elements and standards is crucial. The *elements* tell you what is involved when someone is thinking about X. The *standards*, by contrast, tell you *how well* someone is thinking about X. The previous paragraph mentions at least six specific aspects of that "*how well*": *accurate, clear, relevant, logical, important*, and *deep*. Each of them is a standard of critical thinking.[1]

A basic distinction, one that guides all critical thinking, is the difference between *analysis* on the one hand, and *evaluation* or *assessment* on the other. To put the distinction in very general terms: in analysis, you are addressing *how* something does what it does; in evaluation or assessment, you are addressing *how well* something does what it does. In the purest case, the *elements* are about analysis; the *standards* are about evaluation. (Note that in some contexts, there is a distinction between *evaluation* and *assessment*. In this book, though, they have roughly the same meaning: both of them center on coming to conclusions about the *quality* of something.)

Critical Thinking Standards

clear	precise
accurate	deep
relevant	broad
important	sufficient
logical	fair

Reflecting on the standards in critical writing. Take a few moments to dwell on each of the standards. Think about the role each plays, first as you construct a critical plan for your paper, then as you identify the weakpoints, and then as you develop the paper, turning the plan into actual well-written paragraphs.

- The paper you write needs to be *clear*. It needs to be one where the reader can follow what you are saying and understand what you mean, all the way through. The standard of clarity applies to individual points you make, as well as to the paper as a whole.

- The points you make in your paper need to be *accurate*, as accurate as you (or an unbiased observer) can tell. They need to have evidence behind them. They need to be backed up with good reasoning, observation or experience. The sources you use to back up your points need to be reliable. And, to show the reader that the points you are making are accurate, you frequently need to *give* the evidence, reasoning, and sources that back up the points you are making.

- The points you make in your paper have to be *relevant*. This means they relate directly to the thesis of your paper. Both the main points and the subsidiary points in your outline need to have a bearing on explaining or giving backup for your central thesis. The standard of relevance applies to every aspect of the paper: from the examples and illustrations you give to the sources you use and the way you cite them.

- The paper needs to stress what is most *important*, what is most *significant*. In it, you dwell on essential points having to do with your thesis statement. You expand on those important points and show them as prominent. Though you may sometimes decide to bring up minor or incidental points, you don't dwell on them, even if they are otherwise interesting. Minor points that you bring up are relegated to a minor position, and points that are irrelevant to the thesis are omitted entirely.

- The paper needs to be *logical*. Central to critical writing is having an outline that is *logically organized*. A critical writing paper is one where the reader can follow logically from one point you make to another, where the reader can see how the individual parts fit together logically as a whole.

- The points you make in the paper need to be *precise*. You need to give the necessary details. You don't just speak in loose generalities. You are specific in what you say about the main points and in what you say to back them up. If the points you are making are statistical or quantitative, you give the requisite data. If they are based on exact studies, you give the actual results. If you are describing a piece of literature or other writing, you refer to specific lines or sections. If authors make a point in a striking way, you give the actual quotation. You are precise in how you cite your sources.

- Your paper needs to have appropriate *depth*. In your paper, you take account of the complexities embedded in the topic. Some topics are relatively uncomplicated, while others have multiple complications built into them (such as a paper on important social or political issues). Your paper takes account of the problems that would arise. If the issue requires an underlying theory or framework, you address that as well.

- Your paper needs to have *breadth*. In the paper, you take account of other points of view, other perspectives, and the larger picture, and you do this to the extent required by the issue you are addressing. Some issues intrinsically require that you consider multiple viewpoints (such as writing about an international problem that affects different countries in radically different ways), while some issues are relatively more unitary. The standard of breadth also comes in directly when you spell out "the other side" (as in Chapter 4). Doing so enlarges the scope of your paper by explicitly taking account of how other people might see the issue differently, or how others might disagree with you or find gaps in your account.

- Your paper needs to cover the thesis *sufficiently*. The reader does not feel that the paper is only fragmentary, or that major parts are missing. Instead, the paper is well rounded. It gives a feeling of completeness. The reader doesn't end up saying, "OK. This is good as far as it goes, but really you can't cover that thesis without addressing the issue of X, and you haven't discussed X at all."

- Your treatment of the issues in the paper needs to be *fair*. That fairness applies not just to what you yourself write but to your presentation of research and of "the other side" as well. You do not underplay opposing points of view. You do not present them in biased or slanted language. You give them the credit they are due. As you identify, explain and address the weakpoints in your own position, you consciously try to present objections in their strongest form. Even though you may disagree with them, you strive to explain how people could see them as plausible and reasonable. Fairness is a standard for you, and in your writing the reader can see that it is also one of your values.

A good way to get a feel for how the standards work in critical writing is to take some time to reflect on just one of them. Consider **relevance**. The standard of *relevance* is your main guide in keeping you from wandering off on a tangent, or from engaging in "associational writing."

Often, our minds just seem to work by association of ideas, wandering from one idea to the next. Usually, this is not even noticed by the person who is thinking. You may start off writing about dieting; and that leads you to think about the way slimness is emphasized in our society; and that leads you to the idea that Hollywood stars are almost all thin; and that leads you to think about a particular Hollywood star you saw in a movie last week. Long before the end, the focus in your thinking has been lost. It has rambled from idea to idea, each one less relevant than the one before. When people write in an associational way, the resulting paper will likely go seriously astray. It will be just a string of loosely related thoughts.

Relevance is what can save you. You can use it to monitor your thinking and keep it on track. At each associational step, you can ask yourself, "How is that relevant to the point I'm trying to make?" "Is this really directly relevant to my thesis statement?" "Is it essential? Or is it just interesting but tangential?" Asking questions like these can save you from all the time spent in associational thinking. It can save you from laboriously writing paragraphs that really make your paper weaker, paragraphs you later have to cut.

It is another reminder that critical thinking is not supposed to *add* to your burdens; it's supposed to ease your burdens. Critical thinking makes the writing process *easier* (as well as significantly better). The standards work that way. They are intended not to be additional hoops you have to jump through, but rather a way of making your life (and your writing) more successful, less stressful.

An ideal (an achievable ideal) is to develop a deep habit of relevance. This means monitoring your thinking for relevance in an ongoing way. It takes practice to develop the habit, but after a while it can become almost second nature. You'll find yourself being on track, almost effortlessly attuned to the question you're addressing. A habit of relevance is something that can stay with you all through your life. You might even develop a reputation (at work, for example) as someone whose comments, observations, strategies, decisions—and writing—are worth paying attention to because they are so on target and to the point.

How the Standards Help

The standards are crucial in planning, writing, and revising a critical paper.

- The standards help you avoid pitfalls, errors and flaws.
- They help you with sharpening things up, with focus, with refining.

- They help you with limiting and expanding your paper.
- They help you with coherence, relationship, pacing, and fitting things together.

Avoiding pitfalls, errors and flaws. All the standards help with avoiding pitfalls: of unclarity, of irrelevance, of overlooking important factors.

Accuracy makes a good example. You are going to write a paper, and you come up with an idea you like. The question is "Is it a good idea? Will it make a good thesis statement?" A "good idea" is more than one that is focused and clear. It also has to be reasonably accurate. But often the ideas we get are not accurate—sometimes they're not even close. That's partly because we get ideas based on our previous experience (which may be very limited or even distorted), on news outlets (which are at best highly selective), on what is vivid to us (despite the fact that what is vivid is typically not representative—its unusualness is probably what made it vivid), on social media, on the unexamined norms and folk beliefs of our society, family and social group (despite the fact that we may never have even questioned their validity), and so forth.

For example, suppose you come home and find that your apartment has been burglarized. Valuable things have been taken; maybe the apartment has been trashed. For most people, this is a traumatic experience. Like other victims, you probably feel both angry and unsafe. Then maybe you find that another apartment nearby was also burglarized recently. You might easily think, "Burglaries are on the rise." You might think, "Burglaries are getting out of hand in the U.S." You might say, "Violent crimes are increasing dramatically in the U.S., and as a result we are much less safe than we used

> **Accuracy**: one of the things we learn from the field of history is that our knowledge (or alleged knowledge) rests on *sources*. More strongly than that, *everything* we believe or disbelieve rests on sources. Occasionally, you yourself may be the source—as in personal observation, for example. But everything else is something you learned from others. That ranges from the most ordinary beliefs you have (for example, that you were born on such-and-such a date) to the most profound and far-reaching beliefs: science, religion, politics, the past, or anything that happens or happened outside your immediate vicinity.
>
> So as you write your paper you ask yourself "Do I have this from a reputable source? Is this information I can realistically rely on?"

to be." Notice that this seems like a reasonable thesis statement. Each reformulation becomes clearer and more precise. In the last formulation, you have two main supporting points as backup. You even have concrete examples in the two burglaries that have occurred recently. By broadening it to "violent crimes," you will now be able to use data about other violent crimes in addition to burglary.

But, really, it's not a good thesis statement at all. Burglaries have *not* been increasing dramatically in the U.S. They have been going down: dramatically, in fact, since the 1990s.[2] Having just been confronted with two burglaries, you have an *impression* that they've been increasing—but your impression is way off-base. You do have two examples to use—but two examples are an extremely flimsy basis for drawing a conclusion about burglaries even in your own neighborhood, much less in the U.S. as a whole. In addition, you broadened your thesis statement from "burglaries" to "violent crime." But, of course, burglary by itself is not a violent crime. (The U.S. Bureau of Justice (2017) lists the following as violent crimes: murder, forcible rape, robbery, and aggravated assault.[3]) It may *feel* as if violence has been done to you, but it isn't actually violent. So even the two "supporting points" you started with turn out not to give any support.

> What *might* make a good paper is an account of how you thought and felt after the burglary. You could describe, first, how the assaultive *feeling* of the experience led you to believe that it was (a) violent and (b) an example of a large-scale trend, and, second, how you came to discover the inaccuracy of those conclusions. It would be a paper that nicely highlights intellectual humility and intellectual courage.
>
> More generally, when you hold that something is true (or important, or clear, or deep, or ...), and then discover that there are serious flaws in it, the process of that discovery will often make an interesting and gripping paper.

Sharpening things up, focusing, refining. The main standards that help with sharpening things up are clarity, precision and importance.

There is a sense in which everything rests on clarity. If you say something that is highly unclear, you can't even tell whether it is accurate or inaccurate, relevant or irrelevant, important or trivial. Here is an unclear sentence: "Home is far away." Is that sentence accurate: *Is* home far away? You can't tell. Is it relevant or important? Again, you can't tell. It all depends: *Whose* home? Far away *from what? How far?*

The main tool for making your paper clearer is SEE-I. One of the reasons it helps so much is that, even before you write anything down, it first clarifies *your thinking*. Once you accomplish that, it becomes easier to turn those thoughts into words on the page. So as you plan and develop your paper, you will often be asking yourself:

How can I *state* this more concisely? Can I capture it in in a single crisp sentence?

Will the reader need more *elaboration* here? How can I explain it more fully?

Would another *example* help? Can I give a *contrasting example*?

What is an *illustration* or analogy I could use to help the reader better understand what I'm trying to convey? What else is something that it's *like*?

What parts of it should I staircase?

After the clear thinking, though, you still have to convey it clearly in the writing. A persistent illusion people have is that other people will somehow know what they are thinking, what they have in mind. Suppose you write something unclear, such as "Graduating is good." You may *mean* something clearer: you may mean "Graduating (*from law school*) is good (*in the sense that it increases the chances of financial success*)." If you have that clearer idea in your mind, you may assume that you have communicated it to someone else by saying "Graduating is good." But you haven't. You're leaving it up to the other person to *guess* what you have in mind. In conversation, this is sometimes resolved by the context of the conversation. But in a paper, context is much more limited. Often, the only context the reader has is the one the writer has conveyed in the paper itself.

Something similar happens with precision and importance. You may unconsciously assume that readers will supply the precise details you have in mind but have not written, or that readers will be able to tell the most important aspect of your paper, without your having to tell them. There is an analogy here to counseling. Counselors and therapists often call this tendency "mind-reading." If you are having difficulty with a relationship you are in, one of the causes may be that you expect the other person to "read your mind." It is the expectation (often an unreasonable one) that people you have a relationship with should automatically know what you mean or what you want, without your having to say it. In a paper (and probably in a relationship as well), you have to *say* it.

Limiting and expanding. The main standards you need to consider when limiting and expanding your paper, to improve it, are sufficiency, depth, and breadth.

Again, impressions can be deceptive. If you have very strong convictions that X is true, your impression can be that your reasons in favor of X are *sufficient*. But no matter how strong your *impression* is, your reasons may in fact *not* be sufficient. In addition, even if they are sufficient, that is different from *showing the reader* that they are sufficient.

You have to ask yourself:

- Have I made a sufficient case for this?
- In my SEE-I, have I elaborated sufficiently?

A main problem that students often face in writing a paper is how to make it more sufficient. Sometimes that can be just to reach a certain number of pages, but sometimes it can come from a perception that you have not made your case fully enough. It happens within SEE-I's as well. Sometimes you will realize that an elaboration that contains only one or two sentences is not much of an elaboration at all.

Both breadth and depth help you expand your paper, again in ways that are directly relevant. *Breadth* directs you to look at the issue from other perspectives, or other points of view, or to look at how the issue fits into the larger picture. By focusing on breadth, you can consciously search out significant and relevant perspectives you may have missed. You can then develop them using SEE-I.

Similarly, there are any number of ways to address *depth* in your paper. One straightforward way is to look for *complexities* or *complications* in an issue, or to ask yourself "What is *difficult* about this issue?" Notice how rich a source this is for expanding your paper. You can consciously ask yourself what complexities (or complications or difficulties) there might be in an issue you are writing on. As you identify and then explore these complexities, it will open up deeper parts of the issue, and you can then expand on them in your paper.

Virtually any important or controversial issue has complexities in it. If you can't see what they are, there is a good chance it is because you are so immersed in one way of addressing the issue that you are (at least temporarily) unable to see them. You may

> There are other ways to use *depth* in expanding a paper. An issue can be deep for many reasons: because it connects to something meaningful, for example, or because it has rich implications, or because it taps into an important underlying frame of reference. Any of those can give you a direction you can use to expand a paper and make it better.

already recognize this when it comes to controversial issues such as capital punishment, dieting, or ways to reduce global warming. But if an issue is important or meaningful to people, it will likely have complexities even if the issue is not a controversial one.

An example: There are many engineering studies showing that an alarming number of bridges in the U.S. do not meet minimum safety requirements. So: "Bridges on streets and highways need to be safe." This is a strongly *un*controversial view, one that seems clearly true. It is doubtful that anyone disagrees with it. But numerous complexities arise when you start thinking about the issue more deeply:

- Repairing bridges would require a vast amount of money. How should this be funded?
- Should taxes be raised to pay for these repairs?
- What should we do about bridge repair if voters (or their representatives) are unwilling to vote for increased taxes?
- What other essential public needs should we sacrifice to generate funds for bridges?
- Should bridges be repaired so as to meet current needs or to meet needs for the future?

None of these complexities, notice, show that the original statement is not true. Rather, they focus on depth, rather than on accuracy. They function as complexities *given* that the statement is true. The most rewarding way to look at these complexities is not to view them as burdens for you. Instead, each is an opportunity to expand your paper in a new direction, and to do so in a way directly relevant to developing your thesis. In the end, you may decide not to develop any or all of these complexities in your paper, but at least it will be your choice. A conscious focus on depth (like a similar focus on breadth) is

Notice that questions raised by *depth* are different from those raised by *accuracy*. Similarly, *depth* raises questions that are different from those raised by other standards, such as *clarity* and *precision*. In the bridge-repair example, a question having to do with *clarity* is "What exactly is meant by *safe* in terms of bridges?" Does this mean safe for cars? For boats? Safe from accidents? From people who want to blow them up? From floods? Questions focusing on *precision* are "How many bridges have been found to be unsafe? Are they on federal, state or local streets and highways?"

an essential tool not just for making your paper longer but for making it more interesting and more compelling as well.

Coherence, relationship, pacing, and fitting things together. The primary tools here are the standards of logic and relevance.

The standard of relevance has already been introduced and discussed in part. Focusing on relevance prompts you to ask, not just once but again and again, "How is this point related to that one? How do the points fit together?" Above all, "How is each point, example, and illustration relevant to the thesis statement?"

As always in writing, it is important to keep the standard of relevance in mind as you plan your paper, but, once again, it is also important to communicate that relevance to your reader. If you see a certain point as relevant to your thesis statement, you are very likely to take it for granted that other people will also see it as relevant ("mind-reading" again). You may even assume that they will see it as relevant in the same way you do. This is a natural assumption people tend to make, but it's often not true. Think of how often it happens in your day-to-day life: you do something nice for someone, but they take it in a very different way; you say something intended to be just funny, but other people take it as offensive. They don't see the same relationship between your action and your goal as you intended.

In a paper it is risky to assume that your reader will see relevance in the same way you do. You will often have to *explain* to the reader just how one point is related to another and how each point advances your thesis statement. The standard of relevance is your main way of keeping your thinking and your writing on track.

The standard of logic functions in a similar way. One of the main ways it operates is by helping you see the logical organization of your paper, how all the parts of your critical plan fit together as a coherent whole. You can often envision this with an *outline* of the paper. You can also display the logical organization with a *concept map* (often called a *graphic organizer*).

For example, Elizabeth has written a paper with a *thesis statement* and three *main points* that back it up or explain it. (She also has a further *supporting point* (labeled 1a) to support main point #1.) In addition, Elizabeth has included a short section on "the other side" of the issue. There she describes a "weakpoint": In this case it's an objection someone might make to her main point #3.

An outline of her paper might look like the one on the top of the next page. Logically, she shows the major part of her paper in bold print, and she represents the much shorter section on "the other side" in smaller print.

Outline

thesis statement
    main point #1
        1a. supporting point for #1
    main point #2
    main point #3   <u>"the other side"</u>
                         • weakpoints:
                             objection to main point #3

She does the same with her concept map shown below. (She uses a wavy dotted line to show that "the other side" *opposes* main point #3 rather than supports it.) A logically organized paper gives both writer and reader a satisfying feeling of completion or, if necessary, greater clarity about the tension that remains.

Concept Map

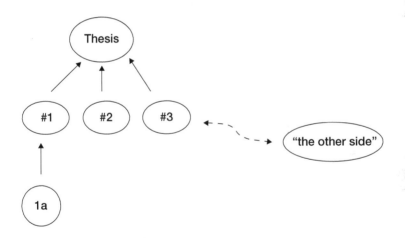

Using the standards implicitly. To a certain extent, we already use the standards to monitor what we say or write or think. They are there *implicitly*. If you are writing a paper about dieting, you are unlikely to spend much time writing about your favorite band, or to say "Dieting is easy and effective for everyone." You filter both of them out because the first one is obviously irrelevant and the second one is obviously inaccurate. You may not use the *words* "irrelevant" or "inaccurate," but you use the concepts themselves.

Typically, though, when the standards are merely implicit, people apply them only in a hit-or-miss way. As a result, they often try to solve problems without being *clear* about what the problem is exactly; they harbor *false* assumptions; they often bring in *irrelevant* information, without realizing that it's irrelevant; they often are satisfied with a *superficial* explanation, even if it is to their advantage to go *deeper*; and so forth, through the rest of the standards.

As with all critical thinking concepts, the real effectiveness comes from using the standards *explicitly*. This means not only monitoring what you write, revising your ideas and words as you go along, but also doing so in a conscious, reflective, reasoned way. The monitoring takes place (a) as you plan your paper, (b) as you turn your plan into a written paper, and (c) when you make any further changes after the draft of the paper is written.

Neglecting the standards often leads people to say things that somehow sound right, even though they aren't. People sometimes say, "Change is good." If you think about it for a minute, you'll see that this can't be accurate. Some changes are good, yes, but can't you easily think of changes that are disastrous? Maybe people mean "Don't refrain from a helpful course of action *only* because it requires change." The standard (in this case *precision*) is left out. People sometimes say (leaving out the standard of logic), "That's the exception that proves the rule"— whereas if there are exceptions, it shows that the rule is *not* entirely accurate: that it is not actually "*the* rule." (Historically, "proving" a rule actually means *testing it*.) "A picture is worth a thousand words," but, again, there have been many thousand-word essays that have said far more than a picture.

Interventions: Enriching Your Paper with Socratic Questioning

The main theme of this book is that using the tools and concepts of critical thinking will make any writing you do better—not just the writing you do for a course in school but *any* non-fiction writing. The techniques, applied thoughtfully, will make your writing clearer, deeper, more logically organized, and more substantial. These techniques begin by focusing your thinking about a topic; they guide you through structuring your writing, including research you engage in; and then they enable you to communicate informed thinking to your reader. This is the main theme. But one of the major sub-themes in this book is that critical writing techniques make your writing not only better but also *easier*. Socratic questioning is one of these techniques. Making interventions in your thinking, using Socratic questioning, makes your writing substantially better, and it also makes the work of writing a good paper surprisingly easier.

Socratic questioning. Traditionally, Socratic questioning consisted of one person, a teacher (Socrates, for example), asking a series of interlinked questions of a group of students, and doing so in a sustained way, with a goal of reasoning through an important issue or concept. The teacher/student aspect of Socratic questioning, though, is not essential to its success; neither is the idea of having only one questioner and a group of responders. In fact, Socratic questioning can take place between just a pair of individuals, or even within just one person. What is essential is that the questions are designed to probe a person's thinking and that all parties are engaged in the process. Engagement means that the questioner is genuinely posing powerful and even challenging questions, and the responder is genuinely trying to answer them. There is also a disciplined aspect to Socratic questioning: skilled Socratic questioners do not ask questions at random. They don't just wait for questions to pop into their heads. Rather, they have developed an ability to ask the kind of questions that lead in fruitful directions, ones that lead the responder down a line of the responder's own reasoning. To a large extent, skilled Socratic questioners can help people reason through topics or issues even if the questioners themselves don't know very much about the topic or issue.

Socratic questioning furnishes you with focused, readily usable tools to make improvements. It is helpful at any stage in the writing process. You can use Socratic questioning even after you've typed the last word into your "final" version—when you read your paper yet again to see if you can make the paper still better. You can use it to re-write parts of a paper your instructor has critiqued and returned to you for improvement. But you can also use it as you plan or write—a section, a paragraph, an SEE-I, your thesis and main points. At any point, you can enrich your paper by making a Socratic questioning "intervention." In the richest sense of the word, all of these count as "revising."

Socratic questioning, as used in this book, is built on the *standards* of critical thinking. What makes it work is that:

a. individual critical thinking standards are used as specific focused questions, designed to probe and stimulate your thinking;

b. the questions are applied to something you have already written or are in the process of writing;

c. in answering the questions you will often bring to light connections you were already making in your mind; and

d. by answering the questions *in writing* you will generate paragraphs that can go directly into your paper and add to its strength and fullness.

Making Socratic Questioning Interventions

Look back at the list of critical thinking standards on p. 151. One of the main ways these standards function is by generating questions in your mind. As you write, you are in effect asking yourself, "Is this *clear?*" "How is this *relevant* to the point I'm making?" "Is this point an *important* one or just a minor side issue?" and so forth. To some extent, something like this may go on even if you're not using the standards explicitly, even if you are not conscious of them at all. But, once again, explicitness is the key because it guides you to conscious reflection. Asking questions explicitly, consciously, reflectively, can transform your writing (and your thinking as well).

The following list contains the most widely usable Socratic questions based in the standards. They are phrased in a way to make them particularly applicable to writing. (Note that, because of the flexibility of critical thinking concepts, the wording of the questions may have to be adapted to fit the specific issues you are questioning.)[4]

The Socratic questions won't help you much if you see them as just one big block. You can't experience how useful they are by just glancing over the list. You have to try them out. (You can use as many of them as you find useful, but a good way to see the power they give you is to try *just one*.)

1. Choose some important part or aspect of your paper. Call it X.
   [It can be one of your main points. It can be a supporting point. It can be a concept or idea that comes up in an important way in your paper. It can be virtually anything: the only requirement is that it should be *important* in your paper. X may be something you've already given an SEE-I for, or elaborated on at length. Usually, it doesn't matter how much or how little you've already written.]
2. Choose a Socratic question to ask.
   [At this point you don't necessarily even have to pick out exactly the right Socratic question. Just choose one that fits with X.*]
3. Answer it. Explain your answer.
   [See how answering it makes the thoughts, and the words, come to you. Give as full an answer as you can. As you do so, notice

*A suggestion is to choose a standard other than clarity. By this time you have already worked quite a bit on clarity with SEE-I.

Socratic Questions

Clarity
- How can I elaborate on this further?
- Can I give an additional example, one that clarifies the point in a somewhat different way?
- Can I give a contrasting example?
- Would another illustration be helpful?

Accuracy
- Why would someone believe this is true?
- What reasons or evidence is this claim based on?
- How can this be backed up?

Relevance
- How is *this* related to *that*?
- How is this relevant?
- What bearing does this have on the overall issue?

Importance
- How or why is this important or significant?
- What are the most significant parts of this?

Logic
- Have I made logical connections throughout my paper?
- How does this make sense?
- How does this form a coherent whole?

Precision
- What are some of the details of this?
- What are some of the specifics of this?

Depth
- What factors make this difficult?
- What are some of the complexities of this?
- What is meaningful about this?

Breadth
- What would this look like from another perspective?
- How could we look at this in another way?
- How does this fit in with the larger picture?

Sufficiency
- How can I make this more adequate for the task at hand?
- What is an additional point I can bring up here?
- What more can I say about this without bringing in extraneous details?

Fairness
- What makes this a fair thing to say?
- How might biases or vested interests be coming into this?
- How might this be viewed less egocentrically or sociocentrically?

Notice how the Socratic questions are worded. In one way, they are open-ended; in another way, they point you in a specific direction and further *open up* the issues you are dealing with. This combination is part of what gives you ways to make your paper better. By contrast, "yes-or-no" questions can often leave you with nowhere to go. For example, if you write something and then ask yourself, "Is that deep enough?" or "Is that precise?" your natural response will be "Yes," or maybe "Yes, I think so," or "I honestly don't know." Asking the question in these words gives you very little insight into how to make it deeper or more precise. But if you ask "What are some complications about this?" (a depth question) or "What are some of the details about this?" (a precision question), the questions send you down a directly helpful path.

how your answer, and maybe the way you explain your answer, adds quality, cogency, and richness to what you've already said.]

4. Write the answer out, including the explanation you've given. [This will probably take at least one full paragraph, maybe more. You may decide to include examples and illustrations.]

5. Import your answer directly into your paper.

Why Socratic questioning works: Transforming the implicit into the explicit. Making an intervention with Socratic questioning enriches your writing. And it does so in a *direct* way, one that can also make writing your paper significantly easier as well. It allows you to revise your paper and make it better, right then and there, at any point in the writing. It does this because, by applying Socratic questioning, you will generate actual additional paragraphs—relevant, significant paragraphs—ones you can then import directly into your paper. The questions bring out and help you develop more fully what may already be hovering in your mind. The power of the questions often comes from taking what is there in your thinking in an un-articulated and barely conscious way—*implicitly*—and making it conscious. It lets you articulate it—*explicitly*—and incorporate it directly into your paper. In the process, it often brings insight as well.

You can feel for yourself how it changes and focuses you when you use Socratic questions *explicitly*. Suppose someone asks you an ordinary question in conversation:

• What were you talking about yesterday with person X?
• What was yesterday's class about?
• What did your supervisor at work say about XYZ?

You just answer the question. It's just automatic. There is probably not even a pause between when the question is asked and when you begin your answer.

But it's entirely different if someone asks you the same question but this time explicitly puts in a standard from the Socratic questions:

- *Be as accurate as you can be*: What were you talking about yesterday with person X?
- *Be as detailed as you can be*: What was yesterday's class about?
- What did your supervisor say about XYZ? *What was the most important part of it?*

When the questions are asked in the second way, there is a distinctive pause before you answer, a pause in which you are *processing* and thinking more critically about the answer.

Moreover, like other critical writing techniques, Socratic questioning applies not just to writing a formal paper for a class but to any kind of writing: an important memo at work, a business report, a research review, a treatment plan, a case study—almost anything. All of these forms of writing may in some respects be different from writing a paper for class. But Socratic questions will substantially enrich any of them.[*]

Think of the critical thinking standards as *habits* you cultivate in yourself, and the difference that would make in your life. Consider *importance*. Imagine the effect it will have if you consciously pay attention to what is important and what isn't. Suppose people you care about say something that is meaningful to them. You ask, "What is important about that to you?" You ask it not as a challenge but because you want to understand their thinking, to show that you care about what they are saying. It is a way of connecting with them on a deeper level.

You can do it with yourself as well: you say or do something that is meaningful to you. You can follow it up, then or later, by asking, "What is important about that? What makes it significant?" Taking ownership of just that one standard—importance—can increase your insight substantially. It can also help you increase your appreciation for what *is* important to you, and reduce the attention you pay to the trivialities that often clutter a person's life.

---

[*] Socratic questions help at any level of expertise. The author of this book sometimes gives workshops for professionals whose writings are published in books and academic articles. Though the participants are accomplished and expert writers, they find that the Socratic questions open up aspects that substantially improve their written work.

Socratic Interventions in Practice: Extended Examples

Example #1. You can get a fuller idea of how a Socratic questioning intervention works by considering an abbreviated example you are familiar with by now. Think back on the paper Michelle was writing on stereotyping (Chapter 3). She made a number of points in her plan, and she developed each point by using SEE-I: elaborating and giving examples and illustrations. (In Chapter 4, she developed "the other side" of the issue as well.)

Picture where she is in the writing. She feels *finished* with the paper. In her mind, she is *done*. But suppose it's a little short in length and that she'd also like to make the paper better. She's nearing the deadline for turning it in.

Here are two of her main points:

- Stereotyping is unfair.
- A consequence of stereotyping is that sometimes people are denied jobs or housing or other opportunities because they have been stereotyped.

Here is one of the Socratic questions (it is based on the standard of *relevance*):

- How is *this* related to *that*?

In her main points, Michelle mentions *unfairness* and *being denied jobs or housing*. So she now makes a Socratic questioning intervention. She asks:

"How is the unfairness related to being denied jobs or housing?"

Notice that Michelle already has an idea that they *are* in fact related. That's why she put those two points into her plan in the first place. The related-ness was probably in her mind only implicitly, but it was there. But she hasn't written out *how* they are related. The intervention brings it out, makes it explicit for her. Here is what she now writes:

The unfairness of stereotyping is related to being denied jobs and housing. It is discriminatory, not to mention illegal, to deny people jobs they are qualified for simply because of their gender or the color of their skin. The fair thing to do is to hire people based on the level of their skill, not on whether they have a certain gender or ethnicity. The ability to buy a house should be based on whether the person can afford it, not on other factors that don't have any effect on the person's ability to pay off a mortgage. For example....

Answering the question generates a paragraph, one she can put directly into her paper. She may fill in her example, and she may decide she wants to refine the wording, but she *has* the paragraph.

The question Michelle asked about relevance—"How is *this* related to *that*?"—is just one of the Socratic questions. She could equally have asked about the *importance* of this or that point, the details of the unfairness (*precision*), the complications surrounding the issue of stereotyping (*depth*),* or the way stereotyping fits into the larger picture of the way people treat one another (*breadth*). The question "How is this related to that?" seems utterly simple—but it is powerful. That is true for virtually any of the Socratic questions. They are powerful in that they provide clear paths for expanding and enriching your paper almost at will.

Moreover, when you ask questions such as "What factors make this difficult?" or "Why would someone believe this is true?" you might well get insights you've never considered before. Asking these questions doesn't give insight automatically, but it's close. If you ask about something that is fundamentally important to you and you become intellectually engaged with the question, you can almost rely on gaining insight.

> Remember: Socratic questioning is about being helpful! At any point you might begin by asking one of the questions. But suppose the question you've chosen doesn't seem to fit well. Or suppose you really don't know how to answer it. Or suppose answering it would take you too far afield, or would take too much time.
>
> That is, suppose the question you choose doesn't work for you: Just choose another one!

> Socratic questioning also helps at the very beginning of your paper, when you are planning it out. From your analysis around the circle you are considering possible thesis statements and other main points. And, without being strongly aware of doing so, you're choosing ones that seem more or less accurate to you, that seem important, that seem relevant. The problem is in the word "seem." Using the standards explicitly, as in Socratic questioning, helps you make a more considered, focused judgment. Having a point *seem* accurate (without really examining it) is different from giving your best judgment—explicitly—that it *is* accurate.

---

*Asking about "complications" is just one way of questioning using the standard of *depth*. There are a number of others. See p. 158.

Example #2.

The second example is from a published editorial by Michael Puglia. It appeared in a college newspaper *The Record*.[5] The article itself has 17 paragraphs, but the excerpt here consists of the first two introductory paragraphs and another paragraph at the end. Note that this is an editorial in a newspaper, and so Michael had to make it brief, and he also had to make the individual paragraphs much shorter than they would probably be in a paper for a class.

Here is the title, the first two paragraphs, and the next-to-last paragraph from the article:

Violence in Video Games a Problem for Developing Minds

We always hear stories about how easily children and adolescents can be influenced. That's why there are restrictions in place on many aspects of everyday life: movies, cigarettes, alcohol and so on. But what about something like video games? Could a harmless disc or cartridge impact a young person to the extent of acting out or worse?

The simple answer: no. Many factors are involved in the way the brain works to cause any individual to act a certain way. However, video games can help provoke someone who is already easily influenced.

...

Ultimately, it is up to the consumer to deem what is and isn't appropriate for themselves. Technology is always advancing and so the graphics will keep getting better. Games are just one of the many variables that determine how a person acts.

The first two paragraphs introduce Michael's *topic*—the relation between video games and acts of violence—and they also give the *thesis statement* of his essay. It is expressed indirectly, in the form of a question and an answer, but it can be written this way:

Video games do not influence young persons to commit acts of violence (though they can provoke someone who is already easily influenced).

In the middle of the article—this part is not printed here—Michael gives four main points. His first one is that many children who are drawn to violent video games do so because those children *already* have a tendency toward aggression. His second main point is that when the graphics in a videogame are highly realistic, the realism may be just as influential as how violent the content is. He transitions into his third main point by raising the question of who bears the responsibility for deciding who can play a game. In partial answer to this, he gives his third main point: that the official ratings of video games do not determine who can play; the ratings (such as "M" for those who are 17 and older) are not legally binding— they are only *recommended*. (In the body of the paper, Michael elaborates on these main points, he gives examples, and he supports them with research he has done.)

So, again, who bears the responsibility? His fourth main point answers that question (it's a *conclusion* he has drawn), and he states it explicitly in the first sentence of the next-to-last paragraph:

> Ultimately, it is up to the consumer to deem what is and isn't appropriate for themselves.

Making Socratic questioning interventions. To see the force of Socratic questioning, imagine that this isn't an editorial in a newspaper. Imagine instead that it is a draft of a paper that a student—call him Jay—is writing for a class. Jay recognizes that he has turned out a well-composed piece of critical writing. His editorial has a clear thesis statement and main points, with strong examples, backup, and references to reputable sources. (Most of these are not in the excerpt printed here.) He also recognizes, though, that as a paper for a class, he needs to expand it and make it more substantial. (As much as you can, exercise your own intellectual empathy. Put yourself in Jay's shoes. Think of this as your own first draft and that you are the one using Socratic questioning interventions to expand this draft into a full paper.) To follow Jay's reasoning, you need to have the Socratic questions in front of you, just as Jay does.

In the example below, you will notice that Jay singles out a number of words and phrases in his essay (those are shown here in a darker shading), and he connects them with Socratic questions he writes in boxes at the margins.

Paragraph 1

We always hear stories about how easily children and adolescents can be influenced. That's why there are restrictions in place on many aspects of everyday life: movies, cigarettes, alcohol and so on. But what about something like video games? Could a harmless disc or cartridge impact a young person to the extent of acting out or worse?

Paragraph 2

The simple answer: no. Many factors are involved in the way the brain works to cause any individual to act a certain way. However, video games can help provoke someone who is already easily influenced.

Precision: Specifically, what are some of the factors involved?
Clarity: I can give some examples of each.

Depth: What are some of the complexities in deciding "what is and isn't appropriate"?
Clarity: SEE-I some of these complexities.

Logic: I just said that the video game does not "impact" a young person to act out. Here I am saying it can "provoke" someone. How do those make sense together?
Clarity: SEE-I what I mean by this.

Next-to-last Paragraph

Ultimately, it is up to the consumer to deem what is and isn't appropriate for themselves. Technology is always advancing and so the graphics will keep getting better. Games are just one of the many variables that determine how a person acts.

Accuracy: How can this statement be backed up? I know that technology keeps advancing and that graphics will keep getting better, but I can strengthen my paper by finding a reputable source that says it: → **R**.

Overall: Expanding the scope of the paper as a whole.
Breadth: How does this fit in with the larger picture? How do video games compare to other forms of entertainment as something that might lead to violence?

Precision: What are some important specific "variables that determine how a person acts"?
Clarity: Give an SEE-I for "variables" like poverty and unemployment. → **Importance**: In comparison, how important are video games as a cause of violence?

Using the Socratic questions to expand the paper. Jay begins by picking out some parts of his essay. He has shaded five of them. In the boxes at the margins he asks himself Socratic questions about those parts—but at this point, they are just *possible* questions he might decide to answer. Some of these he will just pass over: he will pick out the ones he thinks will be most helpful in expanding his paper in the limited time he has available. These are the ones he will actually write on. Here is how he thinks about it:

His first intervention is in the second paragraph when he shades the phrase "many factors" and asked the Socratic question about *precision*. He asks himself: What *are* some of the factors that can cause a person to act violently? Thinking about it now, he realizes he could easily describe some of these factors. He writes down a few that come to mind right away:

- *early experiences in a person's family (such as being the victim of abuse)*
- *being bullied at school*
- *living in an area where violence is an everyday occurrence*

For each of these, he knows he can give an SEE-I to clarify and explain how it could lead someone to be more violent.

He then skips to the last paragraph of the excerpt where he shaded the first half of a sentence: "Technology is always advancing." In the box, he asks about *accuracy*, but he is not questioning whether the statement *is* accurate. He already knows it's true. The Socratic question asks about how he can *back it up*. He decides he can describe his own experience of gaming to support this statement. But he has also read about this in gaming magazines and he can easily find a source to back this up. This is why he also put an **R** in the margin. He'll follow up on this research if he has enough time.

He looks over other parts he has shaded and decides that a good one to focus on is in the last sentence where he shaded "many variables." In his original sentence, he focused on the variables that "determine how a person acts." He now asks himself, "What are some of the 'variables' in our society that lead to increased violence?" Two answers come to mind immediately: poverty and unemployment. He listed those in the box in the margin, but he now thinks of others as well, such as easy access to guns and news coverage that highlights violence.

In that same box, he also brought up the standard of *importance*. He asked, "Compared to other 'variables' in our society, how important are video games as a cause of violence?" This question opens up a whole new line of thought for him. As soon as he asks it, he starts to write about it. This is what he writes:

> The influence of video games is <u>at</u> <u>most</u> a minor cause of vio-
> lence. In comparison to <u>major</u> "variables" like poverty and unem-
> ployment, it's not very important at all. People focus on violence in
> video games even though there is violence everywhere. Violence
> is on the news constantly. It's right here on my own campus.
> It's in date rape and domestic abuse. It's in the wars we fight
> where soldiers become accustomed to living with violence. It's in

> *the number of kids in juvenile detention centers and the violence that occurs daily there. When a kid in juvenile detention has gone through a year of living in violence, he doesn't need video games to make him prone to violence when he gets out.*
>
> *In addition, there are whole neighborhoods where violence is a part of everyday life. When you consider the number of factors that make violence so widespread, video games are the most minor thing in the world to worry about. It's like a distraction that keeps us from facing the real problems of violence in our society. An illustration: Worrying about video games as a cause of violence is like running out of a burning house but worrying you might stub your toe.*

Jay decides that with those new paragraphs, and with one or two more about the other Socratic question interventions he's decided to make, his paper will become more substantial, more detailed, and longer—almost twice as long as the essay he started with, and all of it will be relevant, without padding.

A commentary on Jay's process. If you follow Jay's thought process, you'll see how his ideas are prompted by the Socratic questions. As he responds to them, he comes up with a much larger and more significant point than many of the ones he started with. In his new formulation, it's not just that there are some vague "other factors" that influence people toward violence. It's that, compared to the major causes of violence that he lists, video games are at most minor.

It's not a matter of whether you agree with Jay. It's that his paper is far stronger as a result of asking the Socratic questions, taking them seriously, and then getting the idea for the answer. This is the power of the Socratic questions.

"Expand on this."

A comment instructors often write in the margin of a paper is "Expand on this," or "Explain this more fully," or "Elaborate," and a challenge that often presents itself is *how* to expand on it. This may have come up for you already in the elaboration-part of SEE-I's you've worked on. As mentioned earlier, you

> Notice that in the darker shaded areas, Jay applies Socratic questions in creative ways. He lets himself be open to focusing on whatever in his essay gives him ideas about what he might expand on. He focuses on words or phrases, but also on longer parts of sentences. In the box at the bottom, he even asks a Socratic question that applies to the article as a whole. He didn't decide to follow up on that one, but you can probably see how he easily could have.

may have tried to elaborate "in a paragraph or two" as this book suggests, but your elaboration may instead have turned out to be only a sentence or two.

One major benefit of Socratic questioning is that it gives you a virtually unlimited number of ways to expand on a point and explain it more fully.

Suppose you have written a paragraph. How do you "expand" it? You ask, and then answer, a Socratic question from the standards:

- Why would someone believe this is true? (*accuracy*)
- What are some of the details? (*precision*)
- What is a different kind of example? (*clarity*)

These Socratic questions won't expand the paper for you, of course— you will still have to write the actual paragraphs. But they will lay out for you *what* to write about. Writing an answer to one or more of these, or to any of the other Socratic questions, almost automatically makes the point "expand." Answering questions such as these *is* "explaining more fully."

With Socratic questions, you may never again have a problem with how to expand your paper. In fact, the problem for you may shift from "How do I expand my paper" to "How do I limit my paper?"

Socratic questioning in this book is mainly built on the *standards* of critical thinking. But Socratic questioning can be based on the *elements of reasoning* as well. Moreover, since the standards and elements perform different roles in critical writing, making a Socratic questioning intervention using the elements will sometimes yield different paths for enhancing your paper.

Imagine that you have your finished paper, but you decide you still need to expand it or make it better. You have already used the circle of elements to generate your thesis and main points, but this doesn't prevent you from using individual elements now as Socratic questions to enhance your paper.

For example, a main point in your paper is X. You've given a substantial SEE-I for it. Maybe you've already made some Socratic questioning interventions highlighted in this chapter—interventions based on the critical thinking standards. But now you ask yourself Socratic questions based on the *elements*: "OK. What are some additional *implications* of X?" or "What are some further *questions at issue* that might arise about X?" or "What is an *assumption* that X rests on?"

If you decide to use them, answering questions like these can readily expand your paper and make it substantially better.

The flexibility of Socratic questioning gives you choices. Any time you want to improve your paper, make it richer, expand it, or go into it more deeply, you have the Socratic questions at your disposal. And since Socratic questioning is non-linear, there is no automatic order to them, and they become maximally flexible. The questions are tools, not a set of steps, and they allow both your criticality and your creativity to work to greatest advantage.

Stop for a moment and let yourself appreciate the wide range of choices Socratic questioning gives you about how to improve your writing. They provide a wealth of questions you can ask. You can freely pick and choose among them, asking and answering only the ones you decide to. You can let your eye travel over them until you find one—almost any one—that strikes a chord with you and allows you to make your paper better. Or you may in fact choose not to ask, or answer, any of them. That too is your choice. It will be influenced by how much you want to make your paper better, but it is still your choice.

Writing Longer Papers

Socratic questioning and the standards of critical thinking play a major role in writing longer papers. Often, in upper-level courses you may be required to write papers of 15 to 20 pages or longer. Honors programs in many departments involve writing an honors thesis.

Though all the standards are essential, two of them can play a much more central role in longer papers: depth and breadth. The extended page requirement tells you that you will be expected to address the topic in much greater depth: its complexities and complicating issues, its meaningfulness. You will probably have to explain these complexities not just briefly or in passing but in considerable detail. Something similar applies to breadth: showing the larger picture, addressing other perspectives on the topic and, again, going into these in far greater detail. Indeed, there may also be greater depth and breadth in the way you describe and give voice to how other minds might see the issues differently. And the exercise of the intellectual traits will also be deeper and more expansive. As an example, consider the degree of intellectual perseverance you will need just to plan out your time and research even before you begin writing.

With a longer paper, all the essential concepts and processes of critical writing come in, but usually in a deeper and more comprehensive way. (Indeed, the same concepts and processes would come if you were writing not just a longer paper but a book.) In your logical analysis of the topic using the elements of reasoning, you will probably need to identify more assumptions, implications and consequences; include more information; spell out more interpretations and conclusions; and explore more questions at issue. You will also choose more of your responses as main points or further supporting points in the structure of our paper.

You will still be developing all these points with SEE-I, including staircasing. Your elaboration in a longer paper will usually be fuller, occupying perhaps pages rather than just paragraphs. You may give and explain more examples to capture different aspects of the main points (as Michelle did in her paper on stereotyping, p. 81–82). Because having too many illustrations can be distracting, longer papers are likely to have fewer of them overall, but the illustrations you do include will be structural ones that tie the points of the paper together (see p. 83). For staircasing, you can search for focal points within the elaboration you are giving (and sometimes in the examples as well)—these will be key terms or ideas that illuminate the topic in further ways.

You will end up responding to the Socratic questions as a further way of developing your paper, giving more details, explaining what is important about each point, striving for a more sufficient or complete coverage of the topic than you would do in a shorter paper.

Chapter 5: Practice and Assessment Exercises

1. What would the author of this book say are the main outcomes for Chapter 5?

2. **Putting it together.** A challenge in critical writing is not being so taken up with this or that part that you lose sight of the whole. A good way to reflect on Chapter 5, then, and to see where you are in the process is for you to assemble the whole as you see it so far, and then to reflect on how critical thinking standards and Socratic questioning fit into that whole. Here is one way to do it:

   There were three main themes in Chapter 3:

   a. how to build a logical plan for a paper—the thesis, main points, and any additional supporting points—out of an analysis around the circle;
   b. how SEE-I (and enhanced SEE-I) gives a way to turn the plan into the actual paragraphs of the paper;
   c. how research enters into writing a paper using critical thinking.

Chapter 4 then introduced:

d. addressing "the other side" and critical thinking traits of mind.

Now address each of these from the point of view of Chapter 5:

- How do the critical thinking standards fit with A, B, C, and D?
- How does Socratic questioning fit with A, B, C, and D?

3. **Tell your story.** A section in this chapter (p. 155–156) talks about the way critical thinking standards help you avoid pitfalls, errors and flaws. Describe an experience you had where errors or flaws in your thinking led to serious repercussions for you. Give an SEE-I for it.

4. **Tell your story.** What is a time in your life when your reasoning helped you? What is a time in your life when your reasoning led you astray? Which critical thinking standards were involved in each?

*5. **Write about your own experience.** Look at the page listing Socratic questions (p. 165). Have it in front of you. Does it look like too much to do?

Many people have that experience.

You know from what the book says that asking any of these questions is a choice, not an obligation. It means you don't just have a Plan B; you have Plan, C, D, E... ready at hand. Having ten different friends you can go to in an emergency is not a burden. It's empowering. But even that may still give you the feeling that it is too much to do.

Studies show that having too any choices may feel like a burden and may actually inhibit action.[6]

So the question is: What can you do to help you see them as choices, rather than as a burden?

*6. **Analysis versus evaluation.**
   a. In your own words, explain the difference between analysis and evaluation (box, p. 151). Give an SEE-I for it.
   b. Then, for each of the following sentences, decide whether it counts as analysis or as evaluation:

   - Donald Trump ran against Hillary Clinton for president of the U.S.
   - Donald Trump ran against George Bush for president of the U.S.
   - The U.S. invasion of Iraq was a failure.
   - President Bush advocated that we go to war in Iraq.

7. **Analysis versus evaluation.** For the following, decide whether each sentence is analysis or evaluation. For any that are ambiguous or doubtful, explain how it could form a part of either one:

- A main job of police is to hunt "bad guys."
- Public school teachers are not paid enough for the work they do.
- *Great Expectations* is the most tightly constructed novel by Charles Dickens.

Questions 8–21 have to do with making Socratic interventions or applying critical thinking standards.

*8. Chapter 3 describes a way Michelle could give an SEE-I for her main point that "Stereotyping does harm to people":

> She might describe the frustration, sometimes even the rage, that comes from being stereotyped. She might describe how when someone treats you badly, you might never even know if it was because they were stereotyping you, but you'll suspect it just the same. So when you're a victim of stereotyping, the harm continues into the future. She might bring in emotional, economic, and even physical harm. (She thought of these in her analysis around the circle under concepts.) These different kinds of harm will give her a range of examples as well. Her illustration would focus on things that can harm you in a way analogous to the way stereotypes harm you. (She says it is like getting a virus on your computer.)

Suppose that Michelle writes out this part of her paper. Apply two different Socratic questions that Michelle might apply to this excerpt. Then write out answers that Michelle might give.

*9. Look at the following question. Would it work as an additional Socratic question for Michelle's paper?

Is stereotyping *always* unfair?

*10. During her research on stereotyping, Michelle learns that the word "stereotyping" was invented back in 1794 by a French printer named Firmin Didot, who used it to refer to a kind of cookie-cutter mold used in hand-set printing, and that it was first used in its modern sense in 1922 by Walter Lippmann, a journalist and political writer.[7]

She thinks this would make a nice part of her paper on stereotyping, and it's information she got from a reliable source.

What do you think?

*11. In Chapter 1 James constructed an outline for a paper on sin taxes (p. 8–11). Ask two Socratic questions that he could use to enhance his paper. Choose one of them and then write a paragraph answering the question in a way that James would.

12. Chapter 1 also contained the outline of a paper by Sheila arguing that American universities should be as inexpensive as European ones. Do the same as in the previous question. This time try to ask (and then answer) some Socratic question that you haven't asked before.

*13. In Chapter 2, Kara analyzed Juliet in Shakespeare's play, and she concluded that maybe Romeo and Juliet were not "star-crossed" as lovers. She thought that their tragedy was the result of unrealistic wishful thinking.

Ask two different Socratic questions about the point Kara is making. Answer them as Kara would.

14. **Socratic questioning interventions.** Below are two short excerpts from unpublished student essays. The first is from an art education course and the second is from a course in history.[8]

Approach these excerpts the way Jay approached Michael Puglia's editorial on video games. That is, ask Socratic questions about the excerpt and draw a circle around the part of the excerpt that the Socratic question applies to. You may not know enough about art or history to answer the question in an authoritative way, but you should still be able to envision how answering the Socratic question would enhance and fill out the points being made in the excerpts.

> **Art education**. There are many different kinds of meaning an artist may convey: emotional, historical, expressive, conceptual, cultural, technical, and many others (including, of course, combinations). A Dogon mask can be conveying fierceness or power; a Renaissance painter the sacredness of a religious moment; an abstract 20th-century painting may be saying, "Look, as if for the first time, at the texture of the paint itself"; a Dutch still-life vanitas painting may be warning the viewer to reflect on the shortness of life.
>
> It is at this point that you are going to start to find firmer, more justified answers to the question at issue: What is the artist trying to convey? Your answers are still open to revision, but now they are backed up by the information you derived from close observation, from knowledge of context, and from careful study of the work.
>
> **History**. The negative consequences of nationalism are severe, however. Once a people have reached a level of power such that they have attained self-rule and a measure of national

security (enough power to protect themselves), the ruling culture often turns the very nationalistic empowerment that formerly protected their identity as a people into an elitist license to oppress their own minorities.

15. Put yourself in Jay's mind as he expands and enhances the article on video games (p. 172). Answer some of the questions that he raised there.

    Ask at least one more Socratic question having to do with the article, then write a paragraph answering it.

16. Jay decided not to address the Socratic question he asked himself in the box at the bottom, about *breadth*:

    How does this fit in with the larger picture?

    He relates that general question directly to his article by asking:

    How do video games compare to other forms of entertainment as something that might lead to violence?

    Be Jay. What would he write in response to the second question?

17. Go through two of the other extended examples from earlier in this book. Choose a thesis statement, a main point, an SEE-I, or the way the writer in the example describes "the other side" of the issue, and then ask a Socratic question about it. Finally, write out a response that the writer might give.

*18. Socratic questions are maximally flexible and adaptable. If you choose to, you can apply them to whatever aspects of your paper you think would benefit from expansion and enhancement.

    Consider precision, for example. Two Socratic questions about precision are listed on p. 165:

    • What are some of the details of this?
    • What are some of the specifics of this?

    Apply those two questions to the following single sentence:

    Michelangelo painted the ceiling of the Sistine Chapel.

19. Bare facts often feel like an endpoint rather than a starting point. They sometimes seem to shut down inquiry. But applying Socratic questions even to bare facts can open them up and give you something to research and write about.

    Here is a list of a few facts (from different domains). Since each of these facts is only a single sentence, not all the Socratic questions fit with every one of them. But try applying some of the Socratic questions to the facts listed below (or, alternatively, to bare facts that come up in a course you are taking):

- Genes are the basic unit of heredity.
- Cognitive behavioral therapy (CBT) works by addressing how a person's beliefs, attitudes, and ways of reasoning have a major influence on the person's emotions and actions.
- According to the QS University Rankings, the University of Oxford is the highest ranking public university in the world (2020).
- Elizabeth Bennet is the main character in *Pride and Prejudice*.
- Undocumented immigrants pay $12 billion into Social Security each year.[9]

*20. Think about the standard of importance. Suppose you are making a point in your paper. You have already elaborated on it in a paragraph or two; you've given an example, and maybe an illustration as well. You feel finished, but you sense that maybe you're not. How can you, after all that, still enrich that point more fully? Importance, coupled with one of the elements of reasoning, is ideal for this.

One major thing you can do is to apply one of the elements to the point you are making, and then follow it up with a Socratic question about *importance*. It might look like this:

- A main question at issue (implication, assumption, point of view, ...) related to this point is _____.
- What makes that question (implication, assumption, point of view, ...) important is _____.

Addressing the standard of importance not only helps you expand points in your paper, it also serves to bring home *to the reader* what is important about that point.

Choose some issue you are interested in (one you have not written about before). Make a point about that issue by writing a single sentence about it. Then (as in the question) make a statement involving one of the elements, and then follow it up asking a Socratic question about importance. Write out your answer. (Or, better, write out your answer in an SEE-I.)

21. Write out an SEE-I for a point you might make in a paper. Then ask one of the Socratic questions. Write out how you might answer it in a paragraph.

Try to begin with a full account of the point. Then you'll be able to see that no matter how complete your account is, Socratic questions can still enrich it.

22. **Write about writing. Write about your own experience.** In the view of the author of this book, revising a paper is extremely important. Putting yourself in his point of view temporarily, why does he think it's so important?

    Now how about you? What in your view are the benefits of revising your paper? What are the costs or negative consequences of doing so?

    How much confidence do you have that you would know how to revise your paper to make it better? Suppose someone said to you, "OK. Now revise your paper." How would you go about it?

23. **Write about writing.** Explain what it means to say that we often use critical thinking standards *implicitly*. By contrast, what is the advantage of using them *explicitly*?

24. At the end of the exercises to Chapters 2, 3, and 4 you were asked to plan and write a paper using the concepts and processes of those chapters. Continue working on that paper now by enhancing it with Socratic questioning.

Making It Flow, Making It Complete: Content, Audience, Communication, and Criticality

Fundamental and Powerful Concepts

There are several aspects of writing that have not been addressed in this book, at least not in any depth. These include grammar, spelling, paragraphing and topic sentences, transitions, writing interesting prose, voice, word choice, avoiding awkwardness, addressing the wider rhetorical situation, citing sources, and others as well. Some of these are essential to writing any paper; some are crucially important in one kind of paper but not appropriate in another. Beyond these, when you write a paper for a class or write something important as part of your job or profession, unexpected issues often arise that can't be anticipated in any guide to writing.

The GPS on the next page once again lays out the bare bones of the framework for critical writing—the bold print marks where you are now: ready to work on making your paper "flow." But you will see that it is also about improving your paper. Really, the two are inseparable.

The lower box, as before, lists factors that run through everything. The bold print marks the ones that will be highlighted in this chapter.

The question then comes up: How can you address those issues in your writing? What can you use to guide you in addressing them?

What you need are some tools you can use to think your way through these further aspects, to think your way through them—maybe not perfectly, but well. Those tools are the "fundamental and powerful concepts" in writing.

Fundamental and powerful concepts in critical writing. There are four fundamental and powerful concepts that underlie critical writing:

- *content*: what you are trying to convey or communicate in the paper;
- *communication*: how you will communicate or convey that content;
- *audience*: the reader; the people you will be communicating the content to; and
- *criticality*: the elements of reasoning, critical thinking standards, and traits of mind you will be paying attention to in your writing.

The first three are the fundamental and powerful concepts underlying all writing (including writing that is done well, poorly, or somewhere in between).

> **GPS**
> - topic →
> - analysis →
> - plan →
> - writing →
> - "the other side" →
> - improvement →
> - **flow**

> **Pervasive** aspects
> - research
> - critical thinking standards
>
> - **revision**
> - **fundamental & powerful concepts**
> - **giving credit**

Whenever you write anything, there is always a *content* you are trying to *communicate* to an *audience*. The fourth fundamental and powerful concept, *criticality*, is what makes an ordinary piece of writing into one that is well reasoned. With *criticality*, you use critical thinking concepts and processes—elements, standards, traits of mind, Socratic questioning, and others—to shape all aspects of the writing process.

The idea, then, is that for any issue that arises when you write a paper, any issue you have questions about or concerns about, you should think that issue through using the concepts of *content*, *communication*, *audience*, and *criticality*. Deeply grasping these four fundamental and powerful concepts will allow you to think through issues in your writing long after the course is over.

Moreover, these four concepts should, as much as possible, be the concepts you use explicitly to guide your thinking as you write. Take the concept of *audience*. To call it a fundamental and powerful concept means that *audience* is not just a concept you consider from time to time. And it's not just one important concept among dozens of others. Rather, as a fundamental and powerful concept, it is one of only four, and it is something you use to monitor your thinking and your writing all the way through. It means that whenever you write—a paper for class, a report in your employment after you graduate, a text message to a friend, an entry on Facebook, *anything*—you are asking yourself, "Who is going to read this, and in what context? Who is the audience? How can I best connect with this audience?"

"*Fundamental and powerful concept*" is a specialized term. It doesn't mean the same thing as "important" or even "essential." Rather, it means that those four—the "f&p concepts"— are *thinking tools*, tools that function as keys in thinking things through. As a contrast, consider other concepts that are not fundamental and powerful even when they are essential in writing. *Grammatical correctness* is an example. It is not a "fundamental and powerful" concept: no matter how thorough a knowledge of grammatical correctness you have, it will not enable you to think through how to write a

> An illustration: As an analogy, think about driving. There are many aspects of driving that are essential: braking, checking the rear view mirror, keeping up with traffic flow, and dozens of others. But consider the concepts of "control of the vehicle" and "safety." Those are f&p (fundamental and powerful) concepts. They are concepts that both you and a NASCAR driver use to guide you through *all* aspects of driving. They are not just essential "pieces" of driving: they underlie everything else.

memo to your supervisor, or to write or research a paper on topic X, or to convey your understanding in a response to a question on an essay exam. Though grammatical correctness is essential, it is one essential *aspect* of writing. It can't be used to shape everything. Content, communication, audience and criticality *can*.

The four f&p concepts have been present in this book all along, sometimes explicitly, but always at least implicitly. Thus, constructing your outline is a way of choosing the thesis and main points in the *content* of your paper. Doing so by analyzing "around the circle" brings in *criticality*. SEE-I and addressing other points of view enhances *content*, increases *communication* through clarity, and focuses directly on your *audience*, the potential readers of your paper, and, again, does so with *criticality*. Socratic questioning interventions allow you to expand and refine your *content*, to deepen it, and to *communicate* it more effectively to your *audience*. In fact, take any topic in this book, and you can reflect on how each is structured by the role it plays in creating your content, communicating it to an audience, and using critical thinking all the way through.

In many writing classes, teachers sometimes emphasize the "Six-Trait Writing Process":[1]

- content
- organization
- voice
- word choice
- sentence fluency
- conventions

All of those traits* are important, but only the first one—*content*—is actually a fundamental and powerful concept (though *organization* comes close). Voice, word choice, required level of fluency, conventions, and even organization will be very different in different kinds or genres of writing: a lab report, a personal narrative, a case study in social work, a piece of literary criticism, or a text message to your employer about a sick day you need.

So how do you tell the appropriate way to use organization, voice, word choice, sentence fluency and conventions in your paper? You do that by thinking the questions through in terms of the f&p concepts: you do it by thinking *critically* about how to *communicate* that specific kind of *content* to that specific kind of *audience*.

As an aside, the question comes up: How do teachers themselves decide whether a particular word choice, for example, is effective or not? An answer, of course, is that they have experience and training in writing. But the deeper, underlying answer is that they imaginatively put themselves in the mind of the *audience* and from there they think *critically* about what would *communicate* the *content* effectively to this particular *audience*. No matter who is assessing it, *all* effective writing—from a one-line text message to the *Encyclopedia Britannica*—is based on the same fundamental and powerful concepts.

---

*Note that the "traits" in the Six-Trait Writing Process are completely different from the traits in "critical thinking traits of mind."

The four fundamental and powerful concepts give you a set of lenses through which you can view and then think through other aspects of writing (see, for example, Figure 6.1). They work both for large-scale issues and for very specific issues. This chapter will sketch out—briefly—how to use the fundamental and powerful concepts to

Kinds of Writing

- essay exams
- autobiographical essays to apply for a job or to graduate school
- business memos
- expository, argumentative, narrative... essays
- poems
- tweets, Facebook posts...
- journalism
- legal briefs, lab reports
- fictional writing such as novels, stories and plays

...

Aspects of Writing

- question about style
- margins, font, spacing...
- voice
- paragraphing
- word choice
- formatting citations and references
- describing a character in a story you are writing
- verse forms to use

...

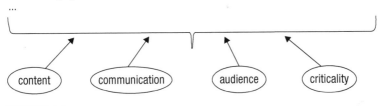

content   communication   audience   criticality

FIGURE 6.1

address three major aspects of writing a paper: grammar, transition sentences, and giving credit to the sources you use in your paper. These center on making the paper flow and on making it complete.

The treatment of these issues in this book is condensed. In any particular case you'll still need to think them through in terms of the fundamental and powerful concepts. This also applies to other aspects of writing that may not be mentioned here at all (*finding your voice* is an example). The suggestion, then, is to think those issues through by asking yourself, again and again, as you write:

> The f&p concepts don't *give you answers*—you may, for example, not know what your audience expects—but these concepts do give you the strongest way to approach getting answers.

- OK. What am I trying to say? What is my content?
- How can I best communicate it?
- Who is my audience? Who are my readers? What do they need or expect?

and the always present:

- How should I use the elements, standards and traits of mind to enhance the paper's criticality?

Rhetoric. As mentioned earlier, rhetoric has to do with *how* you say (or present) something. As you can readily see, it is intrinsically bound up with the fundamental and powerful concepts of both *communication* and *audience*. In a sense, it is even involved in *content* as well: *how* you say something can strongly influence the way your audience interprets the content of what is being said.

As the term is used in most writing classes, *rhetoric* usually refers to clear, fluid writing, writing that is appropriate to the kind of paper; the context in which you are writing; and the specific range of readers you are aiming for. Writing an expository paper for a sociology class will require different rhetoric—a different way of presenting the content—than writing for a literature course. Once school is over, you will be doing other kinds of writing as part of your professional life: important memos, reports, letters and e-mails, and any number of others. Different contexts and audiences may require different vocabulary, different use of evocative or vivid language, occasionally even somewhat different kinds of grammar.

Most of this chapter, on making the paper flow, is in fact focused on aspects of rhetoric.

Making It Flow: Grammatical Issues
How Grammar Works in Writing

Why grammar is important. Some aspects of writing a paper can seem merely technical. They can seem incidental to the critical and creative work of writing a powerful, insightful, well-reasoned paper, of saying something that is worth saying.

Though there is sometimes truth in this, many aspects that may seem minor are not really minor at all. What we call grammar has something to do with meeting widely accepted norms in writing, but it is far from being merely mechanical. Much of it is deeply rooted in critical thinking: specifically, critical thinking about constructing something that *communicates* an important *content* to an *audience*.[2]

Grammar is a good example of this. Though different writing professionals use somewhat different classifications of what is included in "grammar," in the widest sense it applies to a host of roughly related issues. These include punctuation, spelling, syntax, word choice, usage, paragraphing, avoiding awkwardness, and several others.

So how does "grammar" or "grammatical correctness" enter into critical writing?

Grammar and clarity. A good deal of what people call "grammatical correctness" is about *clarity*, one of the basic standards of critical thinking and critical writing. Consider:

Leaving the punctuation out of a sentence even one that is as uncomplicated as this one can make you the reader have to go back and read it again maybe more than once just to make sense of it.

A guess is that you had to go back and re-read the sentence to figure out what it is saying. It's a flaw, often a serious one, to make your reader have to work merely to decipher your sentences.* Making the writing flow is not just something incidental or unimportant: it's something fundamental in communicating with your audience.

Talking about "grammar" or "grammatical correctness" often sounds stodgy or rule-bound. But that's mostly because we don't usually use those *words* when we think or read or talk. They are just not part of our general vocabulary. What people *do* say is something like "I don't get it" or "What do you mean?" Sometimes they just give you one of those confused and annoyed looks that mean "I don't get it and it's your fault." Notice: it's about *clarity*. And a good deal of the lack of clarity in what you write may have its root in grammatical correctness.

Grammar and audience. Your audience expects a level of grammatical correctness. Without it, many people will not take what you say seriously. Maybe they should. It's certainly possible for a paper to contain great insights, be logical, and say things that need saying, and still contain grammatical errors, maybe even serious ones. So maybe people should not judge a paper harshly just because it contains grammatical or spelling errors. But the fact is that many people *do*. This includes not just many instructors but employers, admission officers, and other people as well. Whether they should or not, they *do*. Part of

If you're just texting a friend, it sounds odd to say that "your audience" expects a level of grammatical correctness. But it's true. Different kinds of readers have different levels of expectation. Even when you're just texting a friend, what you write has to be clear enough for your friend to get what you're trying to say. (Try leaving out the spaces between words or writing "me for meet coffee.") In school, as in a profession, your readers are likely to expect a much greater level of the clarity that comes from grammatical correctness.

writing is taking the world seriously as it actually is. It involves being realistic about your audience.

---

*There are exceptions to this. For instance, papers in a technical field can seem indecipherable to outsiders; some literary works (*Finnegan's Wake*, for example) are so packed that single sentences may require multiple re-readings.

Many people are passionate about writing, and often they have strong views about ways of writing that are acceptable or unacceptable in a given context. An obvious example is writing "ain't" or "lol" on a job application—there is a good chance that just that single word choice will disqualify you. Papers for a class are usually written in a style that is at least moderately formal, but sometimes you may not be able to tell in advance what a particular reader may find objectionable, and you may not be able to satisfy all your readers.* Still, as much as possible, taking account of your readers' stylistic preferences is part of respecting your audience.[3]

Writing for your audience also includes taking account of specialized ways of writing. Part of "grammar" is avoiding awkwardness in the writing. There are conventions about how to write in different fields and in different professions. In social science research papers, for example, the writer virtually never says "I." The convention is to avoid all references to the writer; if this is not possible in the context, then you have to use a phrase such as "this writer." In a paper in philosophy, however, there is no prohibition against using "I," and saying "this writer" would sound stilted and irritating.

Impediments to Writing Grammatically

Sometimes, dealing with grammatical issues can be straightforward. There are many strong, reputable, user-friendly websites and handbooks that help you check for grammar. It helps to find a good one and use it regularly.† Your computer already does some of the work, highlighting many misspelled words and at least some grammatical errors. It's not perfect, of course, but it's helpful. In addition, the more you use such guides and consciously focus on the relevant grammatical rules, the more you tend to internalize the grammatical practices you need.

> Writing grammatically is not the goal. It's the means to achieving the goal. But this doesn't diminish its importance. If there is a blockage to your heart, having a stent put in is not the *goal*. The goal is health and a longer life. But this doesn't make the stent any less important. In many contexts, grammaticality is an essential means to achieving the goal of conveying what you are trying to say to the reader.

---

*This book is written in a relatively informal style. One example (among several) is that it sometimes uses contractions: "don't" and "it's," for instance, rather than "do not" and "it is." An informal style is not appropriate for certain forms of writing.

†As of this writing, a helpful, easily accessible website is *The Purdue OWL*, Purdue University Writing Lab, 2017, http://www.owl.english.purdue.edu.

But sometimes, even with the help available, dealing with grammatical issues can be a challenge. It can be daunting. For many writers, that just seems to be a fact of life. Still, there is no way around having to face the challenges. A main way of doing that is to confront some of the impediments that stand in the way of writing a paper that is grammatically clear.

There are many such impediments. Among them are time pressure and the fact that many people don't re-read their papers before submitting them. Sometimes it's simply the result of not looking up essential grammatical rules (or, even more puzzling, not paying attention to the words their computer has highlighted as problematic or grammatically incorrect). But there are deeper, more pervasive impediments that stand in the way for many people, and, making it even harder, some of the main ones operate below the level of our conscious awareness. Here are some:

The feeling of "being finished." A main impediment to dealing with grammatical issues is the feeling of being *finished*. In the critical writing process, "revising" is something you do mostly *as you write*, not something you put off until the paper or the draft is "done." The reason this is important is that when you are "done," you are not at a normal point in the writing. All along, you have been immersed in putting the paper together, sentence by sentence; you've struggled with saying what you want to say; you've reached the last few words of an extended task; and now, suddenly, you feel the relief of being finished. With that feeling of relief, it may not even enter your mind to look back at the paper. And even if it does enter your mind, re-reading the paper to check for clarity, including grammatical clarity, can seem just too much: you're *finished*!

Even if you've been revising—making your paper better—all along, you will still probably have to do some further revision at the end. So you have to do something to hold off that feeling of relief until you've gone through the last steps: re-reading to see whether it "flows," whether it's grammatically correct, whether it's complete. There are strategies for doing this that work for at least some people. One is to consciously include re-reading and checking as intrinsic parts of writing the paper. Writers who do this in effect re-define "finished" so that the relief comes only after these steps have been taken. Another strategy is to stop before you write the last paragraph or two. It's at that point—before you feel finished—that you re-read and revise. Only then do you go on to write the end of the paper.

But, of course, these strategies work only for some people. You may have to invent your own strategy to postpone the feeling of being finished.

The best writers tend to edit and re-edit many times before submitting a paper, and accomplished, published writers almost certainly do this.

Noticing what you don't notice. If you have a question about a grammatical issue you face, it's pretty obvious that you should look it up. You already know that, and you probably also know that sites to help with that are readily available. (After all, just Googling it will often give you a clear answer.) Even if you don't always take the time to look things up, you know it would be better if you did. But one built-in problem in dealing with grammatical issues is that it's sometimes hard to recognize that something even needs to be looked up. You may be perfectly willing to look up grammatical rules when something is problematic in your paper, but sometimes you may just not notice that there is anything problematic to look up. An example for many people is distinguishing "its" from "it's" or "there" from "their" from "they're." (Computer programs sometimes flag these even when they are used correctly.) Each of them has relatively simple rules that you can look up, but until you've internalized the rules, they may continue to slip past you.

If you're not noticing a grammatical issue, the problem becomes far more difficult to deal with. You don't know what you don't know. It's like ingrained "bad habits" about anything, such as not checking your blind spot when you drive or not writing down new passwords when you create them. A good question to think about critically, then, is "How can I get help in noticing what I don't notice?" Only after you notice a problem can you fix it.

> What are some impediments that face *you* in relation to writing in ways that are more grammatically correct?

Practical Guidelines

There is a lot you can do to write in ways that are grammatically correct. The guidelines below are ones you can exercise in an ongoing way as you write or revise. As in almost all critical thinking, they depend on exercising self-awareness and focus:

- Remind yourself to keep in mind the level of grammatical correctness your specific audience expects.
- Remember that there is a striking difference between what seems grammatically clear to *you*, the writer, versus what will seem grammatically clear to the person on the other end, the reader.
- Be aware of your impediments.

- Recognize that what you are doing is difficult. There are real challenges in it. Give yourself credit for your intellectual perseverance and intellectual courage in seeing it through.
- Use a good guide to grammar.
- Take a writing course and engage with it.

Transitions. Beyond questions of punctuation, spelling, syntax and the rest, grammatical issues can include other aspects of making your paper flow—of communicating content to your audience. There are issues of usage, avoiding awkwardness, and some aspects of style. One of the most important of these is *transitions*. Transitional words and phrases are an important part of making the paper "flow."

You use transition words and sentences all the time when you are speaking. Someone says X and you say, "Uh-huh, and ..." or "Yeah, but I..." or "I get it. My own view is ..." Or someone might say, "He said XYZ to me. Like I care!" The "like" is a transition word there, carrying the listener from the "XYZ" to the speaker's reaction to it.

Although these are natural transitions in speaking, you usually can't use "Uh-huh, and..." or the others in writing a paper.* You can, though, give smooth transitions from one idea to another, ideas that make the transition effortless for the reader. Once again, the f&p concept of *audience* is what helps you do this effectively. You have to exercise intellectual empathy and anticipate where readers need a transition to take them from one idea to the next.

For anyone who realizes how important writing is for future success, it can be distressing to see how people sometimes don't engage with their writing courses.

A writing course is a unique activity. It may be that you will never again have the opportunity to get personal feedback, from a professional, on what you write. It works really well only if you engage with it, but if you do, it can bring rewards and improvements you cannot get on your own. It can help you not only with grammar but with several of the unconscious or unnoticed habits of writing that can lead people, later in life, to make negative judgments about your qualifications. Taking a writing course is like having a personal tennis coach, one whose goal is to help you get better at every aspect of the sport. But, unlike tennis, most everyone needs good writing skills to do well in the complex world in which we live.

---

*You *can* use them when writing fiction, or when quoting what someone actually said or wrote.

Though there are many phrases you can use to bridge from one idea to another, one of the richest sources of transitions comes from using the Socratic questions from Chapter 5. Explicitly mentioning the words and phrases from the Socratic questions will often tie thoughts, paragraphs, and sections together in just the right way.

Without transition words and phrases, your paper may just look like a choppy list of points:

- A.
- B.
- C.
- D.

To the audience, it can seem as if you are just giving four unconnected, disjointed points.

But using phrases that come directly from Socratic questioning will often bridge seamlessly from one section or paragraph to the next. The result is likely to be a paper that *shows* readers how the points fit together, and how the paper as a whole is coherent:

- A.
- What makes A difficult is B.
- What is most important about both A and B is C.
- A further complication of C is D.

Even in this schematic version, you can probably see the connections and feel yourself being carried from one point to the next.

Again, transition words and phrases will make your writing flow more smoothly. But there is a deeper reason for them. It's not enough just to *have* a logical structure in your paper. You also have to *communicate* that logical structure to your reader. Transitions are part of communicating clearly. Suppose you say X, and then you say Y. In your mind, X and Y are linked: maybe you think that X happened *because* of Y. Since that *because* is in your mind, you almost naturally take it for granted that it will be in your reader's mind as well. But no matter how "natural" the connection seems to you, it is an assumption you have to consciously counteract. Connections that are present in your mind are not automatically there in the reader's mind. It is another example of the tendency to expect other people to engage in "mind-reading" (see p. 157). You need to *show* people the connections you are making.

You may never have noticed the transition words and phrases in what you've read. That's at least partly because they were effective. The writing flowed so smoothly that nothing called your attention to the words that made it flow.

Paragraphing and topic sentences or ideas. People often have difficulty breaking their paper down into paragraphs. It is a serious impediment to clarity to confront paragraphs that just go on and on, maybe for a full page, drifting from one idea to another without a break. The reader needs to see distinct ideas blocked off into distinct paragraphs. What gives clarity is having paragraphs that focus on a single main idea. For writers, it is often helpful to formulate that single idea in one specific sentence, called the "topic sentence" for that paragraph. But even when it is not captured in a single sentence, the main idea of that paragraph—the single main idea—should be clear. As with using transitions, paragraphing is another aspect of making a paper flow.

The framework for critical writing lays out the logic of your paper, and this logic makes the work of paragraphing flow much more straightforwardly and naturally. That same logic often yields relevant, sharp topic sentences or ideas for paragraphs. Analysis around the circle, the elements of reasoning, and SEE-I all help dramatically with making coherent, smoothly written paragraphs, each of them usually centered on a clear topic sentence. If your analysis around the circle has four main points to it, explaining them will automatically generate at least four separate paragraphs. Using the elements of reasoning, when you explain different *implications* of an issue, or different *assumptions* the issue rests on, each will probably become at least one separate paragraph, maybe more. And you can *create* the transition by writing "An implication of this is…" and "An assumption behind this is…" Each implication, assumption, or response to another of the elements will be the centerpiece of that paragraph—its topic sentence.

Similarly, when you give an SEE-I, the elaboration will likely be two or more paragraphs. With examples and illustrations, if you *explain* them (rather than just mentioning them), each of them may merit its own paragraph. If you then *staircase* the SEE-I, you will likely generate separate paragraphs, each with a relatively straightforward topic sentence or idea. Socratic questioning interventions help with paragraphing also. If you spell out "why someone would believe this is true," or "how this is related to that," or "what factors make this difficult," you will be alerted to begin a new paragraph, one with its own topic sentence.[*]

---

[*]Distinguishing one idea from another often is not exact. For example, in the three paragraphs in this section, the first paragraph sets up the problem (the need for paragraphing and topic sentences or ideas); the second paragraph describes one way of addressing this problem (the elements of reasoning); and the third paragraph focuses on two other ways of addressing this problem (SEE-I and Socratic questioning). You can probably see that the last two paragraphs could have been combined (topic idea: three ways of addressing the problem). But it would have resulted in an overly long paragraph.

Checking on how your paper "flows." When you are making your last revisions, after the draft of your paper is finished, you need to do at least a rough check for any last corrections and to see how the paper flows. A minimal check is to read through the finished paper, making grammatical corrections, paying attention to where the reader will need transitions, and sharpening sentences.

A far better check, though, is to have someone else read it out loud. If they stumble as they read, or have to go back to the beginning of the sentence to find their way, that's an indicator that you may need to do some re-writing. (It won't work so well if you yourself read the paper out loud: since the words are your own, the paper may just seem to flow smoothly to you. But that's *you*. The "flow" you are interested in is not the one in the privacy of your own mind, but rather the flow that communicates itself to your reader.)

It's worth reflecting on something that seems almost paradoxical about the idea of a paper that "flows." When you *read* it, it seems effortless. It's the way a great figure skater moves perfectly across the ice, or a great basketball player casually makes a spectacular lay up. In writing, it shows up in a succinct and well-honed business memo that exactly pinpoints a problem and its solution; in a letter of recommendation that makes you feel as though you actually know the person being recommended; in a fluent, illuminating piece of journalism; in an expressive and well-organized application for graduate school; in a paper for a class that is not only insightful but also a pleasure to read.

The seeming effortlessness of it conceals from us the amount of work it often takes to achieve this appearance of effortlessness. The skater and the basketball player put in literally thousands of hours to get to the point where their performance seems so easy and casual. I have a friend who wrote a technical book of philosophy, and a colleague said to him that it read as if he just sat down and wrote it off the top of his head. My friend said that it had taken him a full year of work to make it sound as if he had written it off the top of his head.

Making It Complete

Giving Credit

An essential part of writing a paper is giving credit to those whose words, ideas or information you use. Notice that the focus is not just on using someone's *words*. It's on ideas and information as well. If you incorporate someone's actual words into your paper, you have to use quotation marks and give credit to the person who wrote the words. (Usually, you use someone's exact words only if there is a point to doing so. Maybe their words are a focus of your paper (such as citing lines of poetry that you will be analyzing), or they have said something in a striking way. Usually, you don't quote someone's exact words merely to avoid stating the point in your own words.) But similarly, if you use someone's ideas, or if you use information that a source has supplied, you have to give credit—whether you are using the writer's actual words or not.

The practical matter of giving citations and references. The main ways of giving credit in a paper are (a) by giving a citation in the text itself, (b) by giving footnotes or endnotes (as in this book), and (c) by including a separate page at the end of the paper listing sources you have cited. (This page is usually titled "Works Cited," or "References," or "Bibliography.") There is no universal rule here that applies across different forms of writing, or in different disciplines or professions, or with different instructors. In some fields or contexts, you may have to give credit in all three ways, while in others you may have to give credit in only one or two of them. Similarly, in some fields you can use either footnotes or endnotes, while in others you must use only one of the two.

"Citations" and "references." The terms can be confusing, and they are used in somewhat different ways by different writing professionals.

Usually, when you *say* that you are using a certain source, you are giving a "citation." (You are *citing* a source.)

When you give a "reference," on the other hand, you give bibliographical information about the source (this usually includes its title, authors, and where and when it was published).

In your paper, citations will usually be given in the text of your paper itself, or they will be indicated with a footnote or endnote number. References are usually given in a separate section at the end of your paper.

There are accepted styles for typing and formatting your sources. The styles can differ dramatically from one field to another. The main "citation styles"—four of them—are MLA, APA, Chicago (including Turabian), and IEEE.[4] Each of them has highly precise rules about how to give citations and references. Once you find the citation style required for the kind of paper you are writing, you can follow the instructions and examples given in a number of reputable websites. ("Research and Citation" in the Purdue Online Writing Lab <owl. english.purdue.edu> is, once again, a helpful one.)[5]

For many people (including the author of this book), formatting references can be frustrating and time-consuming. Still, many instructors require careful adherence to prescribed ways of formatting. There are programs and websites that will format references for you (or at least claim that they will). But, in using such programs, you usually will have to supply a considerable amount of information about the source, and even then you have to use the programs with an awareness of how they can fail to do what you want them to do. (Luckily, you can expect formatting programs to get better. Maybe by the time you read this, engines may be available that will do the formatting in a way you can simply rely on.)[*]

As always, a major guide comes from the fundamental and powerful concepts, in this case *audience*. It enters in two different ways. First, the purpose for giving reference information is to enable readers to find the source you used quickly and accurately, so they can check it out for themselves. Second, the audience also may include your instructors: their goals may include having you learn to write in line with the conventions of a certain field or discipline.

Why pay so much attention to giving credit? If you describe this process to yourself as "having to list references," it sounds as if it's an arbitrary hoop you have to jump through. The point, though, is not to "cite sources" or "list your references." The point is to *give credit*. Giving credit is part of taking your writing seriously.

As a purely practical matter, one that will make your life easier, you should take down the information about sources as early as possible (usually by cutting-and-pasting), and in the required citation style. That is part of "Writing before You Write" (see p. 100). It's beneficial to take down the reference information about a source even if you're not sure you will actually use it. This practice saves you from scrambling frantically to re-find a source you located half an hour ago (or worse, last week). For the same reason, it is also a good idea to bookmark web sources so you can easily consult them later.

---

[*]Note that citations and references in *books* often follow different procedures from those followed in *papers*, and thus they don't generally serve as useful models for your own referencing information. That is in part because books often address more diverse goals and audiences than papers do. Rowman & Littlefield, the publisher of this book, requires that a specific style be used. However, in the extended examples in this book, students were sometimes required to format references in APA style (for example, in Lucia's psychology paper on false memory) or in MLA style (for example, in Sheila's references to universities in Chapter 1).

There are two main goals in giving citations and references in your paper:

- to credit the people whose ideas or words you are using, and
- to give guidance to your readers.

Any reader concerned with intellectual integrity and who values honesty in writing will expect you to give credit to those whose ideas or words you are using. But it's not just an expectation. Many instructors (and other readers) take thinking and writing seriously, and they may actually be *offended* if you take someone's words or ideas without giving credit.

But even more important than meeting the expectations of others is the issue of fairness itself. Fairness is one of the standards of critical thinking, and intellectual integrity is one of the essential traits of a critical thinker. Not giving credit to people when you take their ideas is being straightforwardly unfair. It is doing something wrong to them.

The second goal, giving guidance to your audience, is different. As mentioned above, people who read what you've written need to be able to find the sources you used. They may need to see if, in their view, a given source is reliable enough for them to trust it. They may also want to find out more of what the source is saying about the topic.

Plagiarism. A good practical definition of "plagiarism" is using someone else's words or ideas without giving proper credit (whether doing so was intentional or not). The critical thinking emphasis is on fairmindedness and intellectual integrity. It is not just a way to guard against cheating. Students sometimes think the issue of plagiarism is over-emphasized, and, of course, at times it may be. But the emphasis fits well with the spirit of critical thinking. Unlike the way the world sometimes operates, the emphasis in critical thinking is not just on winning. It is not aimed primarily at merely persuading people to your point of view or merely getting them to follow you. It is on thinking things though and presenting your best reasoning to people, while being open to the idea that at any time you may in fact be wrong about a position you are taking. If the intention is to persuade people, it's to persuade them *critically*: by giving clear, accurate, and relevant reasons why they *should* be persuaded. (Hitler was a phenomenally effective persuader, but as a thinker he was possessed by a host of ideas that were not only horrific but illogical and ridiculous as well.) The focus is on helping yourself and others understand both the positive and negative effects of a particular idea or course of action.

Thus, the emphasis on intellectual integrity is a crucial part of critical thinking.

Taking It Seriously

Engaging with what you write. A key theme in this book is not just writing but also *engaging* with what you write. You can describe engagement in different ways: taking it seriously, leaning in, making it your own. You can call it *writing with intention.* A sense of engagement gives deeper value to many aspects of people's lives, aspects that go well beyond writing a paper. The idea of engagement applies to personal relationships, leadership, playing a sport or a video game—indeed to almost anything. When you do these activities with engagement, with intention, they can give you benefits and a degree of fulfillment that can't be achieved without that engagement.

By contrast, doing something without engagement can be just going along, or going through the motions, or viewing activities as just jumping through hoops, or feeling yourself victimized by having to do the activity. In addition, fear often steps in: activities carry more personal psychological risk when you are serious about them. If you *commit* to doing something, you are putting more of yourself on the line. Regardless of the reason, though, when you don't let yourself engage, you can deprive yourself of what makes an activity meaningful. Either way, it's a choice you have to make for yourself.

Engagement has striking benefits when it comes to writing. Writing works in a way that speaking does not. Thoughts that are spoken often seem just to drift away, but writing with engagement gives the sense of something more permanent and solid, something you can return to later, develop, and learn from. Engaged, critical writing helps you think things through in a reflective, insightful way. Two benefits of writing with engagement can almost seem opposites. It can help you see things "from the outside," but it also helps you "go inward."

A finding in cognitive science is that when we read something, we tend strongly to take for granted that what we've read is true.[6] It's hard to believe that this is so, but it is, and if you look closely, you can see it in your own experience. The exception is when we already have strongly held information or beliefs on the other side (such as scientific, religious, or political beliefs). But for anything else where we are more or less neutral, we simply accept what we read, and we do so without being aware that we are accepting it. If people read, say, that supplement XYZ increases energy or "brain power," they tend to just take that information in. They often do so without even wondering whether the information is reliable. The question just doesn't come up.

> It is only "stepping back" from that information that makes people doubt what they read. If someone asks explicitly, "Do you think that's true?" they will *then* probably question it. At least they'll probably wonder about it. The same will happen if you ask the question of yourself. The explicit focus—the stepping back to ask the focused question—creates the distance you need to evaluate what you read.

Seeing things "from the outside" gives you a chance to step back from yourself and your thoughts. This reflective step, this stepping back, lets you examine your thoughts from different perspectives. It lets you be (temporarily) outside of yourself, looking in. This outside perspective gives more scope for your creativity, and it makes you better able to see biases or unfounded assumptions in your own thinking, ones that get in the way not only of writing a good paper but of enjoying your life as well. Writing critically helps you assess the validity of your ideas. By seeing your words written out, you are in a much better position to use critical thinking standards to evaluate them.

This is the "outside perspective." But writing also allows you to go inward. It helps you go inside yourself in a deeper and longer-range way. Often this means developing who you are, seeing your strengths and weaknesses in a new way, learning from previous experiences—experiences you can almost re-live, even much later, because you've written them down. (Even just having to put ideas into words often makes them clearer and more precise than they were in your mind.) One of the values of keeping a journal, for example, is that it allows you to go back to thoughts you had earlier. In a way, writing allows you to view "past selves," and this process, in turn, allows you to construct your present and future self.

Motivation. Motivation is sometimes a major challenge in writing a paper. How can you get yourself to do the work of writing a paper? How can you motivate yourself to use the processes and concepts of critical thinking in your writing?

Often it seems to people as if motivation is either there or it's not. Either they are motivated to do X or they're not. They can maybe make themselves *do* X, but they can't make themselves *want* to do X. Take running for exercise. I may simply not want to run. End of story. Though I can still make myself go for a run, it seems as if there's nothing I can do to make myself *want* to go for a run. It feels as though what motivates me is beyond my control.

But actually you have a lot more influence on your motivation than you might think. This is especially true from a longer-range perspective. Though there may be nothing much I can do to make myself want to run right now, there are things I can do right now that make it far more likely that, later, I'll end up not just running but wanting to run, actually enjoying it.

If the motivation isn't there right now, one thing that can help is to act "as if." This means acting *as if* you are taking it seriously. It's not just going through the motions: rather, it's "trying on" a level of commitment. It's similar to what happens in performances on stage. If you're acting in a play, or singing a song before an audience, or doing stand-up or improv, the advice professionals give is to *be* the character you are playing, to *immerse yourself* in the song you are singing, to *feel yourself* being funny. Or think about travel writing. Good travel writers don't just say "I went here. I went there." They get involved in telling you about the places: the sights and smells, the history, how different these experiences are from what is familiar. That is what gets the audience to be taken up in the travels.

So, again, how can you motivate yourself to do the work of writing a paper?

Engagement actually helps with this in a substantial way. To the extent that you are engaged with writing the paper—or to the extent that you can get yourself to adopt the attitude of being engaged with it—writing a critical paper can bring rewards, sometimes unexpected ones.

It can bring any number of practical rewards. It will help you get better grades: not just in the current class you are taking but, since it fosters a number of critical thinking skills, in other classes as well. It will help your next paper become substantially better, in part because you've been paying attention as you wrote this one. It makes your next paper not only better but also *easier to write*. Moreover, learning to write critically in school helps you become a good writer in your professional life after you graduate. The explicit focus on elements of reasoning such as *assumptions* and *implications*, or on standards such as *clarity* and *relevance*, will help you bring critical thinking and critical writing into your future work. Making Socratic questioning interventions will give you a wide range of strategies for improving everything you do later.

But in addition to practical rewards, engagement with critical writing often brings with it a host of more intangible and often unexpected internal rewards. As you write about a topic critically, as you take it seriously, you will be creating many ideas of your own, developing them, researching them, making judgments about what is most important in them, striving explicitly for accuracy, clarity and depth. Doing this can make the thinking and the writing your own in a lasting way. The creativity involved in it is almost automatically rewarding.

There can be a genuine sense of accomplishment that comes from doing intellectual work to your best ability. Beyond that, there is a feedback loop between improvement and the resulting sense of accomplishment. Not only can doing the work well give you a sense of accomplishment, but the sense of accomplishment actually helps you do the work better the next time.

You probably know this from your own experience. As you learn a sport, for example, you feel a sense of accomplishment as your skills improve. And this sense of accomplishment in turn helps you improve your skills even more next time.

Obstacles to motivation. A theme in this book is that engagement is rewarding. Being engaged with what we do in our lives is not only beneficial in practice but internally rewarding. So, if this is true, the question that arises is: Why is it often difficult to engage with writing about a topic? Why isn't engagement the natural and automatic response to writing a paper?

> One thing you can do to give yourself the feeling of accomplishment is to recognize how much of your own creativity is involved in writing a paper. It enters in any number of ways: in how you construct your paper, in the thesis and main points you come up with, in how you engage in research. It comes up in the content, in how you communicate, in the ways you take your audience into account, and in all aspects of the criticality you work through. There is a strong sense in which everything in your paper comes *from you.*

Maybe the main reason is that so many factors get in the way of taking things seriously. Obstacles to engagement apply not just to writing a paper but to a wide range of activities in our lives. It is sometimes shocking to realize how much of our lives we live on automatic pilot. A key way to help yourself become engaged with your writing, then, is to address the obstacles that confront you.

Some of these obstacles have deep roots in people, but there are others that seem straightforwardly practical. There are genuine practical obstacles to devoting yourself to writing a good paper, ones imposed by external circumstances.

Time pressure is an example. Your time is limited, and writing a strong critical paper takes time. And this means that, in a sense, you may not be able to afford to become too interested in the topic or in thinking it through. The limited time you have available is a genuine obstacle.

But even genuine practical difficulties like this are often not exactly what they seem. In studies, for example, students (and others) automatically commit what psychologists call "the planning fallacy." When students estimate the amount of time it will take to finish an important task (such as writing a major paper), they make the estimate based on the assumption that everything will go perfectly, that no problems will come up. Their estimate of time is "always too optimistic, no matter how unrealistic" it is.[7] It's wishful thinking.

When people write papers for a class, they often don't budget their time realistically. They often rely on everything going right. They often estimate that it will take less time than it will. (Often, in fact, people don't "estimate" at all: they just begin at some point in time and hope for the best.) And whatever portion of time they think it will take, they tend to begin it *just before* the deadline (rather than a week ahead of time, for example). Notice that any one of these approaches greatly increases the chances of failure or of not doing the project as well as they could (and not getting the rewards they would otherwise get).

What can you do? Some steps are straightforward.

- Make a careful, realistic estimate of how long it will take.
- Allow for things to go wrong (the printer breaking down, running out of ink, sources not being available, unanticipated problems) by allocating extra time.
- Be generous with yourself: give yourself the time you need, and then maybe a little more.
- Recognize that X amount of time is X amount of time: if it will take two days to write the paper, spending those two days now is the same amount of time as spending them in the two days right before the paper is due. So begin as soon as possible.
- Don't use the pressure that comes when you're too close to the deadline as your motivator. There is an addictive quality that comes with the rush of acting under pressure. Panic and pressure, though they may help in an emergency, are not friends to rely on.
- Break the time up into realistic segments rather than trying to do all the work in a single sitting.

Imagine that your instructor assigns you a five-page paper to write. Here are the instructions for it:

The paper must be a minimum of five pages. It must include research and citation of sources. It will be a major part of the grade for the course. It will take at least two days of intensive work to do well on it. It is due exactly two days from now.

Would you feel mistreated? *Two days!* Would you be angry at how dictatorial and unfair your teacher is being? Would you think that he or she was being not only unrealistic but also obviously unfair?

That would certainly be my own reaction. To me, the instructor is obviously being unrealistic, and the students are obviously being treated unfairly.

But what's revealing about the scenario is that it is, in fact, the way many people treat *themselves*. They shortchange themselves. They wait until the last minute; they assume nothing will go wrong. They put themselves through panic and rush. And, on top of all that, their grades suffer and they don't get the satisfaction that comes from engaging with writing the paper.

There are other practical obstacles in addition to time pressure. Often the difficulties that are most apparent are the practical ones. But there are internal obstacles as well: ways of thinking, habits of mind, factors we ourselves bring to the project. Though these obstacles often go unrecognized, they are, in the end, often much more serious as impediments than the external practical ones are. At the least, they typically make the practical obstacles more serious than they would be on their own.

One internal obstacle is many individuals' background conviction that what they have to say is just not important. This is mostly an unconscious conviction, lying in the back of their minds. Being beneath the surface and held unconsciously makes the problem that much more difficult to get past.

It is instructive to notice how willing we often are to mistreat ourselves, and how differently we would act toward someone we really care about. Think about the bulleted list on p. 206, and then picture someone you really care about, someone who has a paper due and comes to you for advice. Here is your advice to the person:

Don't even think about how long it will take you to write the paper. Just begin at the last possible minute, and hope everything

> works out. Rush through the whole thing. You'll feel panicky and pressured, you probably won't get the grade you could have gotten, and you won't get the satisfaction of doing it well. But trust me: that's the way to do it.
>
> You wouldn't give this advice to someone you genuinely care about, yet you yourself may do a version of it in writing your own papers. What does this say about how much you care about *you*?

The way to address this is not by over-inflating your own ego or by thinking that every thought you have is automatically accurate, important, and relevant. A better way to address it is to think of your paper as a chance to make an important contribution. This doesn't mean you must uncover something wholly new about an issue, but you can come at it from a new angle, or you can say it in an insightful way. If you have only one important thing to say, you can say that one thing with conviction, and you can support it with sufficient, compelling, and striking evidence.

A second internal obstacle to engagement is a lack of appreciation for what you have accomplished in writing your paper. Too often, people are massively dissatisfied with what they have accomplished. It's true in art projects, dissertations, books, scholarly articles, performances in sports, almost anything. And it's true not just for students but for teachers, CEOs, and professional writers as well.

This dissatisfaction is probably a natural response to the difference between what we hope for (often unrealistically) and what we in fact accomplish. But when it happens to you, it means you miss a chance to appreciate that though the work is not perfect, it's *something*. It's an accomplishment. It's the product of your best thinking at the time and of your dedicated work; it shows planning and execution.

A third internal obstacle has to do with critical thinking traits of

> What are some of the main practical obstacles that get in the way for you personally when you try to becoming engaged in writing a paper? It is important to recognize that at least some of them may be imposed on you by external circumstances. But the next step is to look for the best course of action for you, given these impediments. And a major part of this step is to explore any internal ways of thinking that you yourself add to the pressure of the actual external circumstances.

mind (see p. 117). These traits—or the lack of them—typically operate below the level of our conscious awareness, but explicitly calling them to mind is often a major help in engaging with the task we face. For any of the traits, facing up to them with intention can make the task far more do able.

Take *intellectual perseverance*. Realizing that you are persevering to get through the task actually *helps you* persevere. Explicit recognition of the need to exercise intellectual perseverance helps prepare you for the rigors of the researching and writing you'll need to do. Writing a critical paper involves facing challenges again and again. It involves frustration and mental discomfort. You may know ahead of time that you will have to list your references and make revisions, for example, but it still may not register with you. Explicitly recognizing that you will have to exercise intellectual perseverance helps guard you against having the challenges come up as unpleasant surprises: "Wait! You mean I still have to list my references?" Or: "What? I'm not done? You mean I still have to make revisions?"

> Most of the things people find worthwhile in their lives involve frustration and mental or physical discomfort. If you have a relationship, play a sport, raise a child, learn an instrument, or play video games, you encounter significant frustration and discomfort (and maybe mental and/or physical pain as well). It's part of the process you accept. So it's clear that it's not the frustration or discomfort itself that's the main obstacle. The main obstacle has to do with *something else* about writing a paper. What is that "something else" for you?

Something similar applies if your paper requires you to exercise *intellectual empathy*. As part of the paper, you may have to describe points of view you deeply disagree with, putting yourself through the thinking process someone else is using. Realizing that you have to muster up that intellectual empathy actually helps you do it. Without this explicit recognition, you may just click into the ordinary hit-or-miss level of intellectual empathy you exercise in your life.

Maybe, on down the line, being intellectually persevering or intellectually empathetic might be something you'll do as a matter of course. They may just be there in a significant way, permeating your thinking about anything. But for most of us, the traits of mind don't come naturally or automatically. To get them to become part of us, we have to take them on consciously and practice them.

Without the explicit focus on concepts and processes of critical thinking, people often learn the wrong thing from their papers. They think, for example, that the key to writing a better paper is to make it longer, or to write only what they think the teacher wants to hear, and so forth.

Take length. In and of itself, making a paper longer is not the point. What the paper really needs is to be more developed. The increased *length* is an *effect* of fuller development, not a goal in itself. When instructors assign a ten-page paper, a five-page paper, or a one-page paper, it's because they have different goals in mind for what that paper should accomplish. Obviously they are not actually motivated by a desire for a certain number of pages. They do it with the goal of prompting a certain level of fullness (in a longer paper) or conciseness (in a shorter paper). Length requirements give you an indication of the kind of topic or the degree of development appropriate for the paper.

The Larger Vision and Looking Ahead

Learning from the experience. When you finish your paper, there may be a temptation to toss it aside. Even if you don't do that physically, you may do it mentally. Instructors who painstakingly write comments on student papers are distressed that sometimes students toss away the paper without even reading the comments.

It's a good idea to resist that temptation. There is no real point in starting the next paper from zero. What you learn from writing a paper is something you can apply explicitly to whatever writing you do next. It sounds obvious to say it that way, but it's far from automatic. Again, explicitness and engagement are the keys. For it to help with your next piece of writing, you have to focus explicitly on learning from this one. Then, in the next piece of writing, you have to consciously focus on applying what you learned from writing your previous paper.

Reflecting on the Paper You've Written

What did you learn from writing this paper?
What did you learn—*about writing*—from writing this paper?
What about the paper or the research was important for you?
Where did you allow your creativity to enter?

What **impediments** did you run into?

- Did you notice those impediments while you were writing the paper or only now when you are reflecting?
- What did you do about these impediments?
- Did you realistically figure out the time you needed to write the paper?
- Did you give yourself enough time? Or did you shortchange yourself?
- If you didn't have enough time to do the job you intended to do, what can you do about it next time?

Which aspects of writing the paper were **most challenging** for you?

- Finding a thesis statement
- Finding your main points
- Organizing the paper
- Doing the research
- Finding reputable sources
- Being clear
- Revising
- Making the paper flow

Elements of reasoning

- Which elements of reasoning did you use to make your points?
- Which did you leave out? Why did you leave these out?

Critical thinking standards

- Which of the critical thinking standards did you consciously pay attention to as you wrote the paper?
- Which of the standards did you *not* consciously pay attention to as you wrote the paper? (In your own best judgment, would the paper have been better if you *had* paid attention to these standards?)
- On reflection, now, after the paper is finished, which of the critical thinking standards did you fall short on? Which did you not consider at all? Which worked out well?

Critical thinking traits of mind

- Which of the critical thinking traits did you bring to bear on the writing?
- Which ones might have helped improve your paper if you had brought them to bear on your work?

Socratic questioning

- What Socratic questioning interventions did you make?
- In your best judgment, to what extent did these interventions make your paper better?
- Did you have trouble filling the required number of pages?

Engagement

- To what degree did you engage with the issue or question you focused on?
- To what degree did you engage with *writing*?
- What is one thing you can do to make your next paper better?

Beyond writing a paper. Being able to write critically is a central part of higher education. Writing—at least engaged writing—increases your understanding of almost anything. This is, of course, important for doing well in school. Beyond school, unless you become an academic, the writing you do in your professional life will not be formal papers of the kind you write for classes. But writing papers using critical thinking develops skills and habits of mind that transfer to virtually any significant, developed piece of writing you do later on—from writing in a profession to an impassioned love letter. If the writing is important to you, and if it extends beyond a paragraph or two, it will almost certainly have the same key features as in writing a paper:

- There will be a central idea that you are trying to convey in the paper as a whole. (That central idea is what this book calls a *thesis statement.*)
- You will be explaining and supporting this central idea (= the *main points* of the paper).
- You will be putting it all together (= your *logical outline*).
- You will be considering objections people might have or aspects people might find missing (*"weakpoints," "the other side"*).
- You will have the opportunity to make the piece of writing better (*Socratic questioning* gives you a virtually unlimited potential for making it better).
- Overall, there will be content you are trying to communicate to your audience, and you will want to carry that out in a well-reasoned way (*the fundamental and powerful concepts*).
- You will be writing as clearly and fluidly as you can.

But on a larger scale, writing critically, with intention, can help you shape the person you are and the person you want to become. You can remind yourself that, though it may not seem like it, you are doing this to make your life richer. In one way or another, this is a main goal you have.

So, a good question to ask yourself is:

How was writing this paper like the way I live my life?

Chapter 6: Practice and Assessment Exercises

*1. **Putting it all together.** Up to Chapter 6, here is one highly condensed way of describing what you have to do to write a paper:

Once you have decided on a topic to write about, you:

- think your way through it and learn about it;
- pick out and organize the main things you want to say about it;
- explain them in the body of your paper;
- figure out how other people might find flaws or gaps in what you are saying;
- enhance and expand the paper.

You probably noticed that the concepts and processes of critical thinking are missing from the description above. Those are the concepts and processes that lay out *how* to do each of the parts listed.

Describe, using an SEE-I, how you would use the process of critical writing to go about each of those parts.

Then move on to Chapter 6 and describe how each of them fits with the fundamental and powerful concepts of critical writing.

Questions 2–10 are related to fundamental and powerful concepts.

2. **Tell your story.** In the Exercises to Chapter 1 you were asked to tell your own story with respect to writing.

At this point, at the end of this book, you have had a set of new experiences of writing, perhaps different from the ones you had before. Describe how you think of writing now, and contrast it with the way you thought of it before.

3. Why is *criticality* one of the fundamental and powerful concepts? That is, why isn't it enough to consider *content, audience,* and *communication*?

*4. (a) Who is Charles's intended audience for his paper on dieting (p. 46–50)?

  (b) Who is Lucia's intended audience for her paper on false memory (p. 52–55)?

5. Go through the other extended examples and decide (a) if the writer had an intended audience in mind; and, if not, (b) who you think their audience was, based on what they thought and wrote.

*6. Suppose you are writing a paper for a course in a specific subject matter (such as history, literature, or marketing...). Who is your audience?

7. Take a piece of writing you have done so far, preferably a full paper you have written. Briefly, state the *content* you were trying to convey in your paper. You may not have been conscious of the *audience* you were writing for, but still, as much as possible, describe the audience your writing seemed to aim at. Finally, address *communication*: To what extent was the way you wrote it congruent with that specific audience?

*8. Wouldn't it be better to add more fundamental and powerful concepts to the list of four? Wouldn't it help to add others such as voice, paragraphing, conventions, rhetoric, footnotes and endnotes, giving credit, and maybe several others? That way, writers would have more concepts in their tool kit, not just the four described in the text.

*9. Choose two of the topics listed below (or some other new topics that are important to you and fit with courses you are taking):

   - dealing with depression
   - PTSD
   - tipping in restaurants
   - dealing with stress
   - political correctness
   - maintaining an adequate exercise program in the midst of a busy life
   - how body image influences your view of yourself and others

   First, prepare for writing by explicitly identifying both the *audience* you will be addressing and the kind of writing you will engage in to *communicate* your content to that audience. Describe each of them with an SEE-I.

   Next, go through the full process of critical writing. The most beneficial response would be to actually write a paper on each of the two topics. Short of that, describe how the book would say to go through the full process of writing about it.

*10. **Write about writing.** There is a footnote in Chapter 6 (p. 192) that says this book is written in an informal style. What kinds of papers would make an informal style unsuitable?

The baseline paper.

11. A box on the first page of this book asked you to start off by writing "a baseline paper" before you began reading the book at all. The three parts of this question focus on the paper you then wrote: the *experience* you had of writing it; your *assessment* of it from your current vantage point; and *writing* a new paper on the topic.

(a) **The experience of writing it.** Without looking back at the baseline paper now, reflect on what the experience of writing it was like for you. Note anything that came up for you as you wrote it. What was difficult? What was easy? What was frustrating? Was it interesting? Were you engaged as you wrote it? Describe the experience.

(b) **Assessing it.** Read the baseline paper now. Assess it. How did you come up with the main things you wanted to say? Did you have a thesis statement? Main points? What important points did you leave out in it? How did you develop the points you were making? Did you address "the other side" of the issue? How did you "fill the pages"? Did you pay attention to standards? To what extent did you revise it? Did you pay attention to content, audience, communication, and criticality?

Do some reflecting on how skills you have learned would make that paper better.

(c) **Writing a new paper.** This time, re-write the baseline paper using the concepts and processes of critical writing. Analyze the topic "around the circle." Create an outline. Use enhanced SEE-I to develop it. Identify and describe the weakpoints. Ask and answer Socratic questions about it.

*12. What would the author say are the main outcomes for Chapter 6?

13. Which important terms or concepts in this chapter do you believe you have a pretty strong grasp of? Which are some you don't understand so well? Which terms or concepts are new for you? What aspects of the terminology of writing are giving you trouble?

*14. **Write about writing.** A good number of exercises in this book required writing. What did you do to achieve an appropriate level of grammatical correctness in what you wrote then?

Before you began reading Chapter 6, did you use any of the practical guidelines on p. 194–195?

*15. **Transitions.** Imagine a book about California. Chapter 3 is on education in that state, Chapter 4 is on wine producing there, and Chapter 5 is on Hollywood movies during the 1990s. So how would you expect Chapter 4 to begin? And how would you expect Chapter 5 to begin?

*16. Take a few of the longer paragraphs in this chapter and identify the topic sentence or idea in them. Do it with the first paragraph on p. 185 and with the paragraph on p. 186 that begins with the word "Moreover." Then do the same with two or three other paragraphs.

17. On p. 200–201 there is a section on "Why pay so much attention to giving credit?"

    Summarize what the author is saying in that section by giving an SEE-I for it.

    Then evaluate it from your own point of view, describing the extent to which you agree or disagree with the author.

18. **Reflecting on your own experience.** How do you motivate yourself to do things that (a) you know you have to do, but (b) you don't want to do?

*19. Give an SEE-I for the concept of *engagement*. The suggestion is to do this without looking back at the text.

    Before you begin doing so, make an estimate of how long it will take you to do it with the level of quality you intend. Afterward, compare your estimate to how long it actually took you.

20. What are some things in your life that you engage with fully? What are some things in your life you almost always do on automatic pilot?

*21. Cognitive science experts often distinguish between our automatic gut responses to problems and our reasoned assessments of them.[8] Both of those have a strong hold on us, and each of them comes to the forefront in different circumstances.

    Look at the section "What can you do?" on p. 206. Each of those is intended as something a person can do to actually carry out the work of writing a good paper.

    Which of those steps rationally make sense to you? That is, to what extent can you see how those steps would be helpful for someone?

    Then address your gut response. That is, for each one, say whether (in all honesty) you believe you will in fact do it for your next paper.

    This is a reflective question, not a judgmental one. It is not saying that there is something wrong in your behavior if you don't do what the steps suggest. It is asking you to reflect on the difference between what seems rational to you and what you do or don't do.

*22. Look at the box about mistreating yourself (on p. 207–208).

    How often do you mistreat yourself that way—not just with regard to writing but with other things in your life? Choose some activity in your life and apply this to it.

23. **Write about writing.** What is your view of writing courses? Do you think about how they will probably help you in doing something that you realize is important in your education and your life?

24. **Reflecting on writing.** Choose some writing you engaged in, preferably a complete paper. Carefully go through the reflection process on p. 210–212.

25. The last sentence in this book asks:

How was writing this paper like the way you live your life?

The idea is that the way you write papers may reflect a general way you go about doing many other things in your life: hurriedly, calmly, rushed, crammed in, optimistically, hoping for the best, with engagement, carefully, generously, feeling victimized, making the most of your experiences.... How much of the rest of your life do you live in ways like this?

Answer the question by writing a paper on it.

Begin by deciding on who the audience will be for your paper, and making a preliminary judgment about the kind of writing you will use to communicate that content.

Begin the content part as usual by analyzing the topic "around the circle." (The sentence is a question. To go around the circle, the topic would probably be "the relationship between the way I wrote this paper and ways I live my life.") Construct an outline you intend to follow.

Then develop the paper with SEE-I's.

Address the weakpoints in your paper: how others might disagree with, or find serious gaps in, what you have written.

Enhance and expand your paper by asking and responding to Socratic questions about what you have written.

26. Near the end of the Exercises for each chapter, you were asked to work on a paper using the concepts and processes of that chapter. Look at that paper now.

Apply the fundamental and powerful concepts to it (and, especially, modify the way you communicated the content in light of the audience you identify for it).

Check it for grammatical correctness. Break your paper into paragraphs that have one major topic sentence or idea.

Make the paper complete by giving citations and a "Bibliography" or "Works Cited" section.

Feel the achievement of it.

Responses to Starred Practice and Assessment Exercises

Chapter 1

*1. The main concepts in Chapter 1 include the following:

- thesis (thesis statement)
- structure
- plan or outline for the paper
- SEE-I
- the framework for critical writing

Though you might reasonably include additional concepts, your own list should include all of these, since the first three are essential concepts in writing, and the last two are processes that enable *critical* writing.

SEE-I will run through everything in the book. Because SEE-I is such an ideal process for understanding anything clearly, it is a major theme of the exercises.

*4. No, it doesn't. [The hope is that you can explain why just *having* the components is not enough.]

*5. Here is an SEE-I that James might give. (The one you wrote won't, of course, be the same as this, but you can compare the two.) Notice that the statement part is James's main point itself:

- The money from sin taxes can be used to pay for medical treatment that abusers of those substances (tobacco and alcohol) bring on themselves.
- In other words, when people buy alcohol or tobacco, there would be extra taxes attached to them. There are already taxes on both those substances, but these new taxes would be in addition. The taxes could even

be heavy ones. Those extra taxes would then be collected by the government and put into a separate fund. Then when hospitals treat substance abusers, that fund would be used to pay for the medical treatment. It wouldn't be humane to just withhold treatment for them. People are entitled to receive medical care even if they are substance abusers.

It may be that there wouldn't be enough money in this fund to cover the cost of medical care completely, but it would cover at least a big part of it. And anything that is covered in that way would not have to be paid for by other people who don't drink or smoke to excess. An alternative is that we could raise the taxes on cigarettes and alcohol enough to cover the cost of medical care for those people completely.

- For example, if a pack of cigarettes now costs X dollars, with "sin taxes" added on it would cost double that amount.
- It's like if you go skiing and you break your leg. Either you have already bought insurance to cover your medical bills or you have to pay the bills yourself. Either way, it's your own responsibility to pay for it.

*6. Here is the paraphrase—the statement—given by Paul and Elder:

> The goal of propaganda is to convince people that other groups of people are inhuman, and therefore not worthy of respect and just treatment.

*8. There are several paths you can follow when you elaborate or explain a point. You already have the *statement* part written out. To elaborate, you might consider:

- re-stating the point in other words,
- giving details,
- describing what are the most important aspects of the statement or of the point you are clarifying,
- describing key implications of the point,
- explaining parts of the statement that may be difficult to understand,
- and several others.

"Socratic Questioning" in Chapter 5 (p. 165) gives a large number of paths to pursue in giving effective and compelling elaborations. You may want to look ahead to that section now.

*9. Neither of those is an *example*. The first one is *elaboration*. The second one is an *illustration* rather than an example. (Notice that the question is not about whether you agree or disagree with James.)

*10. An illustration of *democracy*: It's like a game of tug-of-war with many ropes. Everyone gets to pull on ropes going in different directions, and the outcome depends on which side pulls the strongest. (Your own illustration will, of course, be different, and it might well be better.)

*12. Here is one focal point James chooses:

Main point #2. The money from sin taxes can be used to pay for medical treatment that abusers of those substances (tobacco and alcohol) bring on themselves.

An abuser is someone who uses a heavy amount of those substances and does it for a long period of time. In other words, abusers are people who use the substance to such an extent that it does damage to the person's health…. It's using those substances far beyond the ordinary. So it's not someone who smokes for only a few years and then quits, or someone who has a glass of wine or a beer from time to time. It is someone who doesn't just smoke or drink in a managed, responsible way. My friend's father is an example of that: he smoked all his life, and in the end he died from lung cancer. A substance abuser is like someone who swims too far from shore, knowing that he might not be able to make it back on his own.

Though it isn't marked here, James ingeniously also puts a circle around "medical treatment" and consults a government organization (OSHA) that defines what does and does not count as "medical treatment." If he decides to SEE-I that, it will be a strong factual addition to his paper.

*13. Sheila finds two focal points she considers promising: she could describe the *huge student debt* that students leave school with and the *burden* that imposes on them:

Main point #5. American students leave the university with a huge student debt, one that burdens them for years to come.

*15. SEE-I makes your thinking and your writing clearer, so a short answer is that SEE-I (or SEE and sometimes I) gives you a way to write the content of the paper in a substantially clearer way. Once you have chosen your thesis statement and your main points (Chapters 2 and 3), you will elaborate and explain each of them, you'll give examples to make the points concrete and vivid, and you may give punchy illustrations, analogies or comparisons that will help the reader follow what you are saying in a close and careful way. SEE-I is a main way you can do the work of writing the actual paragraphs that will constitute the body of your paper.

Chapter 2

*1. The three most important ones are closely related to one another:

- the elements of reasoning (as a whole)
- each of the individual elements of reasoning (plus *context*)
- analyzing, or analyzing "around the circle."

The first two are concepts, the last one is both a concept and a process.

*2. **question at issue:** What is the best method for bringing about social change and still coping with the violence that social change arouses?

purpose: Our goal is to bring about important social change.

conclusion: In our protests, we must exercise non-violent resistance.

concept: Non-violent resistance. The last sentence in the excerpt explains the concept.

assumptions:

- All things considered, non-violent resistance is the best way to produce the social change that is so desperately needed.
- Non-violent resistance *will* succeed in bringing about the social change that we seek.

[Note: He is *not* assuming or implying that it will be *completely* successful.]

implications and consequences:

- Protesters *will* have violence perpetrated upon them.
- It is likely that some protesters will be seriously hurt or even killed.

information:

- Law is one important factor in bringing about social change.
- New legal decisions sometimes create tension and provoke violence.

point of view: He is someone who is seeking to promote much-needed social change in the face of violence. He is protesting in order to bring about racial integration, and he is willing to risk violence and even death in order to achieve the social change, but he is unwilling to commit violence in return.

context: Some of the context is described in Question #2. More research will provide a much fuller context for the speech.

*3. A part of the response: The author of the book on traffic identifies three assumptions (though he doesn't use the word "assumptions") that legislators in Finland make:

- that the legislature has the power to "unilaterally impose high costs on breaking the law";
- "that traffic police will actually issue the fines rather than accept what in theory could be a huge bribe";
- "that the public, by and large, feels all this is fair."[1]

*5. Here are some reasonable responses. Notice that though the questions are sometimes singular ("What *is* your main goal?") you can make it plural as you respond ("My main goals *are*…).

main goals:
- Ideally, my main goal to *get rid* of stress in my life.
- More realistically, my goal is at least to cut down on it or make it more manageable.
- Another goal is to do better in school.

question at issue:
- What are some effective ways of dealing with stress? [maybe **R**]
- What are some effective ways of dealing with stress that would work *for me*?

implications and consequences:
- If I deal with stress, a lot of my life will run more smoothly.
- If I don't, it will hurt the quality of my life.

information:
I don't really have much solid information about how to deal with stress. It would help if I found some information in a reliable source (such as cdc.gov).

assumption:
- An assumption I make is that I just don't have time to start dealing with the stress in my life right now. I have too many things I have to do already.

*6. Just a question: When you wrote your "brief account," did you use SEE-I?

*8. Anthony needs to find the topic within the question and analyze that. His topic, he decides, is really money and its relationship to happiness.

So he asks: What are the main *assumptions* people make about money and happiness?

He asks about *consequences*: Does having more money make people happier?

The *question at issue* is the one he started with, but now he makes it more precise by changing it to "Does having money contribute to making a person happier?"

Notice how the greater precision changes it from being an oversimplified, all-or-nothing question. And that greater precision leads Anthony to the *concept*: "money." At first that seems like a ridiculous one to focus on: he says, "I already know what money is. Why concentrate on that?"

But then he asks, "What do I mean by 'money' *in this context*? How much money are we talking about?"

And so forth, around the rest of the circle.

With the focus that the elements bring, he comes up with some new insights about money and happiness. For example, when he answered the question about *consequences*, he decided that he still thinks money can't "buy happiness," but he also thinks that people who are in poverty would be *more* happy if they had enough money to buy things they really needed.

Then, when he gets to the *concept* of "money," he thinks, "Maybe having $2 million doesn't make you happier than having $1 million, but having $100 to feed your family for a while makes you a lot happier than having no money at all."

With those insights, he has the central idea for a thesis of an interesting and original paper.

*12. *Of course* she should list it as a consequence. She'll have to figure out how leaving her boyfriend weighs against other factors, but it would distort all her thinking if she just omitted it. The fact that it's an "emotional part" is irrelevant. *Of course* emotional consequences count. (For that matter, the desire to save money and to attend a highly ranked school both have an "emotional part" to them.)

*14. Here is an SEE-I for analyzing "around the circle":

Analyzing something is a way of mentally taking the thing apart in order to understand it better. In other words, if you want to understand something well—well enough to write a strong paper on it—you can do that by analyzing it "around the circle." It could be an issue, a problem, a decision, almost anything. As you analyze it, you start to see how all its parts fit together, and you even start to see it in a different way. You go beyond just reacting or going with your first impression or without seeing the whole picture.

For example, suppose you plan on being an elementary school teacher. Teachers have an obligation to deal with bullying. They have to realize that they make *assumptions* as they deal with it—and some of those assumptions may not be accurate. They have to realize that they have a *concept* of bullying, and that it may not fit exactly with what their students are doing. They have to realize that they are *interpreting* children's behavior and that a lot of the time they don't have enough *information* about the student's home life. There are certain *questions* they need to be asking. They may know what their overall *goals* are, and they also have to be aware that dealing with it in certain ways has *consequences* that go beyond the classroom. They may need to examine a child's behavior not just from the *point of view* of a teacher but also from the point of view of a parent, as well as from the point of view of the children themselves.

Analyzing something is like the difference between *studying* for an essay exam versus just writing down whatever comes into your mind.

*17. Here are the main outcomes the author would list:

Students will be able:

- to analyze a topic around the circle of elements (and to do so with the moderate degree of clarity, accuracy and depth that is appropriate to starting to learn a new critical thinking process).

In addition, students will be able:

- to explain what constitutes a plan for a paper (thesis, main points structure, outline).
- to give a clear, accurate explanation of how analysis around the circle works and why it is important.

In addition, in an ongoing way students will:

- continue using SEE-I regularly.

*19. There is no definitive answer, of course. An interesting observation is that almost no one ever asks themselves, "How do I go about understanding X?" That question is a reflective, *metacognitive* one, and we seldom even notice those.

Much of the time people try to understand something just by having reactions spring into their mind. Those answers often take into account only a single aspect of the thing, ignoring all the rest. In particular, when people try to understand things, they usually don't pay much attention to their assumptions, interpretations, concepts, or less-than-immediate implications.

Chapter 3

*1. Here is a highly condensed way to think about the process of critical writing. It is far too condensed, and it leaves out many important specifics, but it captures the heart of it.

- Start with something important to write about.
- Think your way through it.
- Find out about it.
- Choose the most important points to say about it.
- Write about them.

There is more to writing a paper than that (for example, there is the rest of the framework to address, and you can't just "write about them": you have to develop the important points with a level of clarity, detail, and depth that the topic requires). But in a real sense that's the heart of it.

*3. The outcomes will be closely related to the responses you gave in question 1.

Here, though, there is something additional to consider. A main thing that distinguishes writing from *critical* writing is explicitly focusing on critical thinking standards. Standards will be addressed directly in Chapter 5, but it would show a commendable grasp of critical writing if you mentioned some of those standards in the outcomes you wrote. For example, you might write the outcome:

Students will be able to construct a thesis statement.

But what you mean by that is:

Students will be able to construct a *clear* and *accurate* thesis statement that is *important* for the topic.

In addition to the three standards italicized, some others are *precise*, *deep*, *logical*, and *sufficient*. Add some standards to the outcomes you have written.

*4. There is often no sure-fire way to tell. But a good, strong way to tell is by closing the book and any notes you may have, and then writing out an SEE-I on your own. That means elaborating on it *in your own* words, inventing *your own* examples, and creating *your own* illustrations.

*5. There is more than one possibility for the **letting it emerge** part of the question. Given the way Charles has thought through the topic of dieting, the most likely thesis statement is one that emerges directly from one of his responses:

- *You have to think long range right from the beginning: when you commit to losing weight, you have to commit to making a real change in the way you live your life, not just for now, but for the future too.*

If that's the one he chooses, he'll have to re-write it, polish it, and say it more clearly: that will be the statement-part of his SEE-I.

*6. **Constructing it.** Here is one reasonable way Lucia could proceed. Her *question at issue*—"What produces false memory?"—led her to the *conclusion* that "There are at least four major ways that false memories can be induced in people." The constructed thesis statement of her paper, then, would be:

Though many factors may lead to false memory, the four major factors are a, b, c, and d.

(For a, b, c, and d she will write in the factors from the four experiments.) The main points in her plan might then be:

Main point 1. The *purpose* of the experiments was to find out how accurate our memories are.
Main point 2. For her second main point she could give a careful description of how each of the experiments was carried out [*information*], including the technical *concepts* Lucia listed, such as control group, etc.
Main point 3. The *concept* of "false memory" that she will derive from her research plus her own thinking about the experiments.

*8. A partial response: Question 8 is much less well defined than many of the others. That's because it is intended to show the undefined way we actually start to think about a possible paper. Even with an insight, you may not know how to proceed.

A good way to begin is to take the thoughts Kevin has had so far and narrow them down into a more definite *topic* he can analyze. Even if you get a good idea—as Kevin has—it may take work to formulate the topic in a way that will help bring out the idea.

A candidate for his topic might be "getting a fair trial."

*9. Kara might re-phrase her thesis statement this way:

> Juliet's risky plan and her own wishful thinking were more responsible for the tragedy of Romeo and Juliet than fate or being star-crossed lovers.

Under her main points she might list some of the "million things" that could go wrong with the plan, and Juliet's "unrealistic" assumption that love will prevail over all obstacles. Juliet's purpose could also be a main point. She might also add another implication of that unrealistic assumption: that Romeo was equally irrational by fatally jumping to a conclusion.

*10. Examples: In addition to examples that might occur to Michelle (or to you), note that an Internet search might yield some especially striking ones that you hadn't thought of.

Illustration. The hope is that you came up with a good illustration of your own. Michelle might search for a good *analogy* to illustrate the point. This might be a comparison to a different situation where a person is denied the means to succeed. She might say, "Not getting a desired job or housing is like running a race, but having to do it without shoes."

*11. With her fourth main point, Michelle will *elaborate* on how it is that people use stereotypes without examining them, explaining how that happens and maybe what she thinks causes it. She'll give *examples* of the unexamined use of stereotypes, trying to find ones that people say casually, almost naturally, without thinking at all about what they are saying. She'll search for a good illustration, perhaps a comparison to other things people say without thinking (profanity might be one).

Her last point was:

> The person who is being stereotyped feels unfairly treated and not given a chance to show what he or she can do.

This point has two different parts in it, so she may put circles around each part just to remind her to do justice to both of them. She will elaborate *both* on how unfair it feels to be stereotyped and *also* on how frustrating it is when you're not even given a chance to see what you can do. Elaborating on each of these might turn out to be the bulk of her paper. She might describe how there are skills you may never get a chance to develop because people did not give you a chance to see what you yourself could do.

She'll give *examples* here too. In fact, this is a prime place for evocative examples. The aim is to give examples that bring home to the reader the seriousness of the feelings, of what it feels like to be stereotyped, the feeling of being "lesser than" that comes from not being given a chance. Probably she'll be able to come up with a good illustration here too (a famous one is "like a raisin in the sun").

Even inside this fourth point, she may consider putting a circle around "unfair" and staircasing it.

*15. There are many possible structural illustrations she could have given. Here is one:

A college education is like streets and highways and bridges. They benefit everyone. Even if you don't use a bridge yourself, you receive goods that are less expensive because they are transported over bridges that are paid for by the public. Imagine that you had to pay a toll every time you used a street or a bridge. Or even worse: imagine that the tolls were so expensive that people had to take out loans just to use them! People who go to college come up with ideas and inventions and technologies that benefit all of us, directly or indirectly.

Can you see why this is a structural illustration?

*16. Giving an example requires some research. Sheila could say:

For example, tuition and fees at public universities in France are only $187–$716 per year for international students. Most public universities (including the most prestigious ones) are free regardless of citizenship[2] (Balan, 2019). The average at American universities is much, much higher: $10,116 per year for residents, and $22,577 for non-residents[3] (Powell & Kerr, 2019).

A contrasting example is what I mean by a university. I don't mean to include private schools or two-year community colleges. I also don't mean include masters or doctoral programs.

*18. Here is an illustration Charles might have given. Notice that it contains what might be called a "contrasting illustration": one that illustrates not just what dieting *is* like but also what dieting is *not* like:

Dieting is not like taking an antibiotic for an infection: with an antibiotic, you take it, the infection goes away, and then you're OK. It's more like taking medication for diabetes. You can't just take the medication, bring your blood sugar level back to normal, and then just coast along, hoping your blood sugar level will take care of itself on its own.

With that illustration, you can clearly visualize Charles's point about dieting.

*19. When you explained the difference, you may or may not have given an SEE-I. Here is an illustration: It's like learning to play basketball. Doing *background research* is like learning to play basketball when you come from a country where no basketball is played. You have to learn even the most basic moves. Doing *focused research* is like getting on a team with a good coach after you have already played a lot of schoolyard basketball.

*22. You should report both. For example, "Experts disagree about point X, but at least some of them claim that X is Y." It wouldn't be fairminded (or accurate) to cherry-pick only sources that support *your* side.

Chapter 4

*1. Some main outcomes: Students should be able to explain the critical thinking traits of mind and give an SEE-I for each of them. Students should be able to explain why it is important to include weakpoints in a paper and be able to identify and describe "the other side" fairmindedly. (An expected outcome is *not* that students will be able to name all the traits of mind.)

*2. Some possible weakpoints in the paper Kara plans to write:
- It is true that Juliet follows a plan that is too drastic and risky and that she could have thought of other plans instead. The reason she didn't think of alternatives, though, is that she is in love. All Romeo and Juliet can think about is being with the other person. So they both make hasty choices. They are star-crossed because love makes them blind to the dangers of the course of action each chooses (focused on a perceived gap in the account).
- Even if Juliet's plan had succeeded, something else just as bad would have happened. They still would never have been able to be married openly. Their families were just too powerful. They were doomed by the warring factions of their families (focused on a possible unforeseen implication).
- You say that she could have come up with some alternative plans, ones that were less drastic. But what *are* those alternatives?
- Juliet's plan was a reasonable one, given the desperate circumstances she was in.

*4. As James looked for weakpoints in his paper, the circle of elements helped focus his thinking. He thought about *concepts* he was using in his paper. One possible weakpoint was the concept *voluntary*. He asks:

> To what extent are smoking and drinking truly voluntary? My own father started smoking as a teenager, but didn't realize what he was getting himself into. Was that voluntary? And then after that it became an addiction. Was it still voluntary?

Similarly, he has often heard that alcoholism is a *disease*. If that is true, he wonders if that shows it is not voluntary. He says, "Diseases aren't voluntary, are they?" But as he considers the issue, he thinks that some diseases do at least have a voluntary aspect to them:

> Type 2 diabetes and high sugar intake are examples. So is catching a disease by sharing needles. Plus, I don't hear people saying that smoking tobacco is a disease.

The weakpoints he has found so far center on his main point #3. But he also discovers "the other side" in a different aspect of the concept "voluntary": Is "voluntary" the *only* crucial factor in whether someone should pay?

Notice how James is thinking critically, both about the paper he is writing and about the issue he is addressing. The various weakpoints he identifies would make a very strong addition to his paper. He would be addressing some of the complexities of the issue.

*5a. James's **thesis statement**:

> We should raise "sin taxes" on alcohol and tobacco and then use the money raised through these taxes to pay for the treatment of people who abuse those substances.

Here are some possible weakpoints about it. (The ones here focus on the self-confrontational question: "What alternatives are there?")

- Instead of raising sin taxes, we could ban advertising of alcohol the way we do with tobacco. That has helped cut down on the number of people who smoke. It might work the same way with alcohol.
- We could make tobacco and alcohol companies pay for medical care caused by the substances they sell.

- We could let things remain as they are now. Though there is a high financial cost to treating those diseases, we manage to do pretty well in paying for them with Medicare and insurance.

*5b. James's **Main point #1:**

> People who don't smoke or drink excessively should not have to pay for medical care for the people who do.

Here are some possible weakpoints:

- Does the burden of paying for stuff like health care fall only on the individual?
- What about humanitarian reasons, like helping someone in need?
- What would happen to such people if they didn't have the money to pay for their medical care—would they just die on the street?

*5c. James's **Main point #2:**

> The money from sin taxes can be used to pay for medical treatment that abusers of those substances bring on themselves.

A possible weakpoint: It's true that the money from "sin taxes" *could* be used to pay for medical treatment. But the government could spend that money on entirely different things, and we would still end up paying for medical care for substance abusers.

*5d. James's **Main point #4:**

> The healthcare costs of tobacco and alcohol in the U.S. are $121 billion per year.

This is a factual statement from a highly reputable source. So it isn't reasonable just to raise objections to it. So you may be puzzled about how you could find another reasonable point of view about it. The self-confrontational questions can help. Consider: "Is there anything else I should be addressing?" Notice that this doesn't lead you to question the statement itself; rather, it shifts your attention to other factors that might be relevant.

A possible weakpoint: Is $121 billion *a lot*? It certainly *sounds like* a lot. But all government spending sounds enormous all by itself. Compared to what? How does that compare with other things the government spends money on?

As James sits with the self-confrontational question "Is there anything else I should be addressing?" he discovers a set of other possible weakpoints. He asks:

What is the cost to society of selling highly sugary drinks? of mining coal? What does it cost us to allow parents not to vaccinate their children against common communicable diseases? Why am I singling out alcohol and tobacco? Doesn't the same argument apply to these others? Should all of these be taxed to pay for medical care they cause?

*6. Here are two ways someone might be on the other side:

- Is changing the way you live your life going to work? How can you go about making such a radical change in your life?
- My plan is to use one of those 50 quick ways to lose weight and *then* change the way I live my life.

*8. One other "weakpoint" also extends her thinking into new areas. She wonders about the concept of *memory* itself. She wonders about our normal memories: To what extent can people rely on the accuracy of their normal memories?

Her own concept of memory, the one she started off with, was that memory was like a recording of the past in your mind: Your mind has a picture of many of the things that happened in your life. You might not always be able to bring that picture to mind, but it's there. She thinks that is the concept of memory that everybody has. She checks the Merriam-Webster dictionary, and it defines memory as "the power or process of reproducing or recalling what has been learned."

Here is her thinking now:

Memory is not a recording of the past. It does not give me a picture like a photograph. It is more like a general story of what happened, but the story can be changed by what happens in the present. (I need an illustration.) (I have an example, but it's probably not a good one to use in the paper. For one thing, it's probably an interpretation, rather than an actual memory: I remember my last boyfriend as being a jerk. But when I look back at what I said in my diary, I didn't see him as a jerk at all. My memory of him changed.)

*9. Neither of those qualifies as a good candidate for "the other side." Both of them merely raise doubts about whether the experiments were carried out accurately and responsibly. There is no evidence that this is so. The "other side" has to be reasonable—and these are just unfounded speculations.

*11. Not really. It is true that in one sense she is finding "the other side" and identifying a weakpoint in the position that there is something wrong with funding Amtrak if it doesn't make money. But it doesn't fit what "weakpoint" means in Chapter 4. In this chapter, what you are looking for is a weakpoint in *your own* position. The self-confrontational questions are *self*-confrontational.

But notice how the self-confrontational questions are useful in responding to things that other people write.

*15. There are many things you could do. One of them is to practice "as if" thinking. Suppose you have trouble being intellectually empathetic to points of view that are diametrically opposed to your own. You can ask yourself, "What would an intellectually empathetic person do in these circumstances?" Then you can consciously act "as if" you were that person. You might even know someone who tends to be intellectually empathetic. You could use that person as a concrete model: What would she or he do in these circumstances?

*16. When they were children, many people held beliefs about their parents that they no longer hold. For example, "My parents were right when they told me XYZ."

This happens in adulthood also. Here are some examples that work for many people:

- A belief I had back when I cared deeply about person X (someone I no longer get along with): "I will always feel close to X."
- People who are divorced: When they got married, many of them sincerely and completely believed that they would never be divorced.
- A time when I felt miserable: "I'm going to continue feeling miserable forever. I am always going to be miserable."
- If I am with X, I will be completely happy.

*23. "Everything happens for a reason." Many people believe this. There could be any number of "other sides": objections to it, alternative views about why things happen, problems with it, unaddressed issues. Here is one: When people think about this, they always seem to focus on big events (such as a car accident or a serious illness). They don't seem to consider small events. Consider a single speck of dust on the floor near where you are sitting. Is there a *reason* why it's there rather than one millimeter to the south? (Of course, it's there because of factors like wind currents and gravity, but neither of those is a *reason*.)

"You can't know the future." It is true that there are many things about the future that you don't know, but there are many things about the future that you *do* know (for example, any calendar will tell you on precisely which days there will be a full moon next year; you know that some people will be born tomorrow). Besides, it is just as true that there are many things about the *past* that you can't know (for example, what Abraham Lincoln was thinking seven seconds before he was shot; how many hours you slept on April 21 of the year you were born; precisely how many calories you took in last year).

Chapter 5

*5. Here are a few things that may help:

- Impose a more structured or linear system on yourself (sometimes an instructor will do this, just as a coach would in a sport). For example: "For now, I'm going to focus on the Socratic question about relevance, importance, and depth. I'll save the rest for later. (But I'll keep open the possibility of changing the system if I have to.)"
- Focus on only one question under each standard.
- Keep yourself from dwelling too intently on the page of Socratic questions as a whole (and especially not on how many of them there are). Instead, you can remind yourself that they are there on p. 165 to consult when you need them.

*6. The distinction between analysis and evaluation is crucial for critical thinking about anything. If you have been asked to write a reaction paper to something you read or viewed, you were being asked to give an *evaluation* of it. If you were asked to describe or explain what is going on in something you read or viewed, you were being asked to give an *analysis* of it. Often people evaluate something without analyzing it first. That is, they make a judgment about whether something is good or bad without clearly understanding the thing. This is always a critical thinking mistake. In the logical sense, analysis *always* precedes evaluation: when you agree or disagree with what someone says (evaluation), you *assume* (often unconsciously, perhaps incorrectly) that you understand what the person means (analysis).

Though the distinction is crucial and basic, it is sometimes difficult to tell whether a piece of writing is part of analysis or evaluation. That is especially true with respect to short excerpts like the single sentences in this question. In this case, the first two sentences are examples of analysis: they are simply describing something. (Notice that the second sentence is analysis even though it is false.) The third sentence is straightforwardly evaluation. The last sentence is a little more ambiguous. Strictly speaking, it is analysis pure and simple. But if it was followed by another sentence that condemned or praised the war in Iraq, it would be part of an overall *evaluation*.

*8. There are dozens of ways the Socratic questions could be applied to her paragraph. Here is one: She picks out the sentence:

> You might never even know if it was because they were stereotyping you, but you'll suspect it just the same.

Then she asks the Socratic question:

> How is this significant?

Her response:

> What is significant about this is that it leaves you constantly second-guessing yourself, and second-guessing why people treat you the way they do. When people are rude to me, I will start to think that it was because they stereotyped me—but it might be just because they were in a bad mood that day. Or they may simply be rude individuals. [She might give a story about her own life as an example of this.]
>
> If I work in an office and there aren't many people of my race or gender or ethnicity in the office, I can start to think that I'm there just as a token representative of my group. How would I even tell if I was hired because of my own qualifications or because they just wanted someone in my group to show that they aren't prejudiced? It can make you feel bad about yourself.

*9. Yes/no questions don't give you scope for enriching your paper. You could get closer to a Socratic question by asking:

> Under what conditions is stereotyping fair or unfair?

That is, in fact, a version of the Socratic question:

> What are some of the complexities of this?

Sometimes yes/no questions can expose flaws, but even then they don't prompt you to explain those flaws.

*10. It is *possible* that it might make a short, interesting introduction to her paper, but it is unlikely. The information about past uses of the word "stereotype" is strikingly irrelevant to what her paper is about.

*11. Here is one possible response. James could ask a question about depth:

> What factors make this difficult?

To give some idea of the flexibility that Socratic questioning gives you, notice that he could ask this question about his position overall, about his thesis statement, and/or about virtually any of his individual main points.

For example, here is a small selection. He could say that there are many difficulties in raising sin taxes on alcohol and tobacco:

- A lot of people are against raising taxes on anything.
- It would be difficult to get it through the legislature.
- It might require a grass roots campaign of gathering signatures and petitions, and that would be difficult to accomplish.
- It would be even more difficult because not that many people agree with me, and their gut response would be to be against "sin taxes." When I asked some of my classmates about whether they would agree, all of them were against the idea, especially before I explained it to them.
- I believe that people would be more open to it when it comes to tobacco, but not to alcohol, because cigarettes and vaping are *addictive*. But a lot of people just enjoy having a beer after work. Why should they have to pay more just because some people abuse alcohol?
- Many legislators themselves enjoy drinking, and so do their constituents.

For any one of these—or for more than one—James could easily give an enhanced SEE-I if he chose to.

*13. Again, there are many different Socratic questions you could ask, and several different parts of Kara's point you could apply them to. Here is one:

> Socratic question: What are the specifics of being "star-crossed"? What is meant by that in Shakespeare's play?

Her response:

> By "star-crossed" Shakespeare means that the death of Romeo and Juliet was "written in the stars," that it was fated to happen. It means that the tragedy was beyond their control, and since they were star-crossed, there was nothing they could do to avert their fate.

Just as with James in the previous question, Kara could expand on her answer by giving an enhanced SEE-I.

*18. Here again is the sentence:

> Michelangelo painted the ceiling of the Sistine Chapel.

You don't have to know much about Michelangelo to see how
adaptable the Socratic questions are. You can get a sense of it by
seeing how the Socratic questions about precision can be applied
to innumerably many aspects of the sentence. For instance, what
are the details or the specifics of:

- how Michelangelo actually carried out the painting of the ceiling?
- how he was commissioned to paint it?
- the artistic problems he encountered in painting it?
- the political problems he encountered in painting it?
- the painting itself?
- this or that figure in the painting itself?
- the use of negative and positive space in the painting?
- the organization of the painting?
- the harmoniousness of it?
- ....

*20. The hope is that combining an element of reasoning with one of
the Socratic questions will make the sentences of your writing
flow much more easily. Notice how this helps you communicate
your point to the audience. What often happens with writers is
that they just *assume* that their readers will see the importance
of a point without its being explained to them (another example
of our tendency to rely on "mind-reading"). By explaining to the
reader *why* the point is important, you are bypassing all those
undermining assumptions. You will not just be thinking in your
own mind that the point is an important one; you will be communicating its importance to the reader.

Chapter 6

*1. Here is a highly abbreviated way of putting it all together, and
then relating the parts of the critical writing process to the fundamental and powerful concepts:

You pick out and organize the main things you want to say
by analyzing your topic around the circle of elements; from that
you identify the main things you intend to say (thesis statement
and main points) and outline the paper; and you learn about the
topic through the research you do. In this way you identify the
content of your paper. You are exercising *criticality* all the way
through the analysis, organization, and research.

You explain your thesis statement and other main points
(plus any additional supporting points) with enhanced SEE-(and-
sometimes)-I. In this way you are exercising *criticality* by focusing

on the critical thinking standard of clarity (and perhaps in not overusing illustrations). This is the main way you are making critical decisions about how best to *communicate* your ideas to your *audience*.

You figure out how people might find flaws or gaps in your paper by identifying the weakpoints and addressing "the other side" of the issue. In doing so, you are expanding your *content*. More important, though, you are addressing the critical thinking standard of depth: facing up to the complexities of the issue and the possible different views your audience may have. (Thus, *criticality*, *communication*, and *audience*.)

You enhance and expand your paper by making Socratic questioning interventions. You are directly exercising *criticality* with respect to critical thinking standards; you are *communicating* more effectively with your *audience*. You are expanding your *content*.

*4(a). There probably is no definite answer. Charles doesn't seem to have an audience in mind as he writes his paper. As he thinks about his topic, he seems to be comparing himself to his fellow students, maybe to those in his own age range, so maybe in a sense they are, at least unconsciously, his audience. (He doesn't seem to be considering people who diet for reasons completely different from his—for example, people who are vegetarian or lactose intolerant.)

(b). In contrast to Charles in the first part of this question, Lucia is writing for a definite audience. She is writing for people who are interested in questions of psychology (specifically, cognitive, experimental psychology) and who have a moderate understanding of it already. You can see this in the way she thinks about explaining what a "control group" is and what a "double blind experiment" is, but she considers it optional. She is writing for someone who already knows how experiments in psychology work.

*6. Though, of course, your instructors are probably the main persons who will actually read your paper (so to that extent they are your "audience"), there is a sense in which your instructors are not the *primary* audience for your paper. Instructors usually read papers *as if* the papers were written for others: usually, for others who are moderately well versed in the subject, perhaps at the level of strong students in the course. (Both Lucia's paper (in question *46) and Kara's paper on Juliet (p. 56–58) are examples of this concept. Kara is writing for someone who is already familiar with *Romeo and Juliet*, not just the story but the play written by Shakespeare. She is not writing for those who have seen only modern movie adaptations of the Romeo and Juliet story. You can see that from the fact that she quotes Shakespeare's lines and does not feel the need to explain the whole plot or delve into the other characters.)

Instructors are too well versed in the area to be your actual audience. Given the knowledge they already have, they may in fact already know what you say in the content of your paper. Often, they are hoping to see a new angle, or a fresh point of view, or a thoughtful way of organizing or synthesizing the material.

*8. There are two distinct problems in adding more fundamental and powerful concepts to the four listed in the chapter. The first problem is that only one of the candidates listed in the question could qualify as a fundamental and powerful concept. For example, though both *paragraphing* and the idea of *giving credit* are important, maybe essential, neither of them will help you think through constructing the paper as a whole. Similarly, *conventions* are just one limited aspect of the fundamental and powerful concept of communication. Of those listed, *rhetoric* is the only one that would qualify as a fundamental and powerful concept. Since *rhetoric* encompasses the full range of how we *communicate*, the two are very closely related.

The main problem of enlarging the set of fundamental and powerful concepts, however, is that doing so turns these critical thinking tools into merely a checklist of details, ones that are relevant in some cases and not relevant in others. By contrast, the four fundamental and powerful concepts are key tools for thinking through *any* piece of writing. They are always relevant.

*9. Just some brief critical writing comments on one aspect of responses you might give: Some of the topics are highly controversial. One example is *political correctness*. With a topic like this, it is probably not possible to write a good paper without addressing the radically different concepts of political correctness that people have in mind, as well as the radically different points of view people have about it.

With some topics, a certain kind of bias can come in unconsciously. For example, your ideas about tipping may be unconsciously influenced by whether you have worked in a restaurant. (Interestingly, this is an example of what is called "biased fairness" (Greene, 83–85). It is based on a sincere desire to be as fair as possible, but because of our own experience, we tilt the fairness in one direction.)

*10. For the expanded examples in this book, we often do not know enough about the context in which they were written to make a firm judgment about the extent to which informal writing would be appropriate or inappropriate. Clearly, though, Lucia's paper on false memory, written about a technical subject in an advanced course, should not be written informally.

An aside: This is a question about *audience* and *communication*.

*12. Some outcomes: students will

- be better able to see more clearly how the processes of critical writing fit together as a whole;
- be able (using enhanced SEE-I) to explain what a fundamental and powerful concept is;
- be better able to resolve unanticipated writing problems and issues by thinking them through using the fundamental and powerful concepts of *content*, *communication*, *audience*, and *criticality*;
- develop some strategies for dealing with grammatical issues;
- give credit to sources they have used in their writing;
- develop strategies to help with motivation and engagement;
- reflect on how writing and critical writing fit with their lives.

*14. A great deal would probably depend on whether you wrote them only for yourself, or if your instructor was going to read them, or if your instructor was going to give you a grade on them.

*15. Somewhere near the beginning, Chapter 4 would probably make reference to education, the topic of the previous chapter. That would help the reader make the transition from one topic to the next.

Similarly, somewhere near the beginning, Chapter 5 would very likely make reference to wine. But it might well make reference to both education and wine. For example, a sentence there might say something like "While both education and wine producing are important to the State, what California is most widely associated with is movie-making, and the center of movie-making has always been linked to Hollywood."

Without such transition sentences, the different chapters would seem choppy and un-integrated with one another.

*16. The first paragraph of Chapter 6: the main topic idea of the paragraph is partly spelled out in the last sentence. It might be expressed this way:

In many pieces of writing, essential but unexpected issues come up that can't be anticipated in any guide.

In the paragraph in Chapter 2, the topic is the fundamental and powerful concept *audience*:

Audience is the concept "you use to monitor your thinking and your writing all the way through."

*19. About the second half of the question: Though it is helpful to give a self-estimate here of the time it will take you, estimating it under these circumstances may not be very reliable. The question explicitly calls your attention to making the estimate, and that probably makes you much more careful in making it than you would ordinarily be.

*21. A personal response: The author of this book has difficulty with several of them. I do each of them sometimes, but at other times I just don't. That usually happens either because it doesn't occur to me at the time or because I think I'll do OK without following these steps. At other times, my gut response is that it just seems too much trouble, say, to make a realistic estimate of how long it will take to write something (even though it takes only a couple of minutes to make such an estimate). Interestingly, research shows that the more stress a person feels or the more things they have on their mind (cognitive load), the less likely they are to do the thing that makes rational sense to them.

*22. A common such experience is driving to get places on time. For many people, it's as if that segment of time is not even part of their life. They simply rush through it. If they could just push a button and get from point A to point B and have the intervening seconds not exist at all, they might gladly push the button. (There is a movie, *Click*, that depicts a man eradicating most of his life by having such a button.)

Bibliography

Ariely, Dan. *Predictably Irrational: The Hidden Forces that Shape Our Decisions* (New York: HarperCollins, 2009).

Aronson, Elliot. *The Social Animal*, 8th ed. (New York: Worth, 1999).

Balan, Robert S. "Tuition Fees at Universities in Europe 2019: Overview and Comparison." *Masters Portal.* (November 18, 2019), http://mastersportal.com.

The Chicago Manual of Style, 16th ed. (Chicago: The University of Chicago Press, 2010).

"Curriculum on Medical Ignorance." *The University of Arizona Medical School*, The University of Arizona. http://www.ignorance.medicine.arizona.edu. Accessed July 19, 2017.

de Villiers, Marq, and Sheila Hirtle. *Sahara: The Extraordinary History of the World's Largest Desert* (New York: Walker, 2002).

Ehrlich, D., I. Gutman, P. Schonbach, and J. Mills. "Postdecision Exposure to Relevant Information." *Journal of Abnormal and Social Psychology* 54, no. 1 (1957): pp. 98–102. doi:10.1037/h0042740.

Elder, Linda. *Liberating the Mind: Overcoming Sociocentric Thought and Egocentric Tendencies* (Lanham, MD: Rowman & Littlefield, 2019).

Elder, Linda, and Richard Paul. *The Thinker's Guide to Analytic Thinking: How to Take Thinking Apart and What to Look for When You Do*, 2nd ed. (Lanham, MD: Rowman & Littlefield, 2016).

Elder, Linda, and Richard Paul. *Intellectual Standards: The Words that Name Them and the Criteria that Define Them* (Lanham, MD: Rowman & Littlefield, 2019).

Elder, Linda, and Richard Paul. *The Thinker's Guide to the Human Mind: Thinking, Feeling, Wanting, and the Problem of Irrationality*, 4th ed. (Lanham, MD: Rowman & Littlefield, 2019).

Festinger, Leon. *A Theory of Cognitive Dissonance* (Stanford, CA: Stanford University Press, 1957).

Goss, Stephen, Alice Wade, J. Patrick Skirvin, Michael Morris, K. Mark Bye, and Danielle Huston. "Effects of Unauthorized Immigration on the Actuarial Status of the Social Security Trust Funds." *Social Security Administration: Office of the Chief Actuary*, No. 151. April 2013. http://www.ssa.gov.

Greene, Joshua. *Moral Tribes: Emotion, Reason, and the Gap between Us and Them* (New York: Penguin, 2014).

Haddad, Yvonne Y. *Contemporary Islam and the Challenge of History* (Albany: State University of New York Press, 1982).

"How to Write a Thesis Statement." *IUB Writing Tutorial Services. Indiana University Bloomington*, April 7, 2014. http://www.wts.indiana.edu.

Kahneman, Daniel. *Thinking Fast and Slow* (New York: Farrar, Straus & Giroux, 2011).

Kaplan, Michael, and Ellen Kaplan. *Bozo Sapiens: Why to Err Is Human* (New York: Bloomsbury, 2010).

King, Martin Luther, Jr. *Our Struggle: The Story of Montgomery* (New York: The Montgomery Improvement Association, 1957).

Long, Vince, and Steve Gardiner. "The InterActive Six Trait Writing Process." *The Literate Learner*, 2017. http://www.literatelearner.com.

Mlodinow, Leonard. *Subliminal: How Your Unconscious Mind Rules Your Behavior* (New York: Vintage, 2012).

New York Times. "Pop Quiz: The SATs; Goodbye Analogies, Hello Anecdotes." August 4, 2002.

Nosich, Gerald. *Learning to Think Things Through: A Guide to Critical Thinking across the Curriculum*, 4th ed. (Boston: Pearson, 2012).

Paul, Richard, and Linda Elder. *How to Write a Paragraph: The Art of Substantive Writing* (Lanham, MD: Rowman & Littlefield, 2019).

Paul, Richard, and Linda Elder. *The Miniature Guide to Critical Thinking: Concepts and Tools*, 8th ed. (Lanham, MD: Rowman & Littlefield, 2020).

Powell, Farran, and Emma Kerr. "See The Average College Tuition in 2019–2020." U.S. News and World Report (September 9, 2019). http://usnews.com.

Puglia, Michael. "Violence in Video Games a Problem for Developing Minds." *The Record*, SUNY Buffalo State, volume CXIX, Issue IV. March 5, 2014, p. 5. Used by permission of *The Record*, SUNY Buffalo State.

Pye, Michael. *The Edge of the World: A Cultural History of the North Sea and the Transformation of Europe* (New York: Pegasus Books, 2014).

Reader's Digest. "50 Easy Ways to Lose Weight." Accessed September, 2014. http://www.rd.com/health/...weight-loss/easy-ways-to-lose-weight-50-ideas.

"Research and Citation Sources." *The Purdue OWL*. Purdue U Writing Lab, 2017. http//www.owl.english.purdue.edu.

Snyder, Howard. "Arrest in the United States 1990–2010." Bureau of Justice Statistics. *U.S. Department of Justice*. Oct. 2012, p. 8. http//www.bjs.gov.

Tardiff, Elyssa, and Allen Brizee. "Tips and Examples for Writing Thesis Statements." The Writing Lab & The Owl at Purdue. Purdue University, February 10, 2014. http://www.owl.english.purdue.edu.

Tavris, Carolyn, and Elliot Aronson. *Mistakes Were Made (But Not by Me): Why We Justify Foolish Beliefs, Bad Decisions, and Hurtful Acts* (New York: Houghton, Mifflin, 2016).

Turabian, Kate. *A Manual for Writers of Research Papers, Theses, and Dissertations*, 7th ed. (Chicago: The University of Chicago Press, 2007).

United States Bureau of Justice. "Violent Crime." Bureau of Justice Statistics, *U.S. Department of Justice*. Sept. 8, 2017. http//www.bjs.gov.

Vanderbilt, Tom. *Traffic: Why We Drive the Way We Do (and What It Says about Us)* (New York: Knopf, 2008).

Weida, Stacy, and Karl Stolley. "Developing Strong Thesis Statements." *Purdue Online Writing Lab*. Nov 23, 2013. http//www.owl.english.purdue.edu.

Workman, Mark, and Jacqueline Raphael. "6+1 Trait Writing." *Education Northwest*, 2017. http://www.educationnorthwest.org/traits.

Writing Tips: Thesis Statements." The Center for Writing Studies, University of Illinois, University of Illinois at Champaign–Urbana, 2013. http://www.cws.illinois.edu.

Endnotes

Chapter 1

1. Note that complete information about sources referenced in the endnotes is contained in the Bibliography. The approach to critical thinking in this book is one that has been developed over the years by Richard Paul, Linda Elder and myself at the Foundation for Critical Thinking (www.criticalthinking.org). It is, by intention, a robust approach to critical thinking. It is laid out and amplified in a wide variety of publications available in the Thinker's Guide Library. A good, concise description of the most central aspects of the approach is contained in Richard Paul and Linda Elder, *The Miniature Guide to Critical Thinking: Concepts and Tools*, 8th ed. (Lanham, MD: Rowman & Littlefield, 2020).

   For learning to think critically within a field or discipline, see Gerald Nosich, *Learning to Think Things Through: A Guide to Critical Thinking Across the Curriculum*, 4th ed. (Boston: Pearson, 2012).

2. For an overview of the elements of reasoning, see Linda Elder and Richard Paul, *The Thinker's Guide to Analytic Reasoning: How to Take Thinking Apart and What to Look for When You Do*, 2nd ed. (Lanham, MD: Rowman & Littlefield, 2016).

3. For a broad view of the intellectual standards extant in human languages see Linda Elder and Richard Paul, *The Thinker's Guide to Intellectual Standards* (Lanham, MD: Rowman & Littlefield, 2019).

4. For a beginning understanding of critical thinking traits or intellectual virtues, see Paul and Elder, *Miniature Guide...Concepts and Tools*, 24–26).

5. For a concise account of the problems of egocentric and sociocentric thinking in human life, see Linda Elder and Richard Paul, *The Thinker's Guide to the Human Mind: Thinking, Feeling, Wanting, and the Problem of Irrationality,* 4th ed. (Lanham, MD: Rowman & Littlefield, 2019). For considerably more depth, see Linda Elder, *Liberating the Mind: Overcoming Sociocentric Thought and Egocentric Tendencies* (Lanham, MD: Rowman & Littlefield, 2019).

6. There are exceptions to this. Some tools of critical writing do not apply directly to some kinds of writing. Fiction, poetry, drama, free-writing and written brainstorming are exceptions. But even with these, the concepts and processes of critical writing often help in part or indirectly. And, in any kind of writing, the concepts of critical thinking are always a rich source of insight.

7. James used two sources in his research. Following MLA format, he cites his sources in the text of his paper this way:

   ("Economic Trends in Tobacco" 2017)

   (Bouchery 2011).

   He makes a separate page titled "Works Cited" at the end of his paper. There, he formats them in alphabetical order using hanging indents:

   Bouchery, E. E., et al. "Economic Costs of Excessive Alcohol Consumption in the U.S., 2006." *PubMed.com. American Journal of Preventive Medicine.* vol. 41, no. 5, November, 2011, 516–24. doi: 10.1016/j.amepre.2011.06.045.

"Economic Trends in Tobacco." *Centers for Disease Control and Prevention*, January 29, 2019. www.cdc.gov/tobacco/data_statistics/fact_sheets/economics/econ_facts/index.htm.

(Again, see p. 198–201 for more about giving credit to sources.)

8. She ends up using two sources, both from the same website. She places an endnote number in the text. Then she gives the full reference to her sources in her "Bibliography," using a hanging indent and putting them in alphabetical order:

Pop, Alexandru. "Times Higher Education Ranking." *Times Higher Education*, Masters Portal (March 15, 2017). http://www.mastersportal.eu.
"Tuition Fees at Universities in Europe in 2017—Overview and Comparison." Masters Portal (January 9, 2017) http://www.mastersportal.eu.

9. Eliot Aronson, *The Social Animal*, 8th ed. (New York: Worth, 1999), 7.
10. Richard Paul and Linda Elder, *How to Write a Paragraph: The Art of Substantive Writing* (Lanham, MD: Rowman & Littlefield, 2019).
11. "Pop Quiz: The SATs; Goodbye Analogies, Hello Anecdotes," *New York Times*, August 4, 2002.

Chapter 2

1. Adapted from "The Elements of Thought." Used by permission of Linda Elder.
2. *Reader's Digest*, "50 Easy Ways to Lose Weight," http://www.rd.com. Accessed September 2014.
3. The figures are from the university library at SUNY Buffalo State (buffalostate.summon.serialsolutions.com, E. H. Butler Library).
4. Lucia is required to reference her sources in APA form (rather than in the format used in this book). She used citationmachine.net to format the references for her. She lists them alphabetically, using hanging indents, on her "Works Cited" page:

Loftus, E. F. (1997). Creating False Memories. *Scientific American*, 277(3), 70–75. doi:10.1038/scientificamerican0997-70.
Loftus, E. F., & Pickrell, J. E. (1995). The Formation of False Memories. *Psychiatric Annals*, 25(12), 720–25. doi:10.3928/0048-5713-19951201-07.

5. Martin Luther King Jr., *Our Struggle: The Story of Montgomery* (New York: The Montgomery Improvement Association, 1957), 6.
6. Tom Vanderbilt, *Traffic: Why We Drive the Way We Do (and What It Says about Us)* (New York: Knopf, 2008), 236.
7. Yvonne Y. Haddad, *Contemporary Islam and the Challenge of History* (Albany: State University of New York Press, 1982), 90.

Self-Assessment: Test It Out #1

1. "Writing Tips: Thesis Statements," *The Center for Writing Studies, University of Illinois*, University of Illinois at Champaign–Urbana, 2013. http://www.cws.illinois.edu.
2. "How to Write a Thesis Statement," *IUB Writing Tutorial Services*, Indiana University Bloomington, April 7, 2014, http://www.wts.indiana.edu.
3. Stacy Weida and Karl Stolley, "Developing Strong Thesis Statements," *Purdue Online Writing Lab*, Nov 23, 2013. http://www.owl.english.purdue.edu.

Chapter 3

1. Tasha's business instructor required APA formatting. She gave two in-text citations: Flanagan (2014) and Amtrak National Fact Sheet (2015). She also gave reference information (in alphabetical order, using hanging indents) for the two sources she used on a page titled "References":

   Amtrak National Facts. (2015). Retrieved from https://www.amtrak.com.
   Flanagan, G. (2014, May 23). "Why the heck is Amtrak still in business after losing money 43 years straight?" Retrieved from https://www.businessinsider.com/Amtrak-profitability-facts-2014-5#ixzz3dBE3eykz.

2. Marq de Villiers and Sheila Hirtle, *Sahara: The Extraordinary History of the World's Largest Desert* (New York: Walker, 2002), 35.

Chapter 4

1. The classic theory of cognitive dissonance was formulated by Leon Festinger, *A Theory of Cognitive Dissonance* (Stanford, CA: Stanford University Press, 1957). A good, readable, overall summary of the theory can be found in Carolyn Tavris and Elliot Aronson, *Mistakes Were Made (But Not by Me): Why We Justify Foolish Beliefs, Bad Decisions, and Hurtful Acts* (New York: Houghton, Mifflin, 2016), 13–42, and in Aronson, *The Social Animal*, 8th ed., 182–218.

2. D. Ehrlich et al., "Postdecision Exposure to Relevant Information." *Journal of Abnormal and Social Psychology* 54, no. 1 (1957): 98–102. doi:10.1037/h0042740.

3. As far as I can tell, no one has a good explanation for why people do this. Some people speculate about possible evolutionary explanations, but so far at least they seem to remain speculative.

4. The critical thinking traits listed are based on Paul and Elder, *Critical Thinking: Concepts and Tools*, 14–15. Used by permission. As in Nosich, *Learning to Think Things Through*, 175–76, I have added intellectual engagement. It is a trait essential to thinking and to writing seriously.

5. A rich source for exploring "what you don't know" comes from the work of Marlys Witte, Ann Kerwin, and Charles Witte at the University of Arizona Medical School. See the "Curriculum on Medical Ignorance," *The University of Arizona Medical School*, University of Arizona, http://www.ignorance.medicine.arizona.edu. Accessed July 19, 2017.

6. Elyssa Tardiff and Allen Brizee, "Tips and Examples for Writing Thesis Statements," The Writing Lab & The Owl at Purdue, Purdue University, February 10, 2014, http://www.owl.english.purdue.edu.

Chapter 5

1. In *The Miniature Guide to Critical Thinking: Concepts and Tools,* Paul and Elder highlight nine Intellectual Standards. They are standards relevant to any domain of thinking. I have added "sufficiency" as a standard particularly germane to writing a paper on a topic. Used by permission of Linda Elder. For a deeper, more comprehensive discussion, see Elder and Paul's *Intellectual Standards*.

2. Howard Snyder, "Arrest in the United States 1990–2010," Bureau of Justice Statistics. *U.S. Department of Justice*, Oct. 2012, http://www.bjs.gov, 8.

3. United States Bureau of Justice, "Violent Crime," Bureau of Justice Statistics, *U.S. Department of Justice*. Sept. 8, 2017, http://www.bjs.gov.

4. The questions are adapted from those in Paul and Elder's *The Miniature Guide to Critical Thinking: Concepts and Tools*. I have contextualized them to issues in critical writing. Used by permission of Linda Elder.
5. Michael Puglia, "Violence in Video Games a Problem for Developing Minds," *The Record*, SUNY Buffalo State, volume CXIX, Issue IV, March 5, 2014, 5. Used by permission of *The Record*, SUNY Buffalo State.
6. Michael Kaplan and Ellen Kaplan, *Bozo Sapiens: Why to Err Is Human* (New York: Bloomsbury, 2010), 59–60.
7. Leonard Mlodinow, *Subliminal: How Your Unconscious Mind Rules Your Behavior* (New York: Vintage, 2012), 149.
8. For both excerpts: used by permission.
9. Stephen Goss et al., "Effects of Unauthorized Immigration on the Actuarial Status of the Social Security Trust Funds," *Social Security Administration: Office of the Chief Actuary*, No. 151, April 2013, http://www.ssa.gov.

Chapter 6

1. Reputable websites give definitions and helpful examples of each (such as Vince Long, and Steve Gardiner, "The InterActive Six Trait Writing Process," *The Literate Learner*, 2017, http://www.literatelearner.com; or Mark Workman, and Jacqueline Raphael. "6+1 Trait Writing." *Education Northwest*, 2017, http://www.educationnorthwest. org/traits give definitions and helpful examples of each.
2. You can get a feel for the extent to which we rely on grammar for clarity by looking at the history of writing. There was a time, not so long ago, when people hadn't yet discovered or formulated basic aspects of writing we now take for granted. Before around the eighth century, writers did not distinguish between capital and small letters; they did not put spaces between words or use hyphens; they hadn't discovered the value of punctuation (Michael Pye, *The Edge of the World: A Cultural History of the North Sea and the Transformation of Europe* (New York: Pegasus Books, 2014), p. 61). Imagine reading something that begins this way:
   FOURSCOREANDSEVENYEARSAGOOOURFATHERSBROUGHTFOR-
   THONTHISCONTINENTANEWNATIONCONCEIVEDINLIBERTYAND-
   DEDICATEDTOTHEPROPOSITIONTHATALLMENARECREATEDEQUAL
3. There are sometimes grammatical complexities in writing for your audience. Suppose you work in a professional setting, such as an office or an organization, and you write a report that says:
   The marketing department gave a presentation to Stephanie and I.
   To many people, this *sounds* right. But a guide to grammar will tell you that the grammatically correct form is
   "...gave a presentation to Stephanie and me."
   The problem is that if you say it this way, your supervisor may think that *you* are the one who is saying it wrong. What can you do? (The unintentionally ungrammatical first line of one of the most famous 20th-century poems is "Let us go then, you and I.")
4. "APA" stands for the *American Psychological Association* (the style used most often in writing in the social sciences). "MLA" stands for the *Modern Language Association* (the style used most often in writing in liberal arts and humanities). "Chicago" refers to *The Chicago Manual of Style*, 16th ed. (Chicago: The University of Chicago Press, 2010). A more user-friendly guide to Chicago style is Kate L. Turabian, *A Manual for Writers of Research Papers, Theses, and Dissertations*, 7th ed. (Chicago: The University of Chicago Press, 2007). Both MLA and Chicago are often used in the liberal arts and humanities. "IEEE" stands for *The Institute of Electrical and*

Electronics Engineers (the style most often used in technical fields). There are helpful websites for all of them, many of them much more up-to-the-minute than references mentioned in a book.

5. "Research and Citation Sources," *The Purdue OWL*, Purdue U Writing Lab, 2017, http://www.owl.english.purdue.edu.

6. This is a consequence of what Kahneman has found to be the strong human tendency to register only the information in front of us—unless we stop and consciously reflect on it—not to question it or even weigh it against background information we have (Daniel Kahneman, *Thinking Fast and Slow* (New York: Farrar, Straus & Giroux, 2011, 84–85).

7. Dan Ariely, *Predictably Irrational: The Hidden Forces That Shape Our Decisions* (New York: HarperCollins, 2009), 297.

8. Joshua Greene, *Moral Tribes: Emotion, Reason, and the Gap between Us and Them* (New York: Penguin, 2014).

Responses to Starred Practice and Assessment Exercises

1. Tom Vanderbilt, *Traffic: Why We Drive the Way We Do (and What It Says about Us)* (New York: Knopf, 2008), 237.

2. Robert S. Balan, "Tuition Fees at Universities in Europe 2019: Overview and Comparison," *Masters Portal*, November 18, 2019, http://mastersportal.com.

3. Farran Powell and Emma Kerr, "See the average college tuition in 2019–2020," *U.S. News and World Report*, September 9, 2019, http://usnews.com.

Index

accuracy
  critical thinking and, 155
  Socratic questioning and, 165
analogy, illustration, 22, 187
analysis
  defined, 37
  versus evaluation, 178–179
analytic writing, 17
analyzing
  "around the circle," 42–58
  critical reading, 60
  extended examples, 46–50, 52–55, 56–58,
    78–79
  practice, 66
APA-style citations, 200n
argumentative writing, 16
arguments
  fairmindedness and, 134–135
  examples, 8–11, 77–84, 170–174
  objections/trade-offs, 126–129
  points of view, bias and, 113–115
  points of view, incorporating other, 135–137
  seeing the other side, 125
  self-confrontational questions, 125
  traits of mind, 121
  viewpoints, addressing different, 129–132
  weakpoints, 115–116, 124–126
assessment
  critical thinking standards, 2–3, 177–183
  flow, content, audience, communication, and
    criticality, 213–217
  paper planning, researching, writing, 103–109
  practice and feedback, xxvi
  self-confrontational questions, 125
  self-reflection, 2–3
  Socratic questioning, 177–183
  See also practice and assessment exercises
    with feedback; self-assessment
assumptions, element of reasoning
  examples, 49, 55, 57, 78
  focus, 38, 49
  identifying, 41
  illustration, 36, 47

audience
  critical writing, 186–187, 189
  grammar and, 191–192, 195

background research
  conducting, 90–92
  defining, 89
  focused research *v.*, 93–94, 107–108
baseline paper, 1, 214–216
bias
  critical thinking, 113–115
  examples, 123–124, 127–134
  fairminded descriptions, 134–135
  other points of view, 135–137
  practice and assessment exercises,
    139–144
  self-confrontational questions and, 125
  stepping back, truth and, 202–203
  traits of mind and, 116–124
  weakpoints, 115–116, 124–126
bibliography, 5. *See also* sources, citing
body of paper
  components, 11
  developing, SEE-I and, 23–25
  development example, 81–84
brainstorming, 101n
breadth
  points of view, 153, 158
  Socratic questioning and, 165

choices, paper development, 86
citations, how to, 199–201
citing sources. *See* sources, citing
clarifying SEE-I
  communication through, 187
  critical reading, 60
  See also clarity
clarity
  centrality of, 156–157
  criticality, SEE-I example for, 22–23
  enhanced, 84–87
  examples and, 5–6
  grammar and, 191